The Squire of Knotty Ash and his Lady

an intimate biography of

Sir Ken Dodd

written by

Tony Nicholson

with

Anne, Lady Dodd

GREAT NORTHERN

Great Northern Books
PO Box 1380, Bradford,
West Yorkshire, BD5 5FB

www.greatnorthernbooks.co.uk

ISBN: 978-1-914227-00-4

Design by David Burrill

Photography:

Book cover:
Stephen Shakeshaft (front)
Ron Davies (back)
Painted portrait – David Cobley

Elsewhere:
David Cobley
Ron Davies
Dmitri Kasterine
John Martin
Peter Rogan
Stephen Shakeshaft
Pete Woods
The Liverpool Echo
The Royal Variety Charity
The Dodd family archive
The Ken Dodd Estate

CIP Data
A catalogue for this book is available from the British Library

Anne dedicates this book to the memory of her beloved father Tom Jones, who continues to be a lifelong inspiration, loved Variety shows and admired Ken's work. Sadly they never met.

Tony dedicates this book to the memory of his grandmother, Millicent Ward, who encouraged his childhood showbiz aspirations, and laughed at his impression of Ken Dodd.
He also dedicates it to his wife Jackie and his sons, Chris & Matt.

© Ken Dodd

Lady Dodd's royalties from sales of this book will be donated to
The Ken Dodd Charitable Foundation.

The mission of the foundation is:

A. To advance the education of the public in the performing arts.

B. To further the development of the public appreciation and understanding of performing arts by the support and encouragement of the work of young artists.

C. To provide for the relief of poverty of persons in the United Kingdom and elsewhere who are in conditions of need, hardship or distress by reason of their social or economic circumstances by providing advice and financial assistance to those in need.

D. To provide financial assistance to any other exclusively charitable organisation.

CONTENTS

INTRODUCTION

Sir Ken Dodd was a national institution. The last of a much-loved generation of comedians who enjoyed a unique place in entertainment history. They learned their craft on the thriving variety theatre circuit of the mid-twentieth century, then embraced the new emerging media of radio and television to become national superstars. Those comedians hold a special place in the hearts of the nation. Tommy Cooper, Bruce Forsyth, Frankie Howerd, Tony Hancock, Bob Monkhouse, Spike Milligan, Morecambe & Wise, Eric Sykes, and of course Ken Dodd were probably the cream of the crop. They represented the unique entertainment link between music halls and the digital age.

Ken Dodd, like all those exceptional comedians, understood the need to be different. Each had a unique style and personality – Ken perhaps more so than most. He specialised in the zany and the eccentric. He described his comedy as surreal and whimsical. His gimmicks, or 'trademarks' as he called them, were outlandish, brightly-coloured costumes, and his iconic 'tickling-stick', which he always said was his jester's prop – something to control his hands when he first came onstage, a little nervous. He didn't want his arms flailing around like a windmill, so his tickling-sticks focussed his attention and gave him something physical to do with his hands. Eventually he didn't need them to control his arms but, by then, they had become an irreplaceable trademark. Ken also capitalised on his unusual looks – his prominent front teeth, his big doleful eyes, his sticky-up mop of long hair, and his expressively flexible fingers. It went further than that though. Ken created his own comedy universe. Many people thought his oddly named hometown of Knotty Ash, of which he spoke often, was fictional. It wasn't. Knotty Ash is a very real suburb of Liverpool. Fans however could be forgiven for thinking it was part of Doddy mythology as Ken would call himself 'The Squire of Knotty Ash and King of the Diddymen'. He would regale us with tales of his loyal subjects – the population of Diddymen working down the jam butty mines, the snuff quarries, and the gravy wells, as well as running the broken biscuit repair works, the black pudding plantations and the moggy ranches.

Ken even invented his own delicious comic vocabulary – marmalise, tattyfilarious, discumknockerated, tatty-bye and plumptiousness being words you won't hear from anybody else. He certainly was unique.

The next generation of comedians revered Ken Dodd as a master of his craft. Jimmy Tarbuck described him as: "Without doubt the greatest stage comedian this country has ever had." In the same interview he also said: "He's the best thing to come out of Liverpool and, God knows, we've produced many!" Russ Abbott commented: "In the business we looked upon him as the Guv'nor, the greatest. There will never ever be another Ken Dodd, because of his individuality and style. In my personal opinion he is a legend and will never be forgotten." Ken's close friend Roy Hudd said: "In the business Ken was a total hero. We all thought he was a master craftsman, and I think we all admired him."

Trends in comedy change all the time, but Ken's style was so unique, so infectiously hilarious, and so timeless that he was able to charm younger audiences and younger comedians as well. Dara O'Briain was a big fan and fondly remembers discussing comedy with Ken after one of his marathon *Happiness* stage shows in Ken's dressing-room at the City Varieties Music Hall in Leeds. Dara described it as: "Genuinely one of the most gorgeous hours that I've spent in this industry… It was hugely inspiring. Spending that night in Ken's company, reinforced for me the love of what I do

– just the sheer joy of performance." Current king of the one-line pun, Tim Vine, described Ken as: "Without doubt one of the greatest comedians that this country's produced. He really did bridge that gap between modern comedy and classic comedy."

Joe Pasquale summed it up when he said: "The word is bandied about a lot, and it's bandied about unnecessarily, but he was a genius, a true comedy genius. Ken was an important ambassador for the industry, for comedy, and for Liverpool. I don't think we'll see his like again."

The word 'genius', which, as Joe rightly points out, tends to be overused in showbusiness circles, was clearly not a florid exaggeration when it came to Ken Dodd. Michael Billington is a highly revered theatre critic, who wrote serious reviews of major works of drama for *The Guardian* for over half a century. He said of Ken: "I've seen two theatrical geniuses onstage in my lifetime. One was Laurence Olivier and one was Ken Dodd. What's the link between them? ... It was that feeling that Olivier and Ken Dodd both belonged on the stage and inhabited the stage. That was their territory. I think one definition of a genius is someone who does things that other people do well, they do exceptionally, to a higher degree. That was true of both Olivier and Ken Dodd." Praise indeed from somebody who has spent more than fifty years reviewing all the grand theatrical knights and dames.

Laurie Mansfield, leading showbusiness agent and Life President of the Royal Variety Charity, has traversed the globe, from the excesses of Las Vegas to the Sydney Opera House, watching the best performers in the world, and he says: "There is nobody who controlled the stage like Ken Dodd. It's a magic he had. You can analyse Ken all you want, but at the end of it all – it was him... and a tickling-stick. I've never known anybody else have such command of a stage. It's always a privilege to rub shoulders with genius, and, in comedy terms, Ken was a giant."

Ken Dodd had a successful career which spanned an incredible seven decades, not only as one of our most accomplished solo comedians, but also as a serious singer. Almost unbelievably one of Ken's ballad recordings was the third best-selling single of the entire popular music explosion of the 1960s, topped only by two of the many mega-hits by The Beatles. Chart expert and music pundit Paul Gambaccini likened Ken's second career to Frank Sinatra's second career as a highly accomplished, award-winning actor. Gambaccini commented succinctly: "Almost any pop star would be happy to have had Ken Dodd's chart career. It just happened to be his sideline."

Ken was always keen to point out that there were two very different Ken Dodds – Ken the performer and Ken the private person. And the real Ken Dodd guarded that privacy all his life. Few people, outside his family and closest friends, knew the real man behind the comedy legend. Offstage Ken was a very different person. A quiet, kind, serious, intelligent, well-read, thoughtful, religious, morally-upstanding thinker with strong views and opinions. Of course the person who knew him best of all was Anne Jones, later Ken's wife: ANNE, LADY DODD. Anne shared his life and career with him for over forty years. In fact she first met him in 1961, so she saw all the incredible highs, as well as the odd darker time of Ken's astonishing life.

Ken used to joke that behind every successful man there's a woman with folded arms, rolling her eyes. In fact the more serious version of that idiom couldn't be more true than in Ken's case: 'Behind every great man is a great woman.'

Friend of the family, comedy actor Ricky Tomlinson, said they were almost like a double act: "She was his right hand. It really should have been Doddy & Anne you know."

Roy Hudd said: "She was terrific and she did bring him such love and such happiness, she really did. Everybody needs somebody like Anne, but there aren't too many like her. She was terrific with him."

Ken's nephew John Lewis saw first-hand the importance of Anne in Ken's life: "Quite frankly I don't believe my Uncle Ken could have retained his fame to that degree and for that length of time without having someone alongside him, who was so close to him, so loyal to him. His confidante, his advisor – although he probably would never admit that – his lover, his partner, his best friend, his everything… She was his rock, there's no doubt about that. She was monumentally important."

Self-effacing and modest, Anne Jones had always been happy to be in the background, and had never spoken about her life with Ken, until recently. However, in an in-depth, much-anticipated BBC2 documentary, viewed by millions at 9pm on Boxing Day 2018, Lady Anne opened up for the first time. That highly successful documentary film, which I was privileged to produce, gave Ken Dodd's multitudes of fans the first glimpse of the human side of one of our greatest comedy stars. Of course there is much more to tell than can be crammed into a seventy-five-minute television documentary, so what you are about to read is the full Ken Dodd story, told properly for the very first time.

Sybil Anne Jones, known onstage by her Equity name 'Sybie Jones', but to her friends as Anne, had been a dancer (a Bluebell Girl no less!), and is an accomplished musician, singer and comedy entertainer in her own right. She usually appeared on the bill in some guise during Ken's many stage appearances. Interestingly Anne told me that other people have said she 'sacrificed' her own career to help Ken build on his, but she says she never felt like that. Anne is nobody's fool and she knew she was unlikely to become a star in her own right, so she was more than happy to play her part, supporting Ken and constantly being at his side, whilst enjoying the reflected glory of his immense fame and success.

In the later years, when Ken was touring his one-night *Happiness* shows, and producing the tour himself, Anne really was indispensable. Theatre owner and impresario Nick Thomas told me: "Not only did she send the invoice in and drive the car and carry the bags and sell the tickling-sticks, she was in the show as well. Two spots, no less! She was absolutely brilliant…"

Close friend of Ken and Anne, actress Stephanie Cole, told me: "Anne was extraordinary, because it takes a hell of a lot to carry a hundred tickling-sticks, a hundred Diddymen, all the merchandising, plus all the stuff that's used in the show, and get it all in the car. It wasn't just a five-minute thing, it took about three quarters of an hour, the 'get-out', if not longer. A fairy didn't wave a wand and magically put everybody and everything into the car and whisk them off to the nearest hotel. It was hard bloody graft actually!"

I haven't known Anne for very long, but it's already obvious that she is one of the most capable women I have ever met. When I asked Anne herself about her role on the road she said, with one of her endearing chuckles: "You've heard the expression 'chief cook and bottle washer' haven't you?!" Then she added warmly: "But I loved every minute of it. Although occasionally I'd be loading a car in the pouring rain or the snow and I'd have to climb on a little stool to put all the bits that go on the roof. And in recent years I remember thinking, oh my goodness what am I doing? I'm old enough to be retired, I shouldn't be doing this! And he's well into retirement age..." Anne paused for a moment, then she carried on: "... And then I'd think, one of these days I won't be doing this... and I'll miss it..." Not for the first time in her reminiscences about life with Ken Dodd, Anne's emotions rose visibly to the surface. Clearly she does miss it.

I am a lifelong Ken Dodd fan. I fondly recall my maternal grandmother, when I was just seven or eight years old, encouraging me to do my Ken Dodd impression. (She would have been very proud of the fact that I am writing this book!) I made a BBC television series with Ken in the late 1980s, so I did get to know him. Anne seemed to find it easy to talk to me when I interviewed her for the BBC2 documentary, so it seemed appropriate for me to be the one to help her tell Ken's story properly for the first time. We sat down with a voice recorder for numerous long fascinating days, and I prompted her to remember everything she possibly could about her incredible husband. I also chatted to some of Ken's family members and his closest friends, but predominantly this is Sir Ken Dodd's astonishing story from the closest possible source – Anne, Lady Dodd.

There have been other books about Sir Ken, but, because he was such a private man, he always declined all offers to cooperate with biographers. Consequently they have had to rely on the very limited information which is already in the public domain. This book will go much further, because of the exclusive and extensive access I have had to personal memories from Ken's closest confidante, the splendid lady with whom he shared his life. In company, long before his knighthood, the self-proclaimed Squire of Knotty Ash would always introduce Anne as "my lady", so the title of this book resonates in every sense.

I have learned a tremendous amount from Anne about the man behind the myth.. I have found myself wondering why he guarded his privacy so protectively, because I discovered that I liked him a whole lot more, the more I learned about the human side of Ken. I'm sure you will feel the same.

The intense privacy was possibly a shrewd marketing ploy. When you think about Ken Dodd all you picture in your mind is the toothy, wild-eyed, fireball of fun bounding on to the stage in a crazy costume, with a string of jokes for every occasion. But it did deprive us of ever seeing the well-read, kind, quiet man of faith, humility and surprising intellect. You are about to meet him for the first time.

Ken always intended to write his autobiography, but, like a lot of things in his life, he never got round to it. He always said though that it would be a happy book. He had no time for dour self-pitying memoirs, or tawdry kiss 'n' tell stories.

Ken did keep copious diary-like notebooks with ideas for gags, notes on performances, revealing private thoughts and autobiographical jottings. Lady Anne has given me privileged access to these personal notebooks to help make this the ultimate and definitive Ken Dodd story. Anne wants this to be the happy book that Ken never found time to write. I will do my best.

In an archive television interview I found recently Ken promised his (never written) autobiography would be entertaining. Thanks to Anne I think this will be a good substitute for the Ken Dodd self-penned book we never got.

Acknowledgements

I would like to thank the following people, listed in alphabetical order, for kindly sharing their memories and thoughts about Sir Ken Dodd for this book:

Russ Abbott	John Lewis
Michael Billington	Laurie Mansfield
Lord John Birt	Miriam Margolyes
Norah Button	Roger McGough
Stephanie Cole	Dara O'Briain
Lorna Dickinson	Joe Pasquale
Paul Gambaccini	Barry Reeves
Lord Michael Grade	Peter Rogan
David Hamilton	Roger Stevenson
Jeremy Hicks	Claire Sweeney
Norma Hornby	Jimmy Tarbuck
Alex Horne	Rod Taylor
Roy Hudd	Nick Thomas
Reverend Julia Jesson	Ricky Tomlinson
Bishop James Jones	Tim Vine

All the above have enriched this biography, but it could never have come to fruition without the major contributor – Lady Dodd herself. My personal and eternal thanks to her for allowing me into the fascinating lives of the Squire of Knotty Ash & His Lady. It has been a privilege.

Anne and I would also like to thank some very important people who have helped to make this book happen, and have made our lives easier:

Simon Beresford, David Burrill, Paul Dodd, Jean Gaddas, Robert Holmes, Laurie Mansfield, Debbie Wady and Mark Wells.

Chapter 1:

IN SICKNESS AND IN HEALTH

Wednesday 28th March 2018 was a cold, wet, miserable day in Liverpool, the sky leaden with ominously grey clouds, and yet it seemed like the whole city had turned out, undeterred by the weather. The streets were lined with tens of thousands of respectfully sombre people. Everyday bustling traffic had been diverted away from the city centre. Miles of barricades and temporary barriers had been erected to control the vast crowds. Uniformed police were out in force to oversee the smooth-running of this peaceful but huge public occasion. What was it that had brought this famous city to a standstill? Sir Ken Dodd. It was the day of his funeral, and Merseyside had united in grief to give their favourite son a send-off the likes of which Liverpool had never seen before. It was probably the biggest and most spectacular funeral the city has ever seen, and will ever see. The colossal Anglican Cathedral was packed beyond its normal three thousand capacity. Massive crowds, who couldn't get in, gathered outside, braving the rain to watch the service on a gigantic screen outside the cathedral.

And it wasn't just Merseyside who were grieving. The entire funeral was broadcast live on national television. That fact in itself is almost unprecedented for anybody other than a former head of state or a senior member of the Royal Family.

All this for a mere jester? Well of course Ken Dodd was anything but a mere jester. There has been a special handful of comedians who the nation has taken to their hearts over the years, and Ken was up there among our all-time favourites. Those life-affirmingly funny people have been loved and cherished, and treated like members of our own families. When Ken Dodd died, for many people it was like losing their favourite uncle. And he was a hugely-admired and respected giant in the entertainment industry as well, helping to define comedy through its many transitions over a staggering seven decades. He had packed out theatres, delighting audiences up and down the land all his life; he'd made literally hundreds of television programmes throughout the major formative decades of the small screen; he had been a best-selling recording artiste as a singer through the heyday of pop music; and, ultimately, he had joined a very small elite band of comedy entertainers who have been honoured with a knighthood 'for services to entertainment and to charity'. What a career.

That's why the British people and other entertainers were grieving that day. Ken was special. But to the people of Merseyside he was beyond special. He was one of their own, and Scousers are fiercely loyal to their own. Ken had made a point of staying in Liverpool when most other successful Liverpudlian entertainers had packed up and emigrated south to enjoy their fame and fortune nearer the capital city. The whole of Merseyside was in mourning for their favourite resident and local hero, of whom they were so justifiably proud.

Seventeen days earlier, at the grand old age of ninety, Sir Ken Dodd had sadly passed away peacefully in the Dodd family home, with his new bride, Lady Anne, at his side. It had been an extraordinary life, a massively successful and fulfilling life, and a somewhat unorthodox life. He'd never married until literally two days before his passing, although he'd been with Anne for almost as long as either of them could remember. Newspaper headlines heralded their eleventh-hour wedding, many with unkind and unfounded theories about the reason for his nuptials. Only one person knows the truth behind Ken's attitude to marriage, and why he finally did choose to tie the knot – his bride, Anne Jones. Here's what Anne told me about those almost surreal few days:

He'd had a long spell in hospital, but I'd brought him home to recuperate, or so I hoped. Ken had always said, "We will get married some time, you know," but somehow it had never happened. However, I found out later, whilst he was in hospital, that he had been talking to Julia Jesson, our vicar, and Ken had asked her if there was a way we could actually have a wedding, privately, very quietly, but in church. Apparently he made a point about saying 'in church'. When I heard about the plans I just said, "We'll talk about it later" ... The main priority, at that time, seemed to be nursing him back to health.

Anne had always been referred to as Ken's 'fiancée of forty years', so I asked her when they actually got engaged. She gave me a sideways look and, with a knowing little chuckle, said:

We were just together. People and the press made assumptions. I was even referred to as Ken's fiancée in court, during the tax case, and we never bothered to correct anybody, but there never was an official day when... Well – put it this way – I certainly don't ever remember him going down on one knee and putting a ring on my finger... although he did give me a beautiful eternity ring a few years ago, which meant a whole lot more to me.

The Reverend Julia Jesson visited Ken quite a few times in hospital, just prior to Ken's passing, where they held some private conversations, which were highly personal and intensely significant regarding his deeply held Christian faith. Obviously she cannot and should not repeat those conversations, however Julia did confirm to me that Ken had started talking to her about the practicalities of holding some sort of very private wedding ceremony in St John's Church in Knotty Ash. Sitting in that same church Julia told me she had been aware that Ken and Anne had been contemplating getting married for quite some time: "When you leave it for so long it's the 'how and when' that becomes the problem. But now Ken was wanting to make real plans. I think he would have liked them to just come in very quietly into church here and make their vows together, within the presence of God, in this building. But that, in the end, wasn't possible…"

Ken simply wasn't strong enough to be moved into the church, but that didn't deter him. If he couldn't get to the ceremony, then the ceremony would have to come to him. Anne was understandably distracted by the whole process of nursing Ken, although she was aware that plans were being made. Their closest friends had started getting all the right paperwork in order, and contacting registrars. Anne picks up the story:

It's almost a mystery to me how it all happened. Different people around me helped organise everything. Licences were applied for, the required paperwork was filled in. Somehow it all happened, and, obviously, I'm very glad it did, and of course Ken was as well. It was just unfortunate it wasn't quite the way he intimated he would have liked it.

A day or so before the wedding a visiting nurse frightened me to death by saying, "I've seen this sort of stage before…" I didn't know exactly what she meant, but you just get that terrible frightening feeling that he's not actually getting better. He hadn't been eating. Somehow that made all the plans seem even more urgent. The forms for the registrars were all filled in on the Thursday, and the wedding actually ended up being quite late on the Friday night. The registrars arrived around nine in the evening, but, even at that late hour, they had paperwork to do and phone calls to make regarding the ceremony. Everything had to be done by the book. They even had to talk to Ken in private to check that he wasn't being coerced into a marriage he didn't want. While they were doing that I phoned Ken's best friend Peter Rogan and his wife Colette and asked them to come right over. It must have been nearly ten o'clock by the time I contacted Julia. I think she was already in her pyjamas, ready for bed, when I called…

Julia confirms that: "Yes, it was quite late and I was thinking about going to bed. The phone rang, and, as a vicar, you always answer the phone when it rings. It was Anne and she said, 'Julia, can you come over please? It's happening now.' I wasn't sure what 'happening now' was, but I said, 'Yes of course.' So I went over and the registrars were already there and Anne said, 'We're going to get married – now!' So that was just wonderful to be present and to be part of such an important event in their lives…"

Two registrars were present to ensure everything was legal and done correctly, as it wasn't in church, or on licenced premises. In fact they had applied for, and been granted, a temporary licence for 'Oak House' to be used for the ceremony. Peter Rogan was there as best man, with his wife Colette. Anne's close friend and personal assistant Jean Gaddas was also present. Peter, Colette, Julia and Jean were the official witnesses to the marriage. In fact Julia was also the final piece of the jigsaw, there to bless the ceremony in the eyes of God after the civil ceremony was over and legally binding.

Very few people knew of the embryonic wedding plans, but Peter Rogan told me: "I knew for quite a long time that marriage was in the offing. So it didn't come at all as a surprise to me when the invitation came and the great day arrived. I had a super role to play. What can be better than being best man for your best friend? It doesn't come much better than that…"

Anne recalls:

Somehow that day is a total mist. Ken was fully with it though. He said his vows, and I said mine, just like any normal wedding ceremony. Then Julia read a short passage from the Bible before blessing our makeshift wedding rings, and blessing our marriage, which was all very beautiful. Ken grinned and put his thumbs up afterwards and he had a little drop of champagne, just enough to wet the whistle, as it were. And then he had a drop of his favourite rosé wine, which he loved, the tiniest drop though really. But we were married…

The actual wedding day was Friday 9th March 2018.

Friends would phone Anne to see how Ken was doing during those last few weeks. Ken's close friend and comedian Roy Hudd told me: "I think the most poignant memory I've got of Ken was when he wasn't well and we phoned Anne one night and she said, 'Oh, I've got a bit of news for you'. I said, 'What's that?' She said, 'We got married yesterday.' That was not two days before he died, but it was wonderful news…"

Anne remembers that call well:

Roy and his wife Debbie were so pleased for us. I gave the phone to Ken so that he and Roy could have a word. I remember Ken saying, "Keep it up lad, never give in…" It was to be the last time they spoke.

News of the wedding soon became public knowledge. Personally I think it was extremely uncharitable and unkind of the tabloid press to suggest that the marriage had been a final cynical way of Ken 'having the last laugh' regarding the taxman. In fact the wedding was heartfelt and beautiful and I'm sure the last thing on anybody's mind were the tax implications. The law says that any spouse receives everything their husband or wife leaves behind, whether it's twenty-odd million or twenty-odd pence. It wasn't as though Ken had discovered some obscure legal loophole. In any case he was far too ill and frail by that point to be devious or vengeful. Ken had left instructions for Anne to be looked after whatever happened, so I believe the marriage was a final romantic gesture, in the presence of Ken's God – far from a cynical one.

In the end Anne is using Ken's fortune for so many worthwhile causes that you could be forgiven for thinking that she is spending it more wisely for the greater good than the Treasury would have done if they had taken a huge amount from Ken in Inheritance Tax. Not only that, inevitably, a considerable amount of Inheritance Tax will have to be paid after Anne's death anyway.

There had in fact been a clue that a grand romantic gesture was on Ken's mind at least three or four weeks before the actual wedding. He was in hospital for Valentine's Day, but he commissioned his nephew John Lewis's wife Linda to custom-make him a special Valentine card, which he profusely inscribed with some very personal and touching tributes to Anne, with love and gratitude for all she had done for him during their happy life together.

There is one more positive hypothesis on the possible thought process in Ken's mind in those last few weeks. Sir Ken knew that the one and only thing Anne couldn't inherit, unless he married her, was his newfound title. He could leave her the house and the money whether there was a marriage or not, but his recent knighthood, of which he was so proud, would die with him if he was single. If there was a wedding then Anne instantly became Lady Dodd. Now that is a gesture which I'm sure did appeal to Sir Ken. I wonder if that is the real reason his desire to get married became more urgent while he was in hospital. Anne agrees that is more than likely, even though it was never discussed directly. Her title was indeed a very special legacy from her loving husband.

Anne picks up the story of Ken's final days:

Having sipped champagne at our late-night wedding, the next morning Ken couldn't even drink a drop of tea, because it made him cough. He wasn't eating either, but he had a peaceful couple of days. He listened to records – all his favourite pieces of music – and he asked to watch a television programme he'd made for Channel 5 the year before, which was called Ken Dodd: In His Own Words.

He was still cracking gags right up to the end. On the day he died a nurse asked him if he was comfortable, and he managed to say, "Well I've got a few bob…"

Julia came in regularly to see him in those last few days, and we all took Communion together…

Rev Julia Jesson commented: "We're all hardwired to live, and so there's always that desire to keep going. But Ken, in his last days, was a deeply peaceful, enormously contented man who knew that he had used all his gifts to entertain and to make people happy, and knew he'd done all he could in this world, so there was, within him, this great sense of peace and contentment."

Julia added: "I think all of us would like to spend our last days at home, with those we love and those who love us. And that was the case for Ken. On the day of his passing, which was a Sunday, I'd popped round after church, at lunchtime, and prayed with Ken and had given him Communion. I could sense that time was running out. Then I had another phone call from Anne, later that evening, asking me to come round. There were just a few of us there when it happened, and obviously I prayed… Ken Dodd died peacefully in his own home, with his new wife Anne beside him, which is the best possible way to go from this world into the next…"

Sir Kenneth Arthur Dodd, OBE slipped quietly away in his beloved 'Oak House' in Knotty Ash, with his ever-loyal Lady Anne at his side, on Sunday 11th March 2018. Anne movingly told me:

It was very peaceful…
In fact, the actual moment, you don't know…
He went to sleep…

Chapter 2:

HOME IS WHERE THE HEART IS

Ken Dodd was brought up and lived virtually all his life in the same house. I suppose it was kismet, as well as a neat completion of the circle of life, that he died, aged ninety, in that same house. Living for ninety years in one home is unusual for anybody, but perhaps even more so for somebody from relatively humble beginnings, who has become famous, rich and successful. I believe that the Dodd family home is key to Ken's life story, and was massively important in the way it helped to shape and enrich his life. I am not going to quote the postal address, out of respect for Lady Anne's privacy, but it is probably the most famous address in Britain, after 10 Downing Street, so I suppose I don't really need to be quite so secretive.

'Oak House', to give it its correct name, was originally built on open land as a Georgian farmhouse in 1782, but now stands back just a few feet from a busy main road. It is a well-known sight for visiting fans, who still pay homage to their much-loved comic hero, and, after his death, lay countless floral tributes on the pavement or against the low brick boundary wall. From the outside I always think the house looks extremely enigmatic. It gives nothing away. It is a large, old, solid, brick-built, sober-looking, double-fronted family home, but, as you look at it, you simply cannot escape the knowledge of who lived there for the best part of a century. One of the greatest joke-tellers and zaniest comedians this country has ever produced. That larger-than-life, colourful, effervescent personality certainly isn't reflected in the look of the building, so one starts to imagine what crazy treasures must be hidden inside. Surely it must be an Aladdin's cave of lunacy and frivolity. The truth is of course not quite as simple as that.

Ken Dodd, perhaps more than any other star I have ever met or heard about, was a master at completely separating showbusiness from his private home life. It's quite surprising really as showbusiness and comedy appeared to be his whole life. There cannot have ever been another comedian, before or since, who was more dedicated to their craft, or took more delight in entertaining legions of fans for as long as humanly possible. Yet, once he was home, the boisterous onstage performer liked to shut the door on that world and become the other Ken Dodd – the offstage, studious, quiet thinker and family man. We will return time and time again to Ken's oft-repeated assertion that there were two quite different Ken Dodds. Like the importance of 'Oak House', it is another crucial factor in Ken's unique story, and very much changes what we thought we knew about him.

Two Ken Dodds? Jekyll and Hyde? Actually I don't think so. I think Ken looked on comedy as a job – the best job in the world, a wonderfully crazy job, but nonetheless a job – and he had remained sane enough to be able to see it as that and separate the craziness from his normal British everyday existence. Of course that meant that only his closest friends and family were allowed over the threshold of 'Oak House', and showbusiness colleagues and associates were kept at a safe distance. Ken would happily meet these people on neutral ground, like his favourite meeting place, the Adelphi Hotel in Liverpool, or on showbiz turf – theatres, TV and radio studios, etc – but they were rarely, if ever, invited to the family home. Of course television cameras were never allowed inside Ken's house either.

You can probably therefore imagine how thrilled I was to be invited to 'Oak House' by Lady Anne when she agreed to cooperate with the affectionate in-depth BBC documentary tribute we wanted to make about Ken after his sad death in 2018. My Executive Producer, Mark Wells, and I were as excited as a couple of little kids on the way to the seaside as we approached the house for the first time. We are both besotted by showbusiness and were therefore acutely aware that it genuinely was an honour to be invited into the Dodd inner sanctum. Not that Anne made a big deal out of it. Far from it in fact. She just invited us in as you would go into anybody's home for a chat and a cup of tea. Anne is terribly nice, kind and welcoming. I want to avoid the word 'ordinary', because she is far from that, but she is totally unspoilt by the riches and the fame she has lived around for most of her life.

So, did the privileged visit live up to expectations? Yes, most definitely. Was 'Oak House' an Aladdin's Cave of lunacy and frivolity? Yes and no. Ken had extended the original farmhouse and had built on a large music studio and rehearsal room which houses all of his many awards, pictures and a plethora of showbiz memorabilia. The room is so massive, a grand piano is dwarfed and sits almost unseen in the far left cluttered corner. (Anne readily admits they were both hoarders.) Dotted around were what I'd hoped to see, but wasn't sure I would – the Great Drum of Knotty Ash sitting soundlessly on the floor by a cream-coloured armchair; the famous floor-length, bright red, 'moggy skin' fur coat draped over a matching sofa; the tall Union Jack hat; a Mexican sombrero with ping-pong balls dangling from it on strings; a large foam-lined carrying case that is home to Diddyman Dicky Mint, Ken's ventriloquist's doll; plus a box full of brightly coloured tickling-sticks – all iconic items fondly remembered by anybody lucky enough to see Ken perform live onstage. Poignantly the only thing that was missing from this unique assemblage of original artefacts from the famous Ken Dodd act was the great man himself.

Mark Wells and I were like a couple of Charlies let loose in the Chocolate Factory, looking round that wonderful room. As a genuine Ken Dodd fan I had seen the marathon five-hour stage show many times, and my favourite part had always been the ventriloquism segment with Dicky Mint. It was a clever, well-honed routine, packed with big laughs and surprisingly heart-warming pathos, so I thought all my birthdays had come at once when Anne took fifty-year-old Dicky Mint out of his case and introduced him to us. She says she nearly laid the doll to rest with Ken (you never call them dummies), but is now so glad she decided against the idea, at the eleventh hour. I'm glad she didn't, although I can understand how she was thinking at the time, and what a touching gesture it would have made. I think it's good that Dicky Mint lives on though and acts as a permanent reminder of Ken's genius.

Ken and Anne had also recently converted an old outbuilding into a library to house Ken's incredible collection of thousands of books on comedy and comedians. Sadly Ken didn't quite live long enough to see the completion of the library, but he was just well enough to christen it by placing the first book in there on one of the many shelves – his favourite novel of all time – *The Wind in the Willows* by Kenneth Grahame.

Outside we were shown a large storage unit which contained many props and costumes from over the years, including a twenty-foot blunderbuss! Those areas were definitely the crazy Aladdin's Cave any Ken Dodd fan would hope existed. The rest of the house is just a large yet cosy family home, which almost could have belonged to a retired schoolmaster or a vicar and his wife.

Anne put the age of 'Oak House' into perspective for me when she told me that she had once pointed out to Ken that it was being built in the run-up to the French Revolution. At that time Knotty Ash must have been a countryside haven of open fields, woodland and agricultural areas, with a tiny human population. Even during Ken's childhood it was still a quiet rural village. Although Knotty Ash lies a few miles east of Liverpool, and still tries to retain its parochial identity, boundaries have become blurred and it has now been absorbed into the ever-expanding urban sprawl of that famous city, which has produced so many national treasures and showbusiness legends.

It would appear that a lot of Ken's extraordinariness came from his father's side of the family. His paternal grandmother, Harriet, gave birth to an eye-watering sixteen children. That was not so unusual in those days, and not all survived to adulthood, but one who did flourish was Ken's father, Arthur Dodd. Somehow Harriet also managed to find time to be a very active member of the local branch of the new and up-and-coming Labour movement, eventually becoming chairman of the Old Swan Labour Party. (Ken used to joke, "With sixteen children there wasn't much she didn't know about labour!") She also became Liverpool's first ever female magistrate. Harriet Dodd was a clever woman. It was Harriet who first bought 'Oak House' as a home big enough for the ever-expanding Dodd family. The large farmhouse and neighbouring farmworkers' cottages had come up as a job lot for auction in 1902. She couldn't afford to buy them, but she brazened it out and made the winning auction bid. The very next morning she sold the cottages, which gave her enough money to pay a deposit to secure a loan to pay for the house. Now that is clever!

Her husband George was a builder by trade, and taught Arthur the ropes of the building trade. In 1919, however, Arthur started his own coal delivery business, but retained those construction skills, which made him very self-sufficient when it came to home maintenance, and also led to him becoming a talented prop maker for his entertainer son Ken, in later life.

Anne remembers, while Arthur was still alive, the ever-present large pile of timber, scrap metal, bricks, window frames and 'useful' bits and pieces in the back yard, covered with a heavy tarpaulin. These were all things Arthur had acquired over the years, which were far too good to throw away and 'might come in handy one day...' and, in fairness, often did. Showbusiness started to blossom from his father's side of Ken's family as well. Arthur himself, as we will see, was a talented musician and was a naturally funny man. Two of his sisters played piano at the local cinema to accompany and dramatise the early silent films. Later they formed a touring musical act called the Dunville Sisters and performed on the variety theatre stage. One of them dated famed music hall comedy star Nosmo King.

Ken never knew his grandparents, but 'Oak House' must have been a bustling, busy home as his many aunts and uncles grew up and matured there. When Harriet and George Dodd died, just a year before Ken was born, it must have been a difficult decision as to which of the numerous offspring got the house. It appears that Arthur bought the house at auction, like his mother before him, so presumably it had been agreed that the house would be auctioned and the proceeds split between the surviving eleven or twelve children. Ken's parents, Arthur and his wife Sarah, were obviously keen to keep the house in the Dodd family and that doesn't appear to have caused any ill-feeling with Arthur's many siblings. I'm sure they were all glad that they could still visit the happy family home of their childhood days.

Kenneth Arthur Dodd was born in Liverpool Maternity Hospital on 8th November 1927. He had an older brother, William, or Billy as he was always known. Billy was two years old when Ken was born. Three years later a younger sister called June came along. Ken used to joke that he was the middle one of three siblings – "One of each!" That joke is probably no longer acceptable in a new era of gender-fluidity, but it's harmless really. Humour in innocent absurdity, something in which Ken specialised.

At the age of two toddler Ken came down with a serious chest infection, which worsened and became double-pneumonia. In those days that was pretty much a death sentence for an infant, and he wasn't expected to live. There appeared to be little that doctors or family could do to help him, other than pray. There was what was referred to as a crisis period with illnesses like that. A pivotal fever-pitch night where the poor child either survived or died. The crisis period of Ken's life-threatening illness came over a weekend. His aunt (Sarah's sister) suggested contacting a local man who was a Christian Scientist. They had nothing to lose, so the man was summoned and he sat praying by Ken's bedside for quite some time that critical weekend. In the end of course Ken did survive. He was too young to remember that troubling period, but the family's stories of how those prayers had perhaps saved him led to Ken believing that he was blessed. Anne says that Ken always carried round a small print of a painting by William Holman Hunt called *The Light of the World*, which portrays Jesus standing at a door with a brightly shining lamp, as a reminder of how he had been saved by prayer. Anne and the family agree that was the basis and starting point for Ken's devout beliefs, and where his strong Christian faith came from, something we will explore later in this book. Anne, understandably, gets quite emotional when she thinks about that critical 'crisis' night when we almost lost somebody who was to attain such importance in all our lives – especially Anne's.

Once little Ken had recuperated and his strength had returned it was back to fun and games in the massive back yard of 'Oak House'. Ken, Billy and June all agreed that they had an idyllic childhood, and a lot of the fun and excitement must have emanated from the large expanse of land at the back of the family home. It also made them the focal point for fun for all the neighbouring boys and girls, so they were very popular children. A whole generation later June's son John Lewis remembers that, as a child, a trip to Nanna and Grandad Dodd's house was never a chore, or even just a dutiful family visit. It was an adventure! It seems that a lot of this spirit of adventure and the endless fun and excitement was instigated by Ken's father, Arthur Dodd.

Arthur was a real character, a coal merchant by profession, but also a part-time entertainer. At one time, during the General Strike, with no coal to sell, he had taken work as a professional musician, playing the saxophone and double bass in a dance band on the Isle of Man, then a fashionable resort for affluent Brits. A talented musician, he also played clarinet, and was always cracking jokes. Arthur was described by Ken himself as "the funniest man I ever knew." When Ken was asked by interviewers about his early comedy influences he always cited his witty father first and foremost, before mentioning more famous comic heroes like Arthur Askey, Max Miller, Tommy Handley and Robb Wilton.

Arthur was always clever with his hands and loved making things, so there are stories of dens and treehouses at 'Oak House' – manna from heaven to any adventurous child. As well as the remnants of farm outbuildings, and thanks to Arthur's thriving horse-drawn coal delivery business, there were carts, coal waggons and stables to play in and around as well. The backyard-cum-garden was so spacious they could create cycle tracks to race round on their bikes. John Lewis even remembers experimenting at driving his mother's car in that huge open space, long before he was old enough to be allowed on a public road. No wonder the Dodds' private adventure playground attracted all the neighbouring kids.

There were two working Shire horses called Prince and Duke and, as they had spare stable capacity, they looked after a neighbour's pony called Nancy. They had a dog called Skippy, and they kept hens, who were presided over by a fearsome cockerel which Ken's sister June insisted was more like a guard dog than Skippy was. There was another puppy briefly, which fell ill. Despite Ken's loving attention, bottle-feeding it milk for several days, it sadly died. That heart-breaking hiccup aside it is easy to understand what a wonderful childhood it must have been for the three Dodd kids. Ken never forgot that magical start in life.

It didn't end there either. As Arthur had such a keen sense of humour, and was so interested in showbusiness, he used to take the whole family to the Shakespeare Theatre in Liverpool every week to see top touring variety shows. Young Ken was entranced. He said that's where he first fell in love with the warm rosy cosy glow of a theatre and the 'rumpty-tumpty' sound of a theatre pit orchestra. Very soon he noticed that the main man in the show, or the 'engine driver' as he often referred to the role, was the comedian. Yes there were jugglers, acrobats, singers, dancers, musicians and magicians, but it was the funny man who was usually top of the bill and the real star of the show. It wasn't long before Ken started wishing it was he who was the 'engine driver', up there getting huge laughs and being loved and adored by hundreds of people in the audience.

Spotting and nurturing their son's love of entertainment, for his eighth birthday, Arthur and Sarah bought Ken a 'Punch & Judy' puppet set, which he used to entertain the local kids in the back garden. He and Billy, who was also a keen joke teller, used to stage 'backyard concerts' and charge their friends and neighbours a pictorial collectable cigarette card to watch the shows, or an old penny for a front row seat. Ken and Billy would, amongst other things, do an impression of famed comedy double act Flanagan & Allen. Ken once joked in a TV interview that any criticism from their audience was responded to with a clod of earth being hurled at the critic's head. Critically acclaimed or not, Ken the performer was already starting to blossom.

The family were extremely close, and vital to Ken as an influence on his future career in comedy. In Ken's private autobiographical jottings he said of his father: "My first influence in humour was my father, who loved to laugh, and he loved to make other people laugh. He was always a supreme optimist. He treated us as his pals as well as his children. He told jokes around the Sunday tea table and shared funny experiences and stories. He would take us all to 'The Shakey', where I saw my first comedians – Sandy Powell, Robb Wilton, Ted Ray, not forgetting, my favourite, Arthur Askey."

Of his older brother, Ken said: "As a small boy Billy was my rock, my guardian, my pal, an influence and an inspiration. Later we would share laughter, jokes and clowning. We were always laughing. When I started performing the whole family offered words of encouragement. The kind of unselfish help and encouragement I received from all of them was what an artiste needs to help them grow." Billy and Ken were to remain incredibly close – in fact Ken was best man at Billy's wedding. John Lewis, their sister June's son, fondly remembers going with Uncle Ken to visit Uncle Billy in the nursing home where he spent his last few months. He loved listening to the two brothers sharing endless jokes, anecdotes and family reminiscences. John says it was a joy to witness the real love and affection between two brothers, built up over a lifetime.

Now, although Arthur clearly was a major influence on his son Ken, and was the instigator of a lot of the fun and laughter at home, we should not underestimate the importance of Ken's mother, Sarah Dodd. Small in stature (Ken used to refer to her as his 'mini-mum') she had a giant personality. Her gentle kindness, caring and endless love, was the lynchpin of Dodd family life. She was the rock, looking out for them all and supporting their every need. She was always encouraging and supported her children in anything they wanted to do, constantly reminding them that nothing was beyond their grasp. The Dodd family ethic was work hard and play hard. Like any good parent Sarah was always ready to talk, and, even more importantly, listen. The most precious thing any mother can give her child is time. Sarah would sit for hours talking to her children and would tell them all about her own childhood and her family. Ken once joked that his mum told him that she didn't care what he did with himself in life, so long as he wore a clean shirt. I think there was a lot more to Sarah's sage advice than that however.

Sarah used to help in the coal business by looking after the books and going door-to-door every Friday evening and all day Saturday, just after pay-day, to collect what they were owed for the coal Arthur had delivered that week. Times were hard, especially during the Great Depression of the 1930s, so people would pay for essentials like coal with what they could afford on a weekly basis. Even the Dodds had their tough times financially, which is how Ken, from a very early age, says he learned the value of money. It's why he always said his conscience would never let him fritter money away, having seen right through his childhood how his parents had to make every penny count, in order that the family wanted for nothing.

Sarah and Arthur Dodd conducted their coal delivery business, like most small businesses back then, by collecting cash from their customers. There were no direct debits or bank transfers to pay for domestic items and services in those days. Ken worshipped his parents and followed their lead in everything he did, so it helps explain his sometimes unorthodox attitude towards his own money.

The coal business must have done reasonably well during Ken's childhood, because Arthur and Sarah bought a small holiday cottage in Penmachno, near Betws-y-Coed in North Wales. It was very basic – no electricity, no running water – but any sort of a holiday home would have been a rare luxury in those days. The boys loved to take their bikes and cycle round the beautiful Welsh countryside, but it probably wasn't much of a holiday for Sarah Dodd, who had to cook for the entire family on an open stove.

Both Sarah and Arthur were avid readers and understood the importance of books. Ken was always extremely proud of the fact that he could read by the time he was four, before he'd even started at school. His lifelong passion for books and reading obviously came from his parents. Ken's thirst for knowledge through books never waned and has rippled down through the decades. It has been one of Anne's proudest moments, since Ken's passing, to unveil a bronze bust of her famous husband, which now has pride of place at the central hub of the circular Picton Reading Room of the Central Library in Liverpool. All his life Ken spent countless hours in that same reading room, poring over any book he could find on his favourite subject – humour and comedy. It is very fitting that Sir Ken Dodd is permanently remembered as the library's most famous, and one of its most frequent visitors.

Ken made a science of the subject of comedy, reading endlessly on why we laugh. He took it very seriously, reading all the great philosophers' takes on the subject of humour and laughter. Ken would often quote them: "Aristotle thought that comedy was like a buckled mill wheel, something that wasn't quite right. I think that comedy is a perception of incongruities, something slightly off-centre." Ken turned one genuine quote on the subject from famed psychoanalyst Sigmund Freud into a gag he used often: "Freud said, 'A laugh is a sudden explosion of psychic energy'… Of course the trouble with Freud was he never played second house Friday night at Glasgow Empire…"

It was during his childhood that Ken first read what was to become his favourite novel, as previously mentioned – *The Wind in the Willows*. He adored Kenneth Grahame's inventive and whimsical world of timid talking moles, suave boating rats, wise old badgers and boastful reckless toads. Ken's love of whimsy and the surreal was evident in his professional stage act, notably of course with the creation of Dicky Mint and the Diddymen. Reading humorous, surreal and imaginative books as a child, like *The Wind in the Willows* and Lewis Carroll's timeless classic, *Alice's Adventures in Wonderland,* gave him a love of words, and their power to be funny, which was to inform the rest of his life.

Ken often referred to his childhood as being a bit like that of *Just William,* the fictional eleven-year-old schoolboy rascal created in 1922 by Richmal Crompton. Before PlayStation and Xbox games consoles, kids' play had to be arguably more creative, so Ken would climb trees, ride his bike, and play make-believe games, like pretending to be a spy, skulking behind trees and writing secret messages in invisible ink. He once said his main talents as a child were falling out of trees, digging holes and setting fire to his coat. I think that sums up the out-of-school lives of most young boys before the digital age.

He and his brother Billy had rival gangs of half a dozen or so mates, long before the word 'gang' took on much more sinister connotations amongst young people. Ken's gang was called 'The Crows', but they had no wish to be villains – the big ambition in those innocent times was to be a hero. Children's books and comics in those days were full of strapping square-jawed hunks bravely perpetrating heroic deeds, and fearless acts of derring-do. With his love of reading Ken particularly enjoyed his comics, or 'tuppenny books' as his mum called them. *The Wizard, The Hotspur* and *The Rover* were Ken's essential weekly reading matter, fuelling his desire to become a hero himself one day. Later in life he would make an ironic joke at his own expense about being "a very intellectual child", reading comics all the time. However I think he did himself a disservice as weekly comics were required reading for all schoolboys of that era, and he did supplement his cheap-thrill comic reading with trips to the library and the acquisition of 'proper' books as well.

On the back page of those 'tuppenny books' there was often a full page advert for a London joke shop called Ellisdons, which offered a mail order service to 'Just Williams' all over the world. Ken would send the required number of stamps or a postal order to purchase itching powder, stink bombs and other items of devilish schoolboy prankery. With his love of pretending to be a spy Ken was particularly taken by an advert for a 'Seebackroscope', which he just had to have. This was a small plastic tubular creation with angled mirrors, a bit like a small stumpy periscope, which, like a rear-view mirror, allowed you to see what was going on behind you, without turning your head. Ken later joked, "… so that you could see if an assassin was creeping up on you – which is absolutely essential for a seven-year-old!"

One day though he saw the Ellisdons advert that would change his life for ever. This time it was not offering cut-price paraphernalia for a budding secret agent, but for a budding entertainer. The eye-catching illustration had a puzzled boy looking at a man carrying a heavy suitcase on his back, with the words "Help!" and "Let me out!" apparently emanating from inside the case. The advert boldly boasted that for sixpence (six old pennies) you could fool your teachers and amaze your friends with a tiny instrument or device called a 'Ventrilo', which you hid in your mouth. The somewhat bizarre, pre-Trades-Description-Act-claims for the gadget were that it enabled you to either warble like a bird, or, "throw your voice into trunks, behind doors, everywhere!" Nowadays that advert would land the mail order prank merchants in court on two separate counts. Firstly the Ventrilo was undoubtedly a choking hazard for guileless minors. (It really is a wonder any of us survived childhood before 'health & safety' became a thing!) Secondly it would be against current trading standards, as it cannot possibly have worked. Nobody can actually 'throw their voice' to another place, with or without a small lethal man-made bird-warbling contraption in their mouth. However, much more importantly, the wondrous sixpenny Ventrilo did come with an intriguing free book on *How to Be a Ventriloquist*.

Young Ken devoured and absorbed the secrets of this fascinating book the moment it arrived. By this time he had already started showing interest in being the 'engine driver' of a variety show, and was asking his dad how you become a comedian. In interviews Ken always recalled that question as: "Dad! … Dad! … How, how do you comede?" With the Dodd family appreciation of books and reading Arthur's answer was simple: "Go to the library and read up on the subject." Which is precisely what Ken did… and actually carried on doing for the rest of his life…

Armed with his 'free' book on ventriloquism and his love and embryonic knowledge of comedy, fuelled by visits to the library, Ken, at the tender young age of nine, decided he was going to be a comedy ventriloquist. Now most parents would either ignore or poo-poo such an announcement, but not Sarah and Arthur Dodd. Instead they went out and bought him his first ventriloquial figure.

In his naivety Ken christened his new stage partner 'Charlie Brown'. It was not the smartest name because the letter 'B' is one of the hardest for a ventriloquist to say without moving his lips, so Charlie couldn't even say his own name in full. Ken, in a clever and hilarious bit of knowing self-mockery, used to take advantage of that simple ventriloquist's rule in later life with Dicky Mint. He would ask Dicky if he'd rather have a big bottle of brown beer and some brown bread and butter, or a shandy. Dicky would say "A shandy!", to which Ken, with perfect timing and a comically relieved expression would say, "Good, good! I'm very pleased to hear you say that!"

Nine-year-old Ken was eager to put cheeky Charlie to work though, so he got his father to write him a script which he could learn and perform. Arthur's script for his son and Charlie started something like this:

Ken: Charlie...

Charlie: Yes!

Ken: You're here?

Charlie: Yes!

Ken: You've arrived... ?

Charlie: Yes!

Ken: Can't you say anything else but 'yes'?

Charlie: Yes!

Ken: What?

Charlie:... No!

Ken: Your name is Charlie Brown?

Charlie: Yes cock...

Ken: Cock?! When you talk to me you'll say 'sir'!

Charlie: Sir?

Ken: Yes!

Charlie: Yes sir cock!

Ken was still using that eighty-year-old script to introduce his Dicky Mint vent' doll onstage right up to his last ever live show in late 2017. I'm sure it was partly that old adage, 'If it ain't broke don't fix it', but it seems likely that it also evoked fond memories of his first steps in showbusiness, and was partly a small personal tribute to his late father.

Ken and Charlie Brown's inaugural performance was at the Knotty Ash Church Hall on Thomas Lane. This was unpaid, but it wasn't long before Ken Dodd was offered his first ever paid engagement in showbusiness, still aged just nine. Again it was with Charlie Brown, but this time at St Edward's Orphanage in nearby Broadgreen, on Christmas Day, after their festive lunch. The Roman Catholic Father Superior paid him 'half a crown', which was two shillings and sixpence, equivalent to twelve and a half pence in current decimalised currency. In those days half a crown was a substantial fee for a nine-year-old. Bear in mind his Ventrilo device, which came with the 'free' book on ventriloquism, had only cost him six old pennies, the equivalent of two and a half pence, so his investment had already paid for itself five times over. His family were so proud of him being paid as an entertainer that his mum Sarah sellotaped all the coins on to a length of string and draped them across the hall mirror, to put his hard-earned fee on show for all to see.

Ken always claimed that his second paid engagement with Charlie Brown came about three months later and was for the parent-teachers' evening at his local junior school. He says the headmaster paid him a shilling for that performance, which he always joked taught him a very important lesson – "how to take a cut gracefully".

There is an enduring myth about comedians of that era that they were all born into abject poverty, with no real education, and showbusiness was the only way out of the slums where they lived. Whilst it's maybe true of some, it's definitely not true of Ken Dodd. His father had a successful business. They weren't especially well-off, but they certainly weren't poor, and had a large comfortable family home. Ken was also pretty well educated, although he occasionally expressed regret at not having gone to university.

His first school was Knotty Ash Primary School, which was just around the corner from 'Oak House', and right across the road from St John's Church where the family went to worship and where Ken was a keen choirboy. Somehow it's hard to imagine Ken Dodd as an angelic little choirboy, although he admitted he wasn't completely angelic. There would be frequent giggling, whispering and flicking of paper pellets from the choir stalls, and they would play a game spotting price tags. When bride grooms knelt to pray at weddings they would often reveal the price tag, which they had forgotten to remove from the soles of their brand new wedding shoes.

Anne, who now plays the organ for St John's Church, says that only recently she discovered, to her slight embarrassment, that there are several scratchings of Ken's initials on the choir stalls, along with those of his fellow choristers, that can clearly be seen to this day.

The whole family were closely associated with various activities at the local church. When he became old enough Ken joined the St John's branch of the Lifeboys, the junior wing of the Boys' Brigade, an organisation aimed at providing fun activities for young lads, whilst instilling discipline, drill procedures and Christian values.

Ken said infant school days were very happy, and he had fond memories of his first teachers – the caring, bird-like Miss Sefton, who always believed there was something exceptional about Ken, and Miss Hill, who was a rather plump, rosy-faced lady with a kindly but matronly air about her.

When he moved up to the junior school Ken's love of pranks and his flair for comedy were starting to come to the fore and he became known for playing the fool. His kindly headmaster there was called William Powell, but Ken had renamed him 'Bonky Bill'. Ken by that stage was an inveterate chatterbox, so he was constantly in trouble. Nothing serious, but he was often reprimanded for talking or flicking ink pellets in class. The junior school was mixed, so it was here that he first noticed girls. His favourite subjects were history and geography, and of course, with his love of books and words, English. If the subject interested him then Ken could do quite well in that subject. In fact the Lord Mayor of Liverpool presented eleven-year-old Ken with a Certificate of Merit in the Duke of Northumberland's Under-15s Essay Competition, for a prize-winning composition he had written on the Lifeboat Service. For a while it made Ken tell people that he was going to be a reporter on the local paper, the *Prescot Reporter,* when he grew up. More importantly it kick-started a love of writing that would be an important and rewarding asset for the rest of his life.

Ken didn't much like rules however, so school discipline was anathema to him. Despite the fact that he lived close by, or maybe because of it, he wasn't a good timekeeper either – something which stayed with him all his life, as we will see later. Ken Dodd was often affectionately referred to in showbusiness circles as 'Liverpool's Latest Comedian'…

At the age of eleven Ken won a scholarship to the much bigger, more austere Holt High School for Boys, which still wasn't too far away from home, but seemed like another world to the Ken Dodd who had enjoyed the cosy warm intimate friendly village feel of Knotty Ash all his life. On the day Ken heard he had passed the scholarship exam and had been accepted to Holt High School he was knocked out by a cricket ball, which he was attempting to catch. Perhaps he should have seen it as an omen.

Ken described his transfer to 'The Holt' as like being thrown into an icy bath. For one thing he was no longer referred to warmly as Ken, Kenny or Kenneth, he was now summoned and reprimanded by aloof, inflexibly formal teachers, who only referred to him as 'Dodd!' He said the first time that happened it was like receiving a slap in the face. He also didn't like the fact that, as a scholarship boy, he had to wear a different colour school uniform to the wealthier fee-paying boys. That offended Ken's sense of fair play and equality.

The one positive thing that did stick with Ken about his first day at 'The Holt' was the sight of his new headmaster who greeted all the new boys in the assembly hall. It was the first time, other than in Will Hay comedy films, that he'd seen a schoolmaster imposingly dressed in a mortarboard and flowing black gown. The headmaster concluded his welcome with some wise words which Ken did appreciate and remembered for the rest of his life: "You new boys have not come here to be educated, you have come here to have your minds opened."

Ken's sense of humour wasn't welcomed at 'The Holt' either. He claims he was thrown out of his first ever lesson by the German master for cracking a joke at the teacher's expense. The teacher had asked if any of them already knew any German, and Ken stood and said: "Dodd sir. I know some German. Das ist ein dummkopf!" The teacher's response was swift and to the point: "Out! Keep your sense of humour Dodd to those who may appreciate it!"

'The Holt' was a boys-only school, so Ken also missed the company of girls. It wasn't a particularly happy time for young Ken.

It is a recurring theme in Ken Dodd's story that he embraced happiness and joy. It is no coincidence that he closed his shows with one of his most famous songs, *Happiness*. So Ken kicked back at anything which robbed him of happiness. I think the sombre academic atmosphere of Holt High School did just that. Ken himself admitted that comedians have a part of them that refuses to grow up, an imp inside them. Holt High School wanted to turn joyful, laughing, happy-go-lucky imps into straight-laced, po-faced men, who were destined to be pillars of society. Po-faced was something Ken was never going to be, even if he did eventually become a (fun-loving) pillar of Liverpool society.

Now this is probably as good a time as any to explore the mystery of Ken Dodd's most recognisable trademark feature – his prominent front teeth. Ken always said he liked to do things differently as a mischievous child. As it was only just a few hundred yards round the corner he'd try walking backwards to infant school, just to see if it was possible. He joked he still had the lump on the back of his head to prove it. He also claimed that he once, at the age of around seven, was dared by equally mischievous friends, to try riding his bike with his eyes shut. He was remarkably successful… but only for a few yards. He then hit the kerb and went over the handlebars, bashing his face on the unforgiving pavement, which led to the displacement of his front teeth. Ken has told that story many times. However Anne isn't convinced that it is true. She says it was just a story he made up for curious journalists, in the same way that Irish comedian Dave Allen never told the same story twice about how he came to lose half of his left index finger. Interestingly though John Lewis, Ken's nephew, and somebody who was particularly close to his Uncle Ken, told me that he believes the bike story was probably true. The only evidence either way seems to be the inarguable fact that when you look at photographs of any of the rest of Ken's immediate family – his mum, dad, brother and sister – none of them have particularly prominent front teeth, so it doesn't appear to be a hereditary trait.

Anne says his unusual dental arrangement never bothered her though, in fact I think she quite liked it. And it has to be said that Ken's face was, in many ways, his fortune. It made him instantly recognisable and allowed him to pull expressions that made the audience laugh before he'd even spoken. Tellingly Ken once told an interviewer that a comic can't be good looking. Curiously though, when he combed his hair properly and looked serious when he was singing, Ken had a dashing quality, which made him look positively handsome. Anne says she fell in love with his soulful eyes.

In the famous years, after one of his many BBC radio show recordings at the Paris Theatre in London, Ken was waylaid at the stage door by one of his regular, loyal, middle-aged female fans who said, in her broad nasal 'Estuary' accent, "Ken! Ken – I stuck up for you last night!" Ken took the bait and politely enquired, "Oh really? And how did you do that Thora?" She replied, "Well, last night, my neighbour, Mrs Nuttall, said she doesn't like you, because you're ugly. But I stuck up for you I did! I said – well he's a comedian, isn't he? – He's got to be ugly!"

Ken said that later in life, when he was a successful entertainer, he went for a dental check-up and his dentist asked what he wanted. He grinned his well-known buck-toothed grin and said, "Well you could straighten these!" His dentist stroked his chin for a moment and said, "Yes, I could do that." Ken, who had of course just meant his request as a joke, was stunned. For a few days he debated whether or not to have his famous gnashers evened up, discussing the matter with his closest associates. He said his agent nearly had a heart attack!

In fact Ken's press agent, George Bartram, once put out a story in the 1960s that they had insured Ken's unique teeth for £10,000. It wasn't strictly true, but the press lap up celebrity stories like that.

With the outbreak of the Second World War in September 1939, thousands of families in the Liverpool area decided to evacuate their children out to rural areas, safely away from the anticipated air raids on Liverpool and other major British cities and ports. Ken was just eleven years old and his parents decided that he would be safer staying with another family out in the country, near Wem in Shropshire. However, the German bombs didn't descend on Liverpool immediately and Ken was very soon incredibly homesick. In no time at all he was begging to come home to the heart of the family he loved more than anything, the Dodds at 'Oak House'. Sarah and Arthur went to visit Ken in Shropshire and Ken pleaded, "Take me home!" How could they refuse?

In fact, because the air raids hadn't happened as expected, by January 1940, almost half of the 8,500 evacuated children from the Liverpool area had returned home, including Ken.

Later that year however the first bombs did drop on Liverpool and, because of its significance as such a major strategic port and Britain's main link to America, it soon became the second most bombed British city, after London itself. The Dodds however gambled on the Liverpool Blitz being aimed predominantly at the docks, and prayed the German bombers wouldn't stray as far inland as Knotty Ash, so they decided to let Ken stay at home. Their instincts were correct. Despite an horrific civilian death toll of 30,000 in Liverpool, due to wartime bombing raids, Knotty Ash remained pretty well unscathed.

The youngest Dodd sibling June fondly remembered the war days when their dad would pick them all up from school in his coal lorry at 4pm, then they would travel with him while he finished his round for the day. Being a girl she had the privilege of riding in the cab with her mum and dad, but Ken and Billy would travel on the back of the truck with all the sacks of coal. Other kids would chase the lorry and mischievous Ken would whack them with an empty coal sack. There were then angry yells from their mothers as a cloud of jet black coal dust engulfed their offspring and their previously clean clothes.

June of course was very much a girl in a boys' world, especially as she was the youngest, but that wasn't as negative as it sounds. Her older brothers looked after her and she got away with things that perhaps they wouldn't. According to John Lewis, June's son, Sarah and Arthur slightly spoilt her as she was the only girl, and so did the two boys. Although there were times when mum Sarah would see Billy and Ken disappearing off, up to some new skylark, and she would shout after them to take June with them. Occasionally there would be understandable laddish groans.

June was a very exacting child and would play meticulously thought-out games with her dolls. One evening Arthur, who enjoyed the odd gambling flutter, had invited a group of friends round to play cards. June was occupying herself in the corner of the same room with her dolls, playing schools. June was the teacher telling all her dolls to behave and be quiet or she wouldn't give the books out for the start of their lesson. She kept repeating, "I won't give the books out until you all behave! ... I'm not giving the books out! ... I'm warning you – I won't give the books out until you are quiet!" Eventually one of Arthur's card school turned sharply and said, "For goodness' sake! Give the ruddy books out will yer??!!"

Ken said of those days that there was always music in the house. His mum played piano, and of course Arthur was a proficient musician – plus the whole family could sing. No wonder Ken always described his childhood as idyllic.

Chapter 3:

WORK HARD, PLAY HARD

Ken had always been a bright student at school, but he hadn't enjoyed his time at 'The Holt', so he left full-time education at the age of just fourteen, as many young people did in those days, and went to join older brother Billy and his father in the Dodd family coal delivery business, and, more importantly, pursue his showbusiness ambitions.

It is surprising that a clearly intelligent young man like Ken left school at such a young age, as you could legally do back then. He was obviously more academically inclined than his older brother. Perhaps he was keen to join the family business, or, more likely, the strict discipline of 'The Holt' really did put too many constraints on such an impish free-spirit. Ken has always said that it wasn't a happy time for him, and he'd also add what fun he had when he started working with Arthur and Billy. I think, in Ken's young eyes, happiness and fun was far more important than education.

Another reason for Ken's early departure from 'The Holt' was because of a clash with his blossoming showbusiness pursuits. The school didn't take kindly to him taking time off, skipping homework, or being distracted by his performances. But, if it had to come down to showbusiness or school, there was only ever going to be one winner in Ken Dodd's world.

Wartime German bombs were still raining down on Liverpool, and Ken had the same angst-ridden uncertainties as any teenager, so this was an unusually troubled time for a happy-go-lucky young Ken. He still enjoyed entertaining, and continued to perform his ventriloquist act whenever he could get the odd booking, but he had faced the hard reality that he wasn't yet old enough to be a comedian. He believed, quite rightly, that a comedian has to have maturity and some authority before an adult will willingly pay to hear them tell jokes. Saucy innuendo from a youngster would sit very uncomfortably, and a lot of comedy comes from the absurdities of life, love, sex, relationships, family, work, making home, and the struggle to make ends meet. An audience, understandably, won't buy into wry observations made by somebody who hasn't yet lived. His dream of becoming the 'engine driver' of a show still seemed out of reach, at least for the time-being.

Ken desperately needed some direction, and someone to offer him some proper guidance. Thankfully fate took a hand and a vivacious young Liverpool lady called Hilda Fallon happened to catch one of his performances as a ventriloquist. Hilda was making a name for herself in the Merseyside area by coaching and moulding promising young performers and then putting the talented ones into a successful juvenile concert party called the Hilda Fallon Roadshow. She approached an excited Ken Dodd after the show and asked if he'd like to join her. Of course Ken's answer was, "Yes please Miss Fallon!" He was very nervous, but went down well when he made his first appearance with Hilda's gang at the Broadway Club in Liverpool.

What Hilda was exceptionally good at was motivating her young protégés. Ken always said that Hilda Fallon was one of the two most inspirational people he ever met in his whole life. (The other was Bill Shankly, the former manager of Liverpool FC.) Hilda certainly was like a fairy godmother to Ken at that pivotal, uncertain period of his teenage years. Unless it was a charity concert, all the young performers got a small fee for performing in Hilda's roadshow troupe, and they were in constant demand at working men's clubs, masonic functions, bar mitzvahs, boy scout fundraisers and Sunday concerts.

Hilda motivated Ken to believe in himself. He said she had the knack of making you feel ten feet tall. It was Hilda who first suggested that he didn't always need the ventriloquist doll, and perhaps he should try cutting his trademark teeth as a solo comedian. (The term 'stand-up' hadn't yet been coined.) Perhaps, most importantly of all, Hilda Fallon taught Ken all the basic performance skills, techniques and stage craft that would stand him in good stead for the next seventy-odd years. It was a huge boost to the confidence of a diffident young teenager and wannabe comedy entertainer. Still only fifteen, Ken Dodd was living the dream.

He used to tell the story of the first time Hilda said the concert party was going to be appearing at a 'club', over the water at Ellesmere Port. He was terribly excited at the news, it all sounded so exotic. The only thing Ken knew about clubs were the posh nightclubs he had seen in glamorous Busby Berkeley Hollywood movies on the silver screen. Suave sophisticated men in evening dress with long elegant cigarette holders, women in flowing silk gowns sipping cocktails as they watched impeccably choreographed glitzy shows. Imagine young Ken Dodd's disappointment when they arrived at the Flatt Lane Labour Club with its predominantly male Scouse audience wearing flat caps, downing pints and chain-smoking Woodbines.

Hilda Fallon had a younger sister called Maisie, who was a similar age to Ken, and was equally obsessed by showbusiness, so she was in Hilda's roadshow as well. Ken would proudly introduce: "All the way from the Metropolitan Opera House in Bootle – Miss Nellie Cloggit!" Nellie was Maisie Fallon and she performed alongside Ken for several years.

In later years Hilda Fallon would also nurture the embryonic talents of fellow Liverpudlians Freddie Starr, screen actress Rita Tushingham and budding *Coronation Street* actor Bill Kenwright, who eventually became one of Britain's most successful theatre impresarios.

Another person who was important to Ken's early career was Heddle Nash, who was a famous operatic tenor. Ken was very proud of the fact that he'd had early singing lessons from him. Hence his frequent boast that he had been operatically trained.

Ken received another boost to his teenage performing career during the war years when he spotted an advert in the local paper for a young performer to act as a 'feed' to comedian Albert Burdon in a forthcoming pantomime – *Cinderella* at the Liverpool Pavilion Theatre. A lot of older performers had of course been conscripted and were away at war. Unfortunately Albert, who was a short man, thought that Ken was simply too tall to play his panto stooge. Sensing Ken's disappointment, and seeing his enthusiasm, Albert instead gave him the odd bit part, including the important job of leading the coach and horses on to the stage to take Cinderella to the ball. Ken's wealth of experience with his dad's shire horses pulling the coal waggons no doubt helped, even if this delivery was of a much more refined and glamorous nature. Ken of course loved his time in his first ever professional pantomime, alongside Albert Burdon, who was a big name in the comedy world in those days.

Anne says that it was this pantomime which particularly caused a clash with Ken's school, who didn't approve of him accepting the work and tried to bar him from doing it. He didn't listen of course and took the booking anyway, leaving school soon afterwards. It's another recurring theme in Ken's life – he hated to be told what he could and couldn't do.

The panto job hadn't been all showbusiness glamour however. It had come during the time when the Nazi bombing blitz on Liverpool was at its peak. His sister June remembered one unnerving night for the family when Ken returned home breathless, dirty and exhausted after fleeing from the theatre after the show, darting from door to door as bombs exploded all around him, dodging shrapnel and falling debris. This wasn't going to deter a young stage-struck Ken Dodd however.

June also recalled Ken having a bad bout of bronchitis around that time. Breathing and chest problems were already becoming a weakness in Ken's otherwise strong constitution. Arthur, his father, had similar problems. It is possible that being around toxic coal dust so much of the time took a toll on their health. Maybe though it was a genetic weakness. Remember Ken had nearly died of double pneumonia at the age of two. Whatever the reason, unfortunately he was plagued with asthma and breathing problems all his life.

After the highly successful, exciting and enjoyable panto season Ken returned to Hilda Fallon's concert party, and remained with them until his late teens. By that age he was no longer a juvenile performer, so he realised it was time to branch out on his own, if he was going to persevere with his showbusiness ambitions. He had learned a lot with Hilda Fallon. Most importantly how to connect to an audience and treat them as friends. Ken always said the first thirty seconds of any performance is vital, because that's when you build a bridge to the audience. A 'silver thread' as he used to quote from Gracie Fields. Ken learned to make eye contact and draw everybody in, no matter where they were sitting. Every audience member was important to Ken. That golden rule stuck with him throughout his career.

Leaving Hilda's roadshow, Ken's thoughts returned to being a solo comedian. The trouble was fresh-faced Ken still felt he didn't look old enough. One thing he tried on several occasions was to get a burnt cork and draw a thick black moustache on his top lip to try to make himself look older, if not wiser.

Ken's shrewd father had always impressed upon him the need to be different. There was no point trying to be another Arthur Askey or another Max Miller. They already existed and who would pay to see a pale imitation? So Ken wracked his brain to find a different and new comedy angle. He already had the unique trademarks of his teeth, his big eyes, and his fly-away hair, but he needed a novel comic style. Ironically, in view of his later renown as one of the most prolific gag tellers in comedy history, he decided he would be the first comedian who never told a joke.

As we have seen Ken had been brought up in a musical household and he already had a good singing voice, so, with some help from his father, he worked on an act that didn't have jokes, but instead lampooned the many serious singers of the day, and also burlesqued the various musical sounds of his much-loved rumpty-tumpty theatre orchestra.

Despite his considerable experience with Hilda Fallon, Ken was still quite an insecure performer, especially now he was going solo. He suffered from nerves before any performance, so he decided that one way forward was to hide behind an onstage character. Some of our greatest comedy performers, like Peter Sellers and Ronnie Barker for example, could create comedy magic when they were hiding behind a character, but went to pieces if ever they had to appear in public as themselves. So Ken decided to create a new persona – a buffoon he could play onstage. As he was planning a musical send-up he decided his costume should be an ill-fitting frock tailcoat with an over-sized flower in the lapel, baggy black trousers, a pair of his big boots from his time as a coalman, his shirt hanging out and the collar sticking up, a wonky black bow tie, long hair all over the place, and a burnt cork moustache. Quite a vision! But what to call this bizarre comic creation? He didn't yet have the confidence to go out as simply Ken Dodd, so he felt he needed an equally bizarre stage name.

Ken had been tickled to see a newspaper advert touting for business: 'Arnold Ramsbottom – Plumber & Artificial Leg-Maker'. He found the juxtaposition of the two disparate skills hilarious. During Ken's childhood his dad had often joked about an imaginary doctor called Dr Chuckabutty, a name Ken found amusing, so Ken christened his new musical comedy burlesque creation: 'Professor Yaffle Chuckabutty – Operatic Tenor & Sausage Knotter'. He was good to go. (Ken himself didn't seem to remember which came first, but the character occasionally appeared as Rufus, instead of Yaffle.)

Ken bought his costumes from second-hand shops in those days and he was amused to find a name label in the frock tailcoat he had bought which clearly said 'The Earl of Derby'. He found it comically ironic that the idiotic Professor Yaffle Chuckabutty was first seen onstage dressed in a jacket previously worn at high society functions by the Earl of Derby.

A major part of the embryonic act was Professor Chuckabutty's rendition of 'The Floral Dance'. This 1911 composition, later recorded by Terry Wogan, was a favourite with the earnest-looking, rotund baritones and tenors of the day, who would appear regularly on the Masonic function circuit. Ken's version though was a wicked parody. His funny walk, over-emphasised facial expressions, deliberately laboured breathing technique, and exaggerated enunciation, causing him to dribble and blow apparently accidental raspberries, made his audiences howl with laughter. It was such a hit that Ken still used his burlesque version of 'The Floral Dance' as a party-piece and an occasional part of his act for the rest of his life.

He also developed a clever routine where he would mime and pull faces to various real orchestral sounds, making it look as though he was producing the sounds from his own mouth. Again this would evolve and remain a part of the Ken Dodd repertoire for decades to come.

This is one of the many reasons for Ken's later shows being so long. He was always very good at developing and introducing new material to the act, but he didn't like throwing out tried and tested material which he knew went down well. Anne says he called those original routines 'old friends'. So, instead of replacing old material with new, the act just got longer and longer.

Another early routine, which stayed with Ken all his life, was created with his father – a zany crackpot version of 'The Road to Mandalay', an old music hall song, based on a poem by Rudyard Kipling. Fans will recall Ken marching up and down the stage wearing his bizarrely ill-fitting khaki shorts, pith helmet, bulging knapsack, trailing pots, pans and buckets, not to mention a third false leg and a kitchen sink.

Very soon the laughs got bigger and more guaranteed, his performances blossomed, and audiences warmed to him, so Ken plucked up the confidence to start doing a couple of jokes between these set musical comedy pieces. The Ken Dodd butterfly was about to emerge from the Yaffle Chuckabutty cocoon.

At this stage Ken was still working in his father's coal business and had no real plans to become a full-time professional entertainer. Nevertheless he was loving every minute of his part-time extra-curricular career as a comedy performer, and of course the additional income was very welcome to somebody who, inspired by his diligent hard-working parents, was becoming canny, thrifty and business savvy.

Sarah, his mother, was the cautious one of the family, something which would rub off on Ken to a degree. She was always encouraging when it came to his showbusiness ambitions, but she felt he needed a safer and more secure way of making a living. Sarah had spotted the nascent business brain which Ken was developing, so it seemed logical for him to start his own business.

Ken was enjoying working with his dad and his brother Billy, delivering coal. He and Billy would banter with the housewives, and they would make each other laugh all the time, cracking jokes and larking around. They were very close. However, even though he was happy in the family business, the young Ken Dodd was ambitious and always had his eye on the next horizon. At the age of nineteen he amicably left his father's coal business and, following his mother's advice, set up on his own, selling pots and pans, soap and cleaning paraphernalia door-to-door.

Ken himself has said that this business departure helped his confidence enormously. At first he'd be clammy-palmed and tongue-tied as he knocked on strangers' doors, but soon he developed some harmless cheeky banter which helped break the ice. "Now missus – what a beautiful day to start your spring-cleaning! Could I interest you in a bucket?"

Ken once told interviewer Michael Parkinson that's where the 'missus' bit started. In amongst his wares were feather-dusters, so that could have been the origins of the legendary Ken Dodd 'tickling-stick', although nobody is quite sure about that. It seems highly likely though that he impishly tickled his lady customers with his feather-dusters, and therefore instinctively reached for a feather-duster from his stock cupboard when he decided he needed a jester's prop to hold. This was to steady his nerves and focus his attention in order to stop his arms flailing around, as he took his first tentative steps on to the stage as solo comedian Ken Dodd.

As he started to make money selling door-to-door he used some of his performance earnings to expand the business. You could be forgiven for thinking that the door-to-door business was merely a way of paying the bills while Ken built up his career as a comedian, but that was not the case at this stage. Quite the opposite in fact. The grand plan at that time was that the selling business was the prime source of income, and the focus of his ambitions, so any cash from performing was mainly used to expand and consolidate upon that. Performance money, for example, was used to buy a large van, which was converted by his father into a mobile shop. The mobile shop was also used of course to take his props and costumes to his evening gigs. Ken even created his own range of cleaning liquids, detergents, disinfectants and bleaches – KayDee Products. One shudders to think of the alchemy that went into the creation of some of those potions.

Ken employed a young boy called Alan Shields to help him with the door-to-door round. Anne recalled, many years later, when Ken was appearing at the London Palladium in 1990, Alan came along to see his old employer onstage. Ken had always felt paternal towards young Alan, so, seeing him after the show as a florid-faced plump middle-aged man, he started telling Alan he should look after himself better and lose some weight. Having just come offstage, high on adrenaline, Ken was still in exuberant performance mode, and pointed across the star dressing-room: "Look at your mother! She looks marvellous for her age!" Anne says his 'mother' should have looked marvellous as the lady Ken was pointing at was in fact Alan's wife. Anne wasn't too sure at first, and asked Mrs Shields if she really was Alan's mother. She replied with a wry grin, "NO! But

Doddy's always joking isn't he?!" Anne says she hastily replenished the lady's glass with champagne to keep her sweet, but Ken was still in full flow on the subject, so she had to quickly get up and walk past him a couple of times, to stamp on his foot, and hiss firmly into his ear, "She's his wife!" before he dug himself into an even deeper hole.

All the time Ken was running his KayDee door-to-door selling enterprise, the coal business also continued to be run from 'Oak House' by Ken's father and brother Billy. In fact Billy kept the coal business going well into the 1980s, long after Arthur's retirement, by which time coal was an unfashionable fuel and hardly used any more. Billy used to joke that he'd had yet another customer slip him an account closure note through the door saying, "Gone gas, Gladys." He used to call them his "Gone-gas-Glad" notes.

Billy was always a great joke-teller and had his brother's same sense of the ridiculous, but, despite endless encouragement from both Ken and their father, Billy refused point blank to ever try to perform comedy onstage. He was probably wise not to attempt competing with his talented younger brother. There is a great difference of course between the chap who is hilarious 'down the pub', and a professional comedian. Billy was obviously smart enough to realise that. Pub wise-crackers rarely make great stage comedians, and, perversely, the funniest professional comics tend not to be the life and soul of the party 'down the pub'.

As Billy approached sixty-five his wife persuaded him to retire and sell the coal business. A party was thrown at 'Oak House', with bunting and banners congratulating Billy on "fifty years' hard labour". Within a week he was so bored that he bought the business back again and kept it going until there were literally no domestic customers any more for coal. All that time the coal truck was kept at 'Oak House', long after it had become Ken's home.

Again I am drawn back to the importance of the house, not just as a family home, but as a communal headquarters for the Dodd family through the ages. Billy had left home, got married and was living down the road, but, after parking up his coal truck at 'Oak House' for the night, covered in filthy black coal dust, he would go upstairs to have a bath and change into clean clothes, so that his wife wouldn't have to see him like that, and have him messing up their bathroom. His mother Sarah was of course used to the grime associated with her husband's business, and was happy that her eldest still treated their house as home. Even after Sarah died in 1968 Billy would use the facilities at 'Oak House', with Anne sometimes cooking him a meal, if she happened to be visiting.

If you think about it Ken never really left home. His father lived until 1979, by which time Ken was fifty-two, so, up to that point, it was still Arthur's house. Prior to Arthur's death Anne remembers the large back yard, not as a garden, but as a working space for the whole family. There was the ever-present coal truck and other paraphernalia needed for the coal business; then there was the tarpaulin covering Arthur's pile of useful odds and ends; later a large metal container arrived for Ken's expanding collection of props, costumes and bric-a-brac; there were the dilapidated outbuildings which were used for storage or as Arthur's workshops; and there were other commercial vehicles as well. Arthur would charge a nominal sum ('ten bob a week') to local businesses to park their trucks and vans. Arthur would never accept decimalised currency and still insisted on referring to 'a bob' (shilling) until the day he died. There are even stories of American military vehicles parked at the back of 'Oak House' during the war.

The metal container for Ken's props had been purchased from Liverpool Docks in the 1980s. Anne had the unenviable task of running along the tops of countless shipping containers to find the one in best condition, in the hope it would be watertight.

When Arthur died Anne took on the mammoth task of turning that grimy grey working area into what is now a beautifully landscaped rose garden with a tree-lined duck pond, neatly manicured lawns, a car port, a large conservatory and a summer house. Anne remembers having to get rid of a huge mound of solid asphalt dumped by a tarmacking business that used to pay Arthur to park out there. Even the old farm outbuildings have now either been demolished or renovated and transformed into useful additions to the house, like Ken's music room and his impressive comedy library.

CHAPTER 4:

TURNING PRO

One cannot deny there was always a tremendous family work ethic in 'Oak House'. All through the early 1950s Ken was working during the day selling door-to-door, then going round the Liverpool pubs, clubs and function rooms several evenings a week, perfecting his comedy act.

Having his mother's cautious and risk-averse nature Ken wasn't ready yet to burn any bridges, so he kept both careers running in parallel. It's clear though that he was already being noticed as an extraordinary performer. Lord John Birt, former Director General of the BBC, hailing from Liverpool himself, once told a journalist: "The morning I took my eleven-plus exam, my father said, 'Last night I was at a club in Liverpool, I saw an absolutely brilliant young comedian and son I've got his autograph for you.' It was a shocking photograph – the Ken Dodd visage we now know, with his hair up and his teeth deliberately prominent. As a ten-year-old child, I thought 'WOW' – and of course I've been thinking 'WOW' ever since..."

It was during that intensely busy and exhausting period that Ken met and started dating a young Liverpudlian nurse called Anita Boutin, of French-Canadian descent. They became engaged in 1953.

Around the same time Ken met yet another important figure in his career development. A well-respected London entertainment agent called Dave Forrester, from a company called Forrester-George, contacted Ken and arranged to meet him at the Adelphi Hotel, near

Lime Street station in central Liverpool. Dave, who had originally come from the north-west himself, told Ken he had heard great things about this young exciting comedian, taking Merseyside by storm, and offered to represent him and take him to the next level, in front of a national audience.

Ken says they had tea and cakes which came to one shilling and sixpence. Dave left the bill for Ken to pay, so Ken thought, "Well if he looks after my money as well as he looks after his own, he's the man for me!"

Dave had brought a contract along for Ken to sign, but when Ken asked Mr Forrester what he thought of his act, Dave had to admit he'd never seen him onstage, he'd just heard good things. Ken picked up the contract from the table and tore it in two, bluntly saying, "Well if you can't be bothered to see me work, I won't be signing any contract!"

That could have been the end of a beautiful friendship, but they parted amicably with a handshake, with Dave promising to see Ken work in the very near future, which he did.

Ken Dodd now had a London agent in the form of Dave Forrester. They never did sign a contract to define their working relationship, but Dave continued to be Ken's unofficial and non-exclusive agent for much of Ken's showbusiness work for the next thirty-five years. In fact I dealt with an elderly Dave Forrester myself in 1987 when I booked Ken to co-star in a series for BBC1. Sadly Dave died the following year.

Gruff-voiced, plain-speaking Dave Forrester was a well-known character in showbiz circles. He liked his whisky and he was an undischarged bankrupt, which meant he wasn't allowed to have a bank account, so his business partner Nancy George had to sign all the legal documents and cheques. Despite his colourful background Dave was a very successful agent/manager. After having been a luxury cinema owner in Chorley, Lancashire he had moved south, taken expensive Park Lane offices in London's Mayfair, and had looked after some of the musical greats of the 1950s. Eddie Calvert ('The Man with the Golden Trumpet'), also from the north-west of England, was probably his biggest earner in those early days. Eddie had a string of instrumental hits back when the charts were still referred to as 'The Hit Parade'. Dave Forrester also represented Anne Shelton and Rosemary Squires, who were both successful easy-listening singers of the same era. Of course as we entered the 1960s Elvis and The Beatles changed the whole popular music landscape and artistes like Calvert, Shelton and Squires quickly became unfashionable. Nevertheless Dave's association with these previously best-selling recording artistes and their record companies, notably a friendship he had forged with top Columbia Records (EMI) staff producer Norrie Paramor, helped comedian Ken Dodd to be taken seriously as a ballad singer, and to get his first recording contract with Decca Records.

Forrester-George also represented other comedy stars – slick patter merchant Ray Fell, double act Hope & Keen, and talented ventriloquist Dennis Spicer, whose rapid rise to fame was cut tragically short when he died in a car accident in 1964, aged just twenty-nine. Later in the 1960s Dave Forrester would sign up another massively successful comedy act from the north-west – top TV impressionist Mike Yarwood. His eye for talent was justifiably respected within the entertainment industry.

In later years Mike Yarwood would often perform an hilarious party-piece for his fellow professionals where he would do a perfect impression of Dave Forrester's distinctive gravelly voice, pretending to be on the phone, trying to sell Ken to an American television executive: "I've got this marvellous comic called Ken Dodd... Yes, he's got big teeth and his hair sticks up – he'd be perfect for American television. He comes on with his tickling-stick... What? Oh, it's like a feather duster thing which he waves around and tickles people with... and he says Nikky-Nokky-Noo, and then he tells everybody how tattyfilarious and discumknockerated he's feeling... Yes, that's right... and he asks a woman if she's been tickled recently... Then on come his Diddymen... What? ... No, Diddymen... From Knotty

Ash… They're little people with fat bellies and big hats… No, not midgets! … There's Mick the Marmaliser and Nigel Ponsonby-Smallpiece, and they dance round Ken singing 'We Are the Diddymen', and… Hello! … Hello…"

Dave Forrester was Jewish and was part of a tight-knit circle of Jewish people who controlled a lot of British showbusiness in those days – notably impresario Val Parnell and the three Grade brothers – Lew Grade, Leslie Grade, and Bernard Delfont (né Grade). This meant he was in a position to get his new talented signings work in some of the country's biggest and most prestigious theatres.

With Forrester-George's backing, plus fiancée Anita's encouragement and support, Ken Dodd decided to take the plunge and become a full-time professional comedian. Dave Forrester was able to open the door to the big-time, which in those days, for variety acts, was the Moss Empire circuit. This was the number one British chain of variety theatres, which all up-and-coming comedians dreamed of playing. Every major town and city had its Empire Theatre at that time, where all the big names in showbusiness would appear. They were very choosy about the acts who performed in them, but the Moss Empire Managing Director was Dave's friend and associate Val Parnell.

If Ken was going to tour the country he wasn't going to be able to continue with his KayDee business during the day, so he had to sell up and 'pack in the day job' – always an exciting, but nerve-wracking turning-point for any entertainer.

Nearly eighteen years after getting his first paid engagement, Ken Dodd, aged twenty-six, made his first fully professional appearance at the Empire Theatre in Nottingham on Monday 20th September 1954. With his name at the bottom of the bill, 'Ken Dodd – Britain's new star comedian', he was nevertheless thrilled to be appearing for a whole week, doing a twelve-minute spot, twice-nightly at this prestigious theatre. After the first week his 'bill matter' changed, and became, 'The Unpredictable Ken Dodd'.

Exciting times followed as he moved from town to town playing two shows a night at all the plush Empire Theatres, including the notorious Glasgow Empire, traditionally the graveyard for English comedians. Ken later dubbed it 'the house of terror'. He had heard all the stories of even well-established English comics dying a death there, leaving the stage in stony silence to the sound of their own footsteps, and being advised by less-than-friendly Glaswegian audience members: "Awa' hayme 'n' byle yer heeed!!" ("Go home and boil your head!" for any non-Glaswegians reading this.) Ken was understandably nervous therefore when he attended his band call on the Monday morning in Glasgow. Ken told the story many times, but this book wouldn't be complete without repeating it.

The manager of the Glasgow Empire, Mr Mathie, addressed the whole cast on that week's bill and asked, "Who are the comedians?" Ken and two others nervously raised their hands. "Right – no football gags, no references to Celtic or Rangers because we need the seats, and you get 'the bird' on Friday! Don't worry about it – all English comics get 'the bird' on Friday night…". 'The bird' being a showbiz expression for being hissed at, and booed off the stage. Not great news for the three English comedians.

When it came to first house Friday night Ken was understandably petrified and tottered on to the stage in his Chuckabutty tailcoat, his shirt hanging out and his unruly hair all over the place, pulling faces to show off his trademark teeth and gesticulating wildly with his bendy fingers, his eyes almost popping out of his head. Somehow he managed to stammer out his opening line, which suddenly seemed desperately unfunny and worryingly disrespectful to this boozed-up hostile crowd: "I suppose you're all wondering why I've sent for you!" As Ken used to love telling it, "This man on the third row uncoiled himself, with half a bottle of whisky in his hand, and yelled, 'Cripes! What a horrible sight!'…"

Much more encouraging was a rave review Ken received in *The Manchester Guardian*, after opening in their hometown, less than six weeks into his first professional tour: "The trammels of gentility still cling to the splendid madness of the down-at-heel comic figure created by Ken Dodd at the Manchester Hippodrome last night. But the bow-tie is awry – the boots are laceless, and the morning suit has lost its glory. Mr Dodd has that glorious gift of comic insanity which is only given to the few…"

When he was selling door-to-door Ken assiduously kept detailed notes of what people wanted, and what people bought, almost making a science of supply and demand. He didn't really see any difference, in that regard, with his change of career. He once told TV interviewer Michael Parkinson, "I swapped my pots and pans round for a laughter round." He still saw it as selling himself to the public, so he took the same scientific approach, keeping copious notes of what jokes people seemed to like, allowing himself to improve every day. He wanted to understand what he was selling so he read every book on the subject of humour he could lay his hands on. That way he could be fairly sure what people wanted and expected from a comedian. This painstakingly methodical approach to the new job worked a treat.

Ken had met a young man called Laurie Bellew, who was doing his National Service in the RAF, near Blackpool, in the mid-1950s. Laurie loved variety, but wasn't a performer himself, however he was good at coming up with comic ideas and gags. Laurie collaborated with Ken on his act and would go along to the theatres, as often as he could, sitting in the stalls, making notes about how each joke went down with the audience around him. He would log everything down in a large ledger, which Ken would study after every performance, and then the two of them would work on improving the gags or moving them around to make the act stronger and stronger. Laurie would keep a note in the ledger where each performance had taken place, and they soon spotted geographical patterns emerging. Ken realised that, for example, in the north they seemed to prefer dry droll humour, whereas on the south coast they appeared to like eccentric and surreal stuff, so he began tailoring his act and doing variations according to where he was appearing.

Lord John Birt, having been introduced as a child to Ken the up-and-coming, way-out new comedian by his Liverpudlian father, was surprised to bump into Doddy when he was studying at Oxford University. Ken was reading up on the philosophy of laughter in the sombre surroundings of the Bodleian Library. As Birt observed at the time, "This is a person who takes humour seriously."

Like most young comedians Ken was hungry for success, and wanted to rise to the top of the bill as quickly as he possibly could. I think there can be little doubt that this scientific approach to perfecting his act was a key factor in him achieving that meteoric rise to stardom, much faster than many of his contemporaries.

Laurie Bellew went into press and P.R. when he'd finished his National Service, but his loyal friendship and association with Ken went on right up to Ken's death. He would continue to write odd gags, but, more importantly, Laurie would help Ken, especially with his television work, throughout the whole of Ken's career.

'The unpredictable Ken Dodd' was enjoying himself, touring up and down the country, polishing his act and rising higher up the bill, but it meant he was away from home a lot, so fiancée Anita decided to stop nursing and go on tour with Ken. She was extremely well-organised and made herself useful, helping with props and sound effects, but, more importantly, keeping a record of which gags he'd done in which towns so he wouldn't repeat himself on the next visit, and also taking over from Laurie Bellew, keeping notes on what sort of jokes went better in different parts of the country. This became the origins of Ken's famous 'giggle map of Great Britain', which he claimed to have drawn up of what sort of humour goes well in different regions. I'm not sure there ever was an actual map, but there is no doubt that Ken, aided first by Laurie Bellew, then by Anita, and later by Anne, did scientifically analyse the regional senses of humour, which was a vital tool to a touring comedian who was determined to make sure everybody saw him at his best. Ken always proudly boasted that he never did the same show twice – he would always adapt and adjust his show for every new audience and every new town.

Another vital cog in the early Ken Dodd machine clicked into place in 1955. Ken met a shy young Liverpudlian man, who reluctantly ran a fruit and veg stall on Liverpool market, whilst dreaming of becoming a great comedy writer. He was called Eddie Braben. Eddie loved comedians and used to hang around the stage door of the Liverpool Empire trying to hawk the jokes he'd scribbled on the back of a brown paper bag from his stall to the great variety comics of the day. 'Cheerful' Charlie Chester spotted his potential and bought some of Eddie's early material. Eddie specialised in writing one-line quickfire gags, so he was a perfect fit for Ken Dodd who, coincidentally, lived not too far away. Ken and Eddie hit it off right away, their young agile comedy brains sparking off one another. Eddie would pop down the road to 'Oak House' on a regular basis and sit for hours with Ken, firing jokes and ideas backwards and forwards. It was a very fertile working relationship and the two men became great friends and kindred spirits. They were a team for fourteen years, which Eddie, in his autobiography, described as fourteen 'ferocious' years. Not ferocious as in acrimonious, but vividly describing the fast and furious exhausting speed at which they worked together, producing reams of comedy material, all tailored for the way Ken told 'em.

Dave Forrester's hunch had been correct and, less than twelve months after Ken's professional debut at the Nottingham Empire, he was appearing in his first ever summer season in 1955 on the Central Pier in Blackpool, alongside trumpet player Kenny Baker, radio comedian Jimmy Clitheroe and fellow rising newcomers Morecambe & Wise, who were still getting used to the responsibilities of topping the bill. An ambitiously keen Ken Dodd, now second on the bill, understandably worked extra hard every night to steal the show, making him a hard act to follow, even for Morecambe & Wise. He got on particularly well with Ernie Wise, but Ern' popped his head round the corner of Ken's dressing-room door at the end of the season and said with a grin, "Hey Doddy – you're not with us next year are you?!"

Blackpool at that time was the variety entertainment capital of Great Britain, our Las Vegas if you like, and Ken soon became a much-loved regular attraction there. Blackpool was famous for its entertainment. More so than any other British seaside resort, and consequently it had more theatres. Factories in the north would close for a week or a fortnight in the summer and all their workers would descend upon Blackpool. Thankfully different towns and cities would stagger the holiday period so that not everybody was off work at the same time. 'Glasgow Fair Fortnight', the last two weeks of July, was a notoriously riotous time in Blackpool, with thousands of hard-working Glaswegian families piling on to trains and charabancs south for fun, laughter, and the odd alcoholic beverage...

Pantomimes and seaside summer seasons, the pinnacle of live British entertainment in those days, soon became lucrative annual fixtures for Ken and, by 1958, he was topping the bill in Blackpool himself. In fact it wouldn't be too long before he was starring in numerous sell-out seasons at the massive 3,000-seater Opera House, Blackpool's top venue.

Under Dave Forrester's guidance things were moving quickly. By 1955 Ken had been brought to the attention of a BBC television producer called Barney Colehan, who booked Ken to make his television debut on a new successful series Colehan was making at the Leeds City Varieties Theatre, called *The Good Old Days*, a nostalgic entertainment show in the traditions of old-time music hall. Of course *The Good Old Days* ran for thirty years and became a firm favourite of Ken's, appearing as he did as one of the main guest stars of the show year after year, and often on their Christmas Special. It was the perfect TV format for Ken, because he was playing to a theatre, and he loved the old traditions of music hall and variety.

It may surprise younger readers to know that in the '50s radio was a more important medium than television for variety stars, so Ken was thrilled, in the same year, to be asked to appear on *Workers' Playtime*, an iconic radio series where variety stars were invited to perform in a factory or a large place of work somewhere in the country. The imported fun relieved the drudgery for the local workers with in-jokes and digs at their bosses, whilst entertaining millions at home who would enjoy the experience vicariously. It was Ken's first exciting foray into radio, which was soon going to become an important part of his comedy career and a stepping-stone to him becoming a showbusiness national treasure. He was invited back time and again to feature in *Workers' Playtime* on BBC's entertainment radio station, the Light Programme, and became a regular star of the show.

Leading showbusiness agent Laurie Mansfield remembers being a big fan. After leaving school in 1959 Laurie had gone to work in the offices of the iconic Cadbury's Chocolate Factory in Bournville, where his family lived. Rather than going into the works canteen he would dash home every lunchtime to listen to *Workers' Playtime*, in the hope that his comedy hero Ken Dodd was featuring. Laurie, who is also a dedicated rock & roll aficionado, believes that Ken Dodd was as important and influential to twentieth-century comedy as Elvis Presley was to popular music. He says that listening to Ken on radio was the driving force that made him want to get into the world of entertainment. To put that accolade into context Laurie is now the showbiz mogul who plays host to the Royal Family every year at the Royal Variety Performance, and sits next to the Queen in the Royal Box.

When Laurie made the move into showbusiness he went out of his way to meet his comedy hero, and was honoured to occasionally do business for Ken. Laurie told me: "I'd have done it for nothing… and you don't hear an agent say that very often… But I would have done it just to be able to say that I'd done a deal for Ken Dodd."

BBC radio producer James Casey, son of the legendary variety theatre comedy star Jimmy James, was also impressed by Ken's star quality during his appearances on *Workers' Playtime* and had a word with his boss back at the BBC in Manchester, Ronnie Taylor, the north-west regional head of light entertainment. By September 1958 they had gone into production with a series created around Ken and its other youthful cast members, namely Judith Chalmers and impressionist Peter Goodwright. The series was called *It's Great to Be Young* and was recorded in the Manchester Playhouse. The show was successful enough to bring Ken Dodd to the attention of a radio-loving nation.

It is important to stress how regionalised comedy was in those days. It's hard to comprehend in this day and age, but, back then, before regional accents were so familiar, and at a time when all the BBC announcers had to have cut-glass plummy accents and speak in what now sounds highly affected 'received English', there was a massive north/south media divide. Northern comedy was considered very different to Southern comedy. Famously the BBC's first reaction to Morecambe & Wise was that they were 'too northern'. Hence the importance for Ken of the north-west regional centre of the BBC, which had made stars of other northern comics like Jimmy Clitheroe, Al Read, Ken Platt and Harry Worth. In London, around the same time, the BBC were making stars of Kenneth Horne, Tony Hancock and the Goons.

Some of the north-west radio shows which were considered too northern were only transmitted on the BBC's regional Home Service North, and were never heard in the south. The split was that pronounced. Ken took a leaf from the book of other successful northern comedians, such as his heroes Arthur Askey and Ted Ray, and played down his regional accent and, by default, his northern roots. Things would change during the next decade when Liverpool became arguably the most fashionable place in the world, especially in the field of entertainment and popular culture, and people would affect a fake Liverpudlian accent, just to appear 'cool'.

There were other minor television appearances for Ken, but, rather surprisingly, he and Dave Forrester turned down two approaches from ITV in the late 1950s to appear on their massive variety entertainment blockbuster, *Sunday Night at the London Palladium*. Ken's reasoning, to the public at least, was that he didn't want to be over-exposed by television. In 1957 he was quoted as saying: "Too many TV appearances can bring about a performer's downfall. However good an artist may be, the public tires of seeing the same face on the screen." However it is well known that Ken was very conscious of the north/south divide, so perhaps a huge show like *Sunday Night at the London Palladium* seemed like too big a gamble – a very public place to risk failure in the south.

Ken also knew that television and radio gobble up comedy material at an alarming rate, as all comedians find when they take to the airwaves. Perhaps he was nervous of giving away his best stage material, which is difficult to re-use when it has been seen by millions from the comfort of their own front rooms. Ken always worked at such a breakneck speed that even a few minutes on TV would use up an enormous number of tried and tested gags.

It has also been said that Ken was anxious about how he came over on television, with his unusual looks, and his larger-than-life, deliberately exaggerated performances. These worked well in big theatres, reaching everybody right at the back, but might seem over-the-top on the intimate small screen in somebody's living room.

Television producer Rod Taylor, who used to work for Forrester-George in the 1960s, told me that Dave Forrester was very shrewd and calculating about such important bookings. Ken had successfully played theatres in the south, even the suburbs of London, but Dave advised Ken not to play the notoriously fickle West End or tackle the make-or-break Palladium TV show "until he was ready and the time was right."

Ken was always keen to stress that Dave was merely his agent, not his manager, and he made his own decisions about the direction of his career. I'm sure though that he heeded Dave's advice, born of long experience, when it suited him.

Nevertheless, as television gained momentum and began to overtake radio as the most prestigious outlet for comedy stars, Ken couldn't resist the ultimate accolade when the BBC offered him his own occasional TV series in 1959. This almost proves the point that over-exposure wasn't Ken's real worry. The first show was transmitted on Saturday 25th July 1959 at 8.20pm. It was a key slot in the weekend schedules, highlighting the faith that BBC TV executives were putting in their new signing.

In those days television producers hadn't learned to harness comedy talent and mould the artists for the new mass medium, so these sort of programmes were basically televised versions of variety theatre shows. It was almost impossible to edit video tape in those early days so the programmes were recorded as though they were live, in real time. Ken's first show was recorded at the cabaret-dining-style Continental Theatre in Bolton. Eddie Braben was the main writer, introducing him to the world of television scriptwriting – a world where he would become King, as the chief writer for Morecambe & Wise at their peak.

The Ken Dodd Show was a success and was followed by others over the coming months. There were still only two television channels in Britain at that time, so viewers really got what they were given, which meant there was no pressure to use gimmicks and scheduling tricks to hook viewers in. With a series like Ken's they would make around one a month and transmit them intermittently, as and when they were ready.

Ken Dodd was on the road to stardom. Anne's view is that fame was almost inevitable because he worked so hard at perfecting his craft. He certainly put in the hours. Fellow comedians had families and other distractions like golf, but Ken lived and breathed entertainment and comedy. Anne says, "Ken was married to the business. Let's be honest about it – that's the word." Of course there were two other major factors – talent and ambition. Ken had both of those in spades and the next game-changing decade would see everything fall into place, making him one of the biggest stars in Britain.

Chapter 5:

THE SWINGING SIXTIES

As we turned the corner into the most colourful and vibrant decade of the twentieth century, Ken Dodd was already a star. He was topping the bill in major seaside shows and pantomimes and had his own series on both radio and television. In between he was still touring round, headlining in all the best variety theatres, and popping up on other television shows like *The Good Old Days*.

The post-war '50s had been quite austere and grey, but there was a new optimism and newfound wealth in the '60s, with young people suddenly finding a voice and shaping the future.

Ken wasn't tempted to move down to London, something a lot of northern entertainers felt compelled to do. He loved the cosy security of family life in Knotty Ash, and he was enjoying an exciting buzz that was starting to emanate from his home city of Liverpool. There was a fresh emerging entertainment scene in the pubs and clubs, born out of the new rock & roll sounds being imported from America. It's no coincidence that Liverpool was the hub of all this excitement. The Liverpool docks were the major link with the States, and all the young kids would hang around the docks when ships came in to buy or scrounge rock & roll and blues records from 'over the other side of the pond', brought over by the transatlantic merchant seamen. These much-sought-after discs were virtually impossible to buy in British record shops. This primal, innovative, energetic music, imported from the USA, was then anglicised by the locals and guitar combos and 'skiffle' groups started springing up all over

Liverpool, emulating the likes of Little Richard, Buddy Holly, Carl Perkins, Chuck Berry, Jerry Lee Lewis, and of course Elvis.

In 1960 Ken was topping the bill in a Merseyside charity extravaganza called *Star Matinee*. There were a staggering sixteen local acts on the bill, with Ken topping the bill at number one. Down the bill at number ten, opening the second half, was a relatively unknown local group called The Beatles. Ken didn't think much to them, as they were still quite raw, and, let's face it, it wasn't exactly his kind of music, but he did remember a knock on his dressing-room door that day. A young, fresh-faced chap with a cheeky grin pressed a business card into his hand and asked if he could help get them some bookings. It was John Lennon.

The Beatles greatly admired Ken Dodd. He was a star in Liverpool long before they were, and they had tremendous respect for comedians. The Beatles themselves were always known for their humour and their wit, and they were in awe of other funny people. Long after their colossal success they would happily appear alongside Ken Dodd, Mike & Bernie Winters, Morecambe & Wise, Peter Cook & Dudley Moore, Peter Sellers, etc.

There is a delightfully informal television interview, which is still available on YouTube, where Irish journalist Gay Byrne chats to Ken Dodd and The Beatles together about the massive emergence of the Mersey scene and Beatlemania. You can see the admiration and respect on the Fab Four's faces when Ken wisecracks and ad-libs with them, even daring to make fun of the coolest cats on the planet. You can see that they are loving every minute of it. Paul McCartney paid tribute to Ken the day he died, saying that The Beatles met him on various occasions and always ended up with tears of laughter in their eyes.

It should also be remembered that not only was Ken Dodd a major Liverpudlian star before The Beatles were, but he'd had a successful chart career before them. By the time they first appeared in the British charts Ken had already had three singles in the top thirty. The most successful was 'Love Is Like a Violin', which reached number eight in 1960.

Despite his dedication to perfecting his comedy Ken was also a very good singer and had a knack of picking songs which worked well for his pitch-perfect velvety voice. In the early '50s the most popular music had come from balladeers and crooners, a tradition which dated right back to operatic singer Enrico Caruso and, later, Mario Lanza, who popularised the form by singing operatic style ballads. This evolution into soulful ballads went on well into the Swinging Sixties, with massive hits by people like Engelbert Humperdinck, Solomon King, Des O'Connor and of course Ken Dodd. These balladeers could compete in the charts and often outsell the more obvious '60s pop phenomena like The Rolling Stones, The Who, The Beach Boys, The Kinks and even The Beatles.

Ken had fourteen Top Forty singles in the Swinging Sixties. The Rolling Stones had fifteen. No wonder pop pundit Paul Gambaccini said that any singer would have been more than happy with Ken Dodd's chart career, and that was only his sideline.

Ken of course took his singing very seriously and had his voice trained by professionals. The first important London meeting Dave Forrester set up for Ken, when they realised there was a serious singing career to be had, on top of all his comedy success, was with lyricist and song publisher Jimmy Phillips (aka John Turner). Dave had met Jimmy through Eddie Calvert, when they were recording his massive hit *Oh, Mein Papa* in 1954. He was very good at finding songs for artistes. Ken liked Jimmy straight away. Influenced by the success of popular tenor David Whitfield, Ken suggested that he should perhaps record a version of the pseudo-operatic Spanish song *Granada*. Jimmy didn't think that was the right choice of song for the 'hit parade', but asked Ken to listen to a shellac demo disc of a beautiful French melody which had recently come his way, called 'Mon Coeur Est Un Violon' (literally 'my heart is a violin'). There were two sets of English lyrics – 'Violets & Violins' and 'Love Is Like a Violin'. Ken loved the song and recorded it as 'Love Is Like a Violin' on Decca Records, breaking into the 'Top Ten' in July 1960.

Paul Gambaccini notes that around that time there were other comedy performers, like Charlie Drake, Tommy Cooper and Bernard Cribbins, in the charts, but that was with comedy novelty records. Here was a hugely successful zany comedian having a hit with a serious record. Now that was a novelty.

During the '60s Ken did actually dabble in the then fashionable world of the comedy or novelty record, notably with 'Where's Me Shirt?', 'The Nikky Nokky Noo Song' and 'The Song of the Diddymen'. Strangely, despite his renown as a comedian, these were nowhere near as successful as his seriously plaintive ballads, not even registering in the charts.

Through Dave Forrester's friend, EMI music supremo Norrie Paramor, Ken later met his musical mentor, collaborator and long-time friend and record producer Norman Newell. This happy meeting caused Ken to switch to Columbia Records, where he had even greater chart success from 1963 onwards. Wheels within wheels, as they say. Agents can be very good at putting the right people together.

Ken, with new recording collaborator Norman Newell, was good at spotting the right songs for his voice and for his act. In 1963 he came across an American country & western album by Whisperin' Bill Anderson, and immediately fell in love with the title song called 'Still'. Ken recorded it with Geoff Love & His Orchestra. This was to be his first single for his new record company – Columbia (EMI). It only just scraped into the Top Forty, but it did stay in the British charts for ten weeks in 1963. Ken liked the song so much however that he played the rest of Whisperin' Bill's album to see if there were any other hidden gems which hadn't been heard in Britain. There, buried on Side 2, Track 5, was another Bill Anderson country & western composition called 'Happiness'. The rest, as they say, is history.

One day, a few years later, Ken was doing a record-signing for fans in the basement of a major London store and an American voice called out, "Mr Dodd! Mr Dodd!" Ken looked up and the man said, "My name's Bill Anderson, and you have made me a lot of money…" So, coincidentally, the two men did meet, albeit briefly.

In 2012 Whisperin' Bill Anderson came to London to record a

special BBC4 in-concert TV programme. Here's how he introduced his rendition of the song which had never been a hit in America: "When you write a song you have no idea where it might end up. Every once in a while one will get recorded by somebody who is the last person in the world you think might record one of your songs… Anybody here ever heard of a funny man by the name of Ken Dodd? How tickled I am! I never would, in all my life, have thought that this song would make it across the Atlantic Ocean. And that he would end up making a record out of it, and it would become part of his signature…" Bill then performs a very endearing countrified, acoustic, slower tempo, half-spoken version of his song 'Happiness'. You can find it on YouTube – it's worth a listen.

I asked Anne if she felt Ken was ever disappointed that he wasn't taken more seriously as a singer. Let's face it, despite his immense success, nobody ever answered, "A famous singer," to the question, "Who is Ken Dodd?" Anne says he enjoyed singing enormously, and was very proud of his chart success, but he was most proud of his achievements in comedy, so it was never a frustration for him.

It's at this point that this book gains fresh impetus, because it was right at the end of 1961 when Anne Jones first met Ken Dodd, so we have more personal insights from Anne after that time.

Sybil Anne Jones was born in 1941 into a middle-class family in the north-west of England, one of four siblings. Her mother, Erika, was German by birth, but had left Germany before the Second World War to marry Anne's English father, Tom Jones, who was a lawyer. Even though it was the mid-1930s, well before the war, their courtship was during the rise of the Third Reich, and Erika, at the tender age of just twenty, had to make an appointment at the Gestapo headquarters in Berlin to seek permission to marry an Englishman. They married in 1936, in England.

Anne had always been keen on dance, especially ballet. Her

godmother used to take her to the ballet from the age of six or seven and Anne was entranced. There was no history particularly of music or dance in the family, but whenever Anne heard music she felt she wanted to dance. By the time she was in her teens she was taking ballet classes at school. She enjoyed it so much she used to go to dance classes all day every Saturday as well. Anne knew she didn't have the perfect physical attributes to be a professional ballet dancer, but she loved it with a passion. If her father had to go on business to London all Anne could think about was that he was going to the home of the Sadler's Wells ballet school. Accepting that she wasn't going to make it as a ballerina she expanded her repertoire and learned 'character dancing' as well. This is a subdivision of classical dance, derived from European folk and traditional dancing, which has been adapted for theatrical performance onstage.

Anne had also taken piano lessons as a child. Unfortunately her first piano teacher was a strict disciplinarian who took a very academic and rigid approach to learning music, rapping Anne's knuckles with a ruler if she couldn't play her scales correctly, or recognise notes on the keyboard. The cantankerous old lady's house stank of cats and she frightened poor Anne to death with her sharp attitude, so she didn't learn very much and couldn't wait for her lessons to be over. Anne wasn't interested in musical rules and theory, she just wanted to play tunes, so she soon gave up. Fortunately her mother encouraged her to try again with a different teacher.

Anne had changed schools around the age of twelve or thirteen and her new school had a totally different approach to teaching music. At first Anne was terrified, as she had been before, in case she forgot her scales or failed to identify a note. Her new teacher noticed that she was shaking with fear. Very soon this kindly female music teacher made Anne relax and said she didn't have to learn everything so rigidly. She quickly taught Anne to understand how scales were constructed. As soon as Anne understood that basic concept everything else fell into place, and her playing came much more naturally of course. Bad teachers have an awful lot to answer for, in my opinion. In no time Anne was looking forward to piano lessons, rather than dreading them, and she very soon was one of the only pupils good enough to be playing solo piano at annual school concerts. By the age of fifteen Anne Jones was a proficient pianist and a competent, and extremely enthusiastic, stage dancer.

At Manchester High School she did well academically and undertook a sixth-form secretarial course with languages, as many young educated women were encouraged to do in those days. Despite the gender-skewed nature of her sixth-form schooling Anne still says that the most useful thing she ever learned was shorthand and typing.

Anne left full-time education at eighteen and took an office job with nationalised airline BEA, at Manchester Airport. However she was still besotted by dance and continued to attend dance classes as well. One day, still only a teenager, she was walking past the Manchester Opera House where the Bluebell Girls were appearing. The Bluebell Girls were arguably the most famous all-female British dance troupe in those days, renowned for their glamour, statuesque elegance, glitzy pizazz, and their perfectly synchronised routines. They had been founded by former dancer Margaret Leibovici, née Kelly, (known in the showbiz world simply as 'Miss Bluebell'), who ran the troupe in a very exacting way. Here's how Anne remembers that life-changing day:

I was on my way home from my weekly dance class and was carrying my bag with my shoes and dance things inside. I had recently read in a newspaper about a young girl who had met 'Miss Bluebell', and had been granted an impromptu audition, landing her a dream overnight job as a Bluebell Girl. On an absolute whim, and I still can't think what made me do it, I knocked on the stage door and asked to see Miss Bluebell. It was so exciting for a young girl with no theatrical experience just to go in through the stage door of this famous theatre. The stage doorkeeper told me that Miss Bluebell wasn't in the building, but he said she was staying at the Midland Hotel in the centre of Manchester. With all the bravado and self-

confidence of youth I walked across town to the Midland and asked if Miss Bluebell was in her room. The receptionist pointed across the foyer, and there she was, the great lady herself, talking to her troupe dance captain. Somehow I plucked up the courage to walk across, nervously apologising for interrupting, and asked how I could go about getting an audition. Miss Bluebell looked me up and down and then noticed my bag. She said, "Well if you've got your things with you dear, come to the theatre with me now." In a daze I went with her and the dance captain back to the Opera House, wondering what on earth I was doing.

"Go with the girls dear and they'll get you ready," she said when we got to the theatre. One of the dancers, Berry Cornish, who became a lifelong friend, then took me to a dressing-room and kitted me out in fishnet tights, a black daringly high-cut leotard, and stiletto heeled shoes, which was terrifying as I'd never danced in high heels before. The girls then dragged my hair up on top of my head and plonked a beehive wig on top, which made me look an inch or two taller, and told me I was ready. I'd never felt less ready for anything in my entire life, but, I'd got this far, so it was too late to back out now. Petrified I tottered down to an open space at the back of the stalls where Miss Bluebell was patiently waiting on the back row. She first instructed me to do a few chaînés. In a panic I mouthed to the other girls, "What's a chaîné?" One of them mouthed back, "Pirouette!", so I did a few of those. Next she wanted to see me do some high kicks. It's a wonder I didn't break my neck in those heels! Then she asked me to come and sit with her on the back row and asked me a bit about my family background. Suddenly, quite casually, she said, "Would you like to start work in Paris next week?" I couldn't believe it. My first reaction was to say no. "Ooh no, I can't. I haven't told my parents. No, I can't." Miss Bluebell asked where I lived, and if it was very far. When I said it was only about ten miles away she offered to come and talk to my parents in person the following day, which she did. After her reassuring visit I used that old ploy of saying to my mother, "Daddy says I can go if you'll let me go," and saying to my father,

"Mummy says she'll let me go if you let me go." By the end of the day I'd somehow persuaded them to let me become a Bluebell Girl.

I didn't actually end up dancing in Paris. At Miss Bluebell's suggestion I took a female friend as a chaperone, and we went along to stay with her in her Paris apartment. She wanted me to watch the show, so that I could get a feeling for life as a Bluebell before I joined the line-up. It frightened me to death to be honest. The theatre was packed and the atmosphere was highly charged at this slightly risqué girly Parisian extravaganza. All the Bluebells seemed so sexy, so beautiful and so impossibly tall in their huge headdresses and high heels. The revealing cut-away costumes were quite daring, and there were even topless mannequins posing in the show, not that we were expected to do that, but it was still very daunting for a young naïve girl. It was just too much for me. It seemed terribly exciting, especially when we went backstage after the show, but when Miss Bluebell asked me at breakfast the following morning whether I felt ready to join the show, I said, "No, no thank you." It's a wonder she didn't kick me! Instead she said, "Well dear, in that case, what about twelve weeks in Rome on a television show?"

How could I say no to that? So that actually became my first job as a Bluebell Girl. Ten of us on a live weekly variety show called Giardino D'Inverno (Winter Garden), *featuring in three dance numbers and a song, which we had to learn in Italian of course. The series started in January 1961, and was one of the first of its kind ever to be broadcast in Italy. Not many Italians had television sets at home then, so the cafes and restaurants would be packed with people trying to watch the show. We became minor celebrities in Rome while we were there, and I had my first very innocent minor fling with a gentlemanly local boy, who sold Olivetti typewriters, whilst studying for a law degree. He'd been in the Italian Olympic water polo team in the Rome Olympics the year before, and he took me to the enormous Olympic-size pool to teach me to dive. He wasn't successful – I still can't dive! But I did learn rudimentary Italian, which has proved very useful over the years.*

At first I'd been shy of meeting the other girls in the troupe, because I thought they would all be terribly sophisticated and worldly-wise. In fact they were a smashing bunch who made me very welcome. My new roommate Marguerite and I had so much fun together. The first night in the hotel I returned from the bathroom down the corridor and Marguerite had disappeared. I was really puzzled by her absence, but got into bed and put my book on the lace cloth covered bedside table. Suddenly the 'table' moved! I just about leapt out of my skin! What I didn't know was that Marguerite was an excellent acrobat and could bend right over backwards and hold her ankles. I saw the funny side when I recovered from the shock, and we became the best of friends.

We had to work really hard though, receiving extra help from dance captain Charmian, as we had to learn and perfect three new routines every week for the live television broadcast. It was unbelievably exciting for a young girl. There were international star guests on the show every week, like Maurice Chevalier, Connie Francis and jazz ace Lionel Hampton. I couldn't believe my luck to find myself having communal lunch with these superstars in between rehearsals. It still seemed impossible that an ordinary girl from Wilmslow was doing all this. Miss Bluebell took me under her wing and was quite maternal towards me, being very kind and understanding about my shyness.

Anne, in her usual modest, self-deprecating way, told me that she thinks Miss Bluebell was keen to give her a job because her father was a lawyer. The girls came from literally all walks of life, but Miss Bluebell, ever the businesswoman, did find that when she happened to engage daughters of professionals, like doctors, lawyers and vicars, it attracted more press interest. However there is no way that a dance troupe with the reputation of the Bluebell Girls would have signed up Anne unless her dancing was up to scratch, and unless she looked the part.

At that time though snobbery was at its peak in Britain. As Anne recalls:

When you grow up you only know the world around you, but I quickly realised that I'd had quite a privileged upbringing, compared to some of my new friends in the troupe.

In those days people still looked down on you if you went onstage as a dancer. However my father, despite his public school and Oxford education, was terribly proud of me dancing on television. He wrote to me in Rome to tell me that somebody in our local pub had seen the extensive regional publicity surrounding my signing and asked if he was the father of Anne Jones, the famous Bluebell. He thought that was marvellous – and so did I...

After the television stint in Rome, Anne was offered a summer season with the Bluebells at the Glasgow Alhambra Theatre in *The Five Past Eight Show*, supporting singer Eve Boswell and star Scottish comedian Jimmy Logan. Jimmy said they should all join Equity, the performers' union, to guarantee getting the correct rate of pay. There was another Anne Jones already registered with Equity, so Sybil Anne Jones registered her stage name as 'Sybie Jones', a name she would often use when performing in Ken's shows.

The Glasgow show was a cleverly packaged glossy variety spectacular, put together by the Howard & Wyndham Theatre Group and director Richard 'Dickie' Hurran. The idea was to move the production around the country, changing the star from time to time, in order to refresh the show and make it more relevant to that particular locale. In Glasgow Jimmy Logan had been the ideal headlining act, but in Manchester Ken Dodd was a bigger attraction. So the Jimmy Logan show morphed seamlessly into the Ken Dodd show when the *Five Past Eight Show* package, including the Bluebell Girls, moved to the Manchester Opera House for the Christmas season.

It was the last few weeks of 1961 and impressionable twenty-year-old Anne Jones was about to meet thirty-four-year-old Ken Dodd for the first time. Here's how Anne remembers the first time she set eyes on the man who would become the love of her life:

I'd heard of Ken Dodd, but I don't think I'd ever seen him on television and definitely not onstage. I knew his hit song 'Love Is Like a Violin' from the radio, so when we heard Ken was taking over the show in Manchester, me and a couple of the other girls made up a silly parody version. We'd been warming up at the Opera House one morning just after we transferred to Manchester, and then all of us Bluebells moved down off the stage and sat in the front stalls to let Ken rehearse. I still hadn't met him or even seen him at this point. He bounced out on to the stage and ran through a few of his opening lines – "How tickled I am! Have you been tickled missus?" and he was doing all these slightly cheeky lines straight down to us on the front row, and making eye contact with us girls. He was wearing a very smart, expensive-looking beige knitted sweater. Strangely, given his normal look, his hair was cut quite short, but it was thick and full. I thought, 'He looks nice.' I'm not sure whether I fancied him straight away, but I can still remember exactly how he looked that day. Perhaps I did fancy him, but hadn't yet realised it. I have no idea what he thought of me, but he did start singling me out and speaking to me fairly soon into the run. Every time Ken bumped into me he always called me 'Gladys', so I invented an equally mundane pet name for him, but it was all just in fun. Hardly love at first sight though, and we all knew he was engaged to Anita, who was usually with him in the theatre.

I do clearly remember the first time I made a real impression on Ken, and not necessarily a good one. There was a big production number – Ken singing 'Love Is Like a Violin'. It had been a top ten hit just a few months before, so it was a major feature in the show. The designer had built this massive prop violin, which stretched almost across the whole stage, and Dickie Hurran decided to drape a couple of us girls in glamorous costumes on either end of the violin, as Ken crooned his famous signature tune. I still don't know whether the stagehands had put something on there deliberately, but one night my end of the violin seemed very slippery and, while Ken was in full song, I slid gracefully off the thing and landed on my bottom with a *thump on to the stage. He never let me forget that!*

We did become friends during that Christmas season and even more so as the show moved on to Birmingham, with Ken still topping the bill.

After Birmingham the next contract with the Bluebells was going to be in Japan. You'd think that was a terribly exciting prospect for a young girl wouldn't you, but I didn't really want to go. Sadly I'd lost my father, at the age of just fifty-three, while we were away from home in Glasgow, and I deeply regretted not seeing more of him during that time.

My father Tom loved variety theatre, and he'd been looking forward to our forthcoming Christmas show at the Manchester Opera House. It's a great sadness to me that he died that August and missed meeting Ken by just four months. I did learn from my mother though that my father had been a fan of Ken, and he'd been to see him onstage, a few years earlier, at the Manchester Palace. I have fond memories of my father singing music hall songs, whilst shaving. He also loved Gilbert & Sullivan, and we would all sing his favourite songs on Sunday afternoon drives in his old Morris. Happy times.

Many years after my father died my brother Dick bought me Harold Hobson's autobiography. He was the distinguished Sunday Times *drama critic. It turns out Hobson was at university with my father, and they had been great pals. He mentions the great fun the two of them had together in his memoirs. In fact they shared a love of touring variety shows, and they were also great practical jokers. Some of Hobson's words gave me an insight into a side of my father I'd never really known: "... equally delightful was Tom Jones, a man of infinite kindness and inexhaustible fertility of fantastic imagination, he was expert at the invention of that rare kind of practical joke which injures and humiliates no-one..." How well he would have got on with Ken! Hobson goes on to tell of other madcap escapades they got up to as typical students, and adds: "Besides these amiable vagaries, Tom also had a liking for conducting his conversations in Latin." That explained why my father had actively encouraged me to pass 'O' level GCE Latin. I thought it wouldn't ever be any* use, but Ken would often come across a word in one of his beloved thesauruses, which were all over the house, and ask me if it had a Latin root. So Latin did come in useful after all. Thank you father!

I was no longer a Bluebell Girl, but I'd stayed in touch with friends at Manchester Airport, so they encouraged me to go back to BEA. It was secretarial work at first, on the ground, but when I became twenty-one I was eligible to apply for an air stewardess job, which I got, jetting off all round Europe. It was regarded as a glamorous job in those days.

I didn't want to stop performing altogether though. Ken and I stayed in touch and he was always encouraging about my showbusiness career. I'd started learning to play the guitar and I could do a few impressions, so he helped me put an act together for the clubs. You needed an hour's worth of material for the working men's clubs – three twenty-minute spots. It was mainly singing, but I'd throw in a few of my impersonations. I even appeared on Opportunity Knocks with Hughie Green in the mid-'60s. I had a couple of different stage names as a club act. First I was Sheree Starr, then I went out simply as Annabel, singing more folksy and country songs. All this time I was still working for BEA at Manchester Airport, so I was doing the clubs just as a money-making hobby really, but Ken was very supportive. We'd talk on the phone quite regularly. He always kept in touch – even when I was flying all over Europe with the airline, and that was long before mobile phones of course. The other cabin crew would tease me when we checked into a foreign hotel – "There's a message for you Anne from 'guess who'..."

Looking back I think I was a bit of a loner when I was with BEA. Maybe it was because I was having to be discreet about Ken, but I didn't go out drinking with the other cabin crew – I have never been a big drinker. I didn't want to discuss relationships really, so I was quite happy going off on my own. If we were in, say, Berlin I'd take myself off to the opera. I'd lots of friends but I kept myself to myself I suppose.

It was difficult because I'd fallen for Ken, but he was engaged.

I didn't have any other boyfriends in the '60s, so I was always really pleased if our diaries matched and we got a chance to see one another. Ken was always a great listener. In the very early days, just after he and I had met in Manchester, my best friend from schooldays, Pat Stubbs (neé Jackson), threw a big 21ˢᵗ birthday bash at the farm where she lived with her parents in Cheshire. I'll always remember the date, 4ᵗʰ February 1962, because it ended up being such an important turning point in my life. Pat invited Ken along to her party as a celebrity guest, and he turned up with his writer pal Eddie Braben. Naturally enough Ken and I got chatting, and I think I told him my whole life story, all about my previous relationships, such as they were, and he just sat and listened. He asked me all about my life and my family, and he really was listening because he remembered it all later. It wasn't the usual 'me, me, me,' thing that you get with a lot of stars, so I fell for him. But I couldn't forget that he had a long-standing fiancée, which made life complicated.

I knew Anita of course because she had often been at the theatre with Ken when we were doing the show together. She was a nice person. I wasn't proud of the fact that I'd fallen in love with somebody who was engaged. You can't help it though, can you? Love finds you. You don't go looking for it.

Anne finds it a little difficult to talk about that period, and she says she and Ken rarely spoke about those early days getting to know one another, but I think it was almost inevitable that they would fall in love. Heterosexual male entertainers of that time had many temptations when they were away on tour with glamorous chorus line girls, and Ken had always enjoyed the company of women. Anne's dad had died tragically young so perhaps she was subconsciously in need of a father figure in her life. Ken was charming, sensitive, witty, intelligent and kind. Anne was beautiful, funny, and endearingly naïve. It's no wonder they got on so well and their relationship blossomed. Anita Boutin and Ken had been engaged from quite a young age, but they hadn't got married, so perhaps deep down they both knew that things weren't quite right between them. Ken was loyal though and didn't want to split from Anita, who had been incredibly supportive in his formative years as a professional entertainer. Life can be complicated.

Despite complications in his personal life, the 1960s was a fantastic time for Ken Dodd. Beatlemania had kicked in during 1963, and the whole Mersey Sound was rocking the world. London was swinging, Britain was cool, young people were having a ball, and Liverpool was regarded as the most fertile breeding ground on the planet for popular culture. Ken had already made it in his own right, long before The Beatles conquered the world, but it didn't do any entertainer's career any harm to say they came from Merseyside during that exciting colourful decade. A young Jimmy Tarbuck burst on to our television screens from the London Palladium, finding overnight fame, not only sounding like a Beatle, but looking like one as well. Ken had always been proud of his home city, so he embraced its newfound fame and glory, which probably helped him reach his dizziest heights in the mid-'60s.

Perhaps at long last the north/south divide was becoming a little more blurred. It hadn't gone, but the Fab Four had proved to southerners that not all northerners wear clogs, flat caps and mufflers, race whippets and breed homing pigeons. Ken was still regarded as a northern comedian, but perhaps now was the time to test the water 'down south'. He was a national star thanks to television and radio, but he hadn't yet conquered the all-important West End of London, despite having successfully played all over the country, including several theatres in the capital's suburbs. It's hard to imagine what a brave move it was at the time, but in 1965 Ken took the ultimate plunge by agreeing to star in a run at the London Palladium, then the undisputed number one British venue for the very best international variety entertainment. 'The temple of showbusiness' as Ken called it. It was a bold decision, and he was understandably nervous about it. What if it failed? Would his success so far all tumble down around him? There were those who had their doubts and thought he'd never crack London. However Dave Forrester, his previously cautious agent, at long last thought Ken was ready for the biggest challenge of his career.

Of course he needn't have worried. The show, entitled *Doddy's Here*, was a triumph. The show opened with the famous revolving stage revealing Ken in a yellow Rolls Royce. His extreme first night nerves were buoyed by a rousing welcome from a huge number of Liverpudlians who had made the journey south in coaches to support their local comic hero on his opening night at the Palladium.

It's no exaggeration to say he took London by storm. The sell-out run was so successful it just kept getting extended, week after week. Showbiz supremo Lord Michael Grade said, "I was a young reporter in my late teens, and I'd heard Ken on the radio, so I bought tickets to go to the Palladium to see him. I sat there and was just paralysed laughing. In fact I went four or five times to see him, again and again."

Serious theatre critics, like Michael Billington of *The Guardian*, and Jonathan Miller writing in the *New Statesman,* gave *Doddy's Here* well-deserved rave reviews. Famous stars took their seats to witness the phenomenon for themselves, even Harold Wilson, the Prime Minister, came along. This made Ken the comedy toast of London. Bill Shankly took the Liverpool FC squad to see the show before their nerve-wracking 1965 FA Cup Final match at Wembley Stadium, which they won, helping keep the astonishing profile of Liverpool up in the stratosphere. Legendary '60s playwright John Osborne brought the entire cast of *Meals on Wheels*, a comedy play he was directing at the Royal Court Theatre, to see Ken work at the Palladium so that they could watch and learn from a master of stagecraft and comic timing.

Even Bob Hope, Jack Benny and Bing Crosby took a break from busy visits from the States to see *Doddy's Here*. Afterwards Bob Hope was asked by the press what he thought of the show. He said, with his usual mock grandiose wit, "Oh, it was just great... Every laugh was like a knife in my side..."

In the end Ken broke the record for the longest uninterrupted Palladium run by a solo performer. That record still stands to this day. There is some dispute as to exactly how many weeks it was however. Ken and his friends and colleagues have always said it was forty-two weeks, although the Palladium archivist thinks it was slightly less, due to a short break, but I don't think I will get too many arguments by sticking with the much-quoted figure of forty-two incredible weeks.

Lord John Birt, former Director General of the BBC, was another fan: "Ken was the greatest comedian of his time. He came to the London Palladium for forty-two weeks – a London theatre, not a Liverpool theatre. To my knowledge nobody had ever done that and it's hard to imagine anybody ever doing it again."

It was a staggering feat, but physically and mentally exhausting. He had been performing the show twice-nightly, every night except Sunday, with an additional matinee on Saturday, making an astonishing thirteen shows a week. Most current comedians would think that sort of gruelling schedule completely unworkable, and yet Ken managed it for the best part of a year.

When you're riding on the crest of a wave and you are young and out to prove yourself it's hard to say no to work, so Ken agreed to a week on radio, during the Palladium run, to present and guest host *Housewife's Choice*, which was one of the most popular daytime shows on the BBC Light Programme, as it was still called in those days. (Two years later it would be re-branded as Radio 2.)

Not being used to this kind of free-wheeling, off-the-cuff radio presenting, Ken went in every morning well prepared with a mountain of scripted comedy material that he and Eddie Braben had sweated over. In the end the powers-that-be had to have a quiet word with Ken and remind him that it was supposed to be predominantly a music request show and that he should reduce the amount he was speaking between records. The normal fourteen music tracks per hour had been reduced by Ken to ten per hour. There were sufficient letters of praise for Ken's brief tenure however to justify him doing so much talking. Typical Ken though.

The trouble was this extra radio work meant a lot of preparation, plus early mornings for Ken at BBC Broadcasting House, after a late finish from his second house at the Palladium the night before. Body and soul can only take so much and it did take a toll on his health, with a doctor eventually treating him for mental exhaustion. When the record-breaking Palladium run was over, on the doctor's advice, Ken treated himself to a much-needed week of total rest and recuperation in Forest Mere, a luxury health spa in Hampshire.

One of the spa treatments was an unappetising vegetable diet to clear out the system. Ken remembered thinking it wasn't really working and went for a leisurely walk in the wooded grounds. Suddenly he realised he needed to get back to the distant main building very quickly indeed! The diet was working after all...

Undeterred by this brief health hiccup, Ken went straight into a marathon pantomime season of *Humpty Dumpty* at the Birmingham Hippodrome. And they were marathon panto runs in those days, starting at Christmas and sometimes going on until Easter.

Ken had one particularly memorable anecdote from that panto season. George Bartram, his press agent, was based in Birmingham, but, weeks into the run, he had hardly seen Ken, despite the fact the Hippodrome was just round the corner. George phoned him and suggested they get a meal together between the afternoon matinee and the evening performance. Ken said he couldn't leave the theatre, but there was a restaurant inside, where they could hide away, hopefully incognito. Ken found a quiet corner and had his back to the other diners, to maintain his privacy. The trouble was George Bartram had a rather loud voice and a broad Brummie accent. Ken kept telling him to keep his voice down, because he didn't want to attract attention their way. Suddenly George boomed like a foghorn, "Do you know Ken, in all these weeks you've been 'ere, we've had practically no social intercourse at all!" Much to Ken's embarrassment the entire restaurant turned to stare, having misheard the statement.

Ken had to take a flat in London for part of the long Palladium season, in Kensington in fact, and he spent some of those months in a Mayfair hotel, so it was probably the longest period of his life where he was living away from Knotty Ash. He did manage to get home to 'Oak House' every Sunday though, as that was his one day off.

There was one very special night when Ken's mum and dad travelled south to see their boy triumphing at the Palladium. Sarah and Arthur Dodd were photographed proudly boarding the train at Liverpool Lime Street for a 'local boy makes good' story for the Liverpool press. Sadly Sarah died in 1968, but Ken was thrilled that she had seen him star in his own record-breaking show at the London Palladium, as well as his first appearance in the same theatre, by Royal Command.

If you had to pick one year that was the pinnacle of Ken's achievements in showbusiness you would have to say 1965. Ken himself said that year changed his life and put him at the top of the tree. On the strength of his phenomenal season at the Palladium he was invited to appear in front of the Queen on that year's televised *Royal Variety Performance*, which was a much bigger deal at that time. It was compered by fellow Liverpudlian Jimmy Tarbuck. Ken was rightly praised as one of the show-stealing stars of that particular line-up. The Variety Club of Great Britain made him their showbusiness personality of the year, and he also had his own prestigious BBC television special in prime time on Christmas Night, years before Morecambe & Wise had ever done such a thing. He was extremely proud of a letter from the BBC congratulating him on record-breaking viewing figures for that show.

The Queen was obviously rapidly becoming a Ken Dodd fan because he received an invitation to perform at one of the private functions at Windsor Castle for the Royal Family – their Christmas party. It must be quite unnerving because the acts perform in close proximity to the Queen and the other Royals. Ken remembered that as he sang 'Happiness', the Queen was joining in and tapping the arms of her chair in time to the music. Wouldn't it be nice if we could all invite our favourite acts to come along to entertain us in our own living rooms?

The other astounding achievement which happened for Ken Dodd in 1965 was his runaway chart success with 'Tears'. It was his eighth Top Forty hit single, but it was the first to go to Number One. It stayed there too, for five long weeks, and remained in the charts for nearly six months. I still find it an incredible fact that it was the third best-selling single, in this country, of the entire Swinging Sixties, a decade renowned for its hugely popular chart music. 'Tears' is the solitary non-Beatles single in the '60s Top Five bestsellers, and was only outsold in Britain by two Beatlemania blockbusters: 'She Loves You' and 'I Want to Hold Your Hand'. Incredible!

The '60s continued to be a good time for all Liverpudlian entertainers, especially The Beatles and Ken Dodd. Ken returned to the London Palladium in 1967, 'The Summer of Love', with *Doddy's Here Again*, and continued to consolidate on his success down south and nationally with more television and radio series. As Anne says he was married to the business, so it didn't bother him that he never stopped working.

Despite the fact that it was a complicated time on a personal level, Anne has very fond memories of the 1960s:

I would visit 'Oak House' as often as work permitted. Mr and Mrs Dodd were very welcoming. It always was Mr Dodd and Mrs Dodd, by the way, never Arthur or Sarah, that's just how it was with that generation. You had to respect your elders, but they were very friendly and kind to me. Mrs Dodd was lovely, just delightful, and a very good cook. Ken would joke that I only came for his mum's dinners.

Men weren't much help in the kitchen in those days, in fact they could be a positive hindrance. I remember Mrs Dodd telling me that Mr Dodd would occasionally come into the kitchen, while she was cooking, to play her a piece he'd been practising on his saxophone. One day he came in to play her a tricky piece he'd just mastered, just as she was taking a big Sunday roast out of the oven. As she opened the oven door the steam engulfed Mr Dodd and his prized saxophone, but still he played on, all steamed up, getting in her way as she carried the heavy dish with hot bubbling fat to the table. She was very encouraging to all of them, but there are limits!

Mrs Dodd was terribly proud of Ken and she loved doing things for him, like helping him pack a case with all his clean clothes when he was working away. In the early days of television, when everything was live, Ken would phone home right after the show and ask what they thought. Mrs Dodd would just tell him it was wonderful. It didn't matter if anything had gone wrong, or wasn't quite as good as it should have been, she'd always say it was wonderful and marvellous.

Mr Dodd was very funny, always clowning around and being witty. He had a real twinkle about him and a great sense of humour. In fact I don't think he realised just how funny he was. He was probably a bit more honest than Mrs Dodd with his comments about Ken's performances, but he was always tremendously supportive. He was very clever with his hands too and kept making props for Ken long after the fame came along. I remember in the '60s, when all the groups, especially The Beatles, were at their peak, Mr Dodd made Ken a fake electric guitar. It looked just like the real thing, but when Ken ran on, pretending to be a pop star singing, "yeah, yeah, yeah!" and hit the guitar strings for a dramatic opening chord, the whole thing would fall apart, which got a huge laugh because it was so unexpected. It was held together with magnets, so it was easy to reassemble after the show. Mr Dodd was very clever that way.

Later in life Mr Dodd became a bit set in his ways, but he was always nice to me. I'd go down to the bookies and put a little flutter on the horses for him. He loved all that. It got a bit difficult though in the 1970s because he refused to accept decimalised currency so I'd have to convert all his complicated scribbled instructions for accumulator bets from pounds, shillings and pence when I got to the betting shop.

I became extremely fond of Mr Dodd in his later years and I would sometimes stay over to look after him when his failing health became *a major issue, towards the end of the 1970s. Because of this I was sometimes the one who could get him to listen and see reason. He'd got to the point where he didn't want any upheaval so he was quite obstructive when Ken decided to get central heating installed into 'Oak House'. I suppose a former coal merchant didn't really approve of gas central heating! Anyway I was the one who managed to persuade him that Ken was only doing it to make living more comfortable for him, so in the end he agreed and he stopped grumbling.*

When I visited the house in the '60s Eddie Braben would usually be there. If it was winter Ken and he would be either side of a roaring fire, throwing ideas at one another, making each other laugh out loud, and furiously scribbling things down. They bounced off each other so well. It was a joy to watch.

Ken and Eddie were very close in those days. In fact Ken always said he was responsible for Eddie meeting his second wife. Tragically his first wife had died very young, but he met his second wife Deidree while she was one of the George Mitchell Singers in Ken's 1964 show at the Royal Court Theatre in Liverpool. Eddie had phoned a topical gag about Harold Wilson through to Ken in the theatre wings, during the show. Ken quickly scribbled it on to the back of his hand and then said, "I've got to go! I'm on! Speak to this girl!", and thrust the phone at Deidree, who happened to be standing there, waiting to go onstage. Eddie liked her voice so much he came to the theatre the very next night to meet her and see if her face was as appealing as her voice. It was love at first sight, and they married after a six-month whirlwind romance.

In many ways Ken and Eddie were ahead of their time. They would come up with some really way-out notions for gags and sketches. Sometimes I'd think, 'Is that funny?', but I knew better than to interfere. They had a lovely relationship. Like a lot of comedy writers Eddie was a frustrated performer himself, but he was quite shy. They had developed a great way of working together. Ken might have the kernel of an idea and then Eddie would work it up, instinctively knowing how Ken would perform it. It was a shame when they stopped working together, and that rift wasn't how it has often been portrayed. It has been said that Ken sacked Eddie or that they fell out and Eddie stormed off. Neither of those versions of the story are true.

Eddie had been a bit upset when he discovered that Ken had received a pay increase for writing for some series or other, and he hadn't, but Ken was the star of the show and I think Ken thought that Eddie was perfectly capable of negotiating for himself. This would be around 1968 or 1969. Coincidentally, at the same time, Morecambe & Wise had been abandoned by their writers Sid Green and Dick Hills. Eric and Ernie had just moved over from ITV with Sid and Dick and had made their first series together for the BBC, then poor Eric had that heart attack. The writers thought he would never work again so they went back to ITV. Eric was always hurt by their callousness. Apparently they never spoke to Eric and Ernie about it – they just went. Of course Eric did recover and wanted to get back to work for the BBC, but they now didn't have writers. Bill Cotton was in charge in those days and he could be quite ruthless and manipulative, so he took advantage of the temporary upset between Ken and Eddie and persuaded Eddie to have a go at writing for Morecambe & Wise. Of course the rest is history, but I know Ken felt very let down and blamed Bill Cotton. It all became a bit unpleasant and he never really forgave Bill. Ken certainly didn't want to get rid of Eddie, as has been said, because they were right in the middle of writing a series together.

Ken and Eddie stayed in touch as friends – Christmas cards, birthday cards, and the odd phone call, but Eddie was too busy with Morecambe & Wise to write with Ken any more. Of course it left Ken with a major hole to fill.

He urgently needed new writers, so Ken put an advert in The Stage *and other trade papers, anonymously of course. Well we were inundated with literally hundreds of replies, but, unfortunately, most of the jokes they sent were not suitable for radio or television, or were plagiarised old jokes that had been around for years. Some* of them even sent bits of Ken's own material, not knowing who they were sending them to.

It was all a bit overwhelming. I remember I helped by sending out acknowledgements to all these hopeful comedy writers, thanking them for their interest, and promising to contact them again if any of their material was ever used. Ken did appreciate the efforts of these total strangers and of course understood how difficult it is to create good original comedy, but it was like sorting the wheat from the chaff – and there was an awful lot of chaff! In fairness there was the odd gem, which he paid for and used, and there were a couple of writers who Ken felt were worth contacting and working with, but nobody quite replaced the magic he'd had with Eddie Braben, and of course none of them lived close enough to have that daily face-to-face contact, which had been so productive.

Norman Beedle and Steve Tombs were probably the best finds from that advert. Norman was a funny man from Hull, a real character with that Yorkshire droll wit. He worked with Ken quite a lot after that, and there were others, but some of them were sporadic and hit and miss, not nearly as prolific and dedicated as Eddie had always been.

John Pye was another regular writer from the 1970s onwards. John and his wife Jennifer ran card shops as their main source of income, but they loved coming along to the shows and they became close friends of ours. John would even have small walk-on parts in the stage shows as Ken's butler, and Jenny would help run our theatre merchandising.

Another thing that I remember about visiting 'Oak House' in the '60s were the dogs. Ken had always liked dogs. His close friend Peter Rogan once said, "Ken Dodd without a dog would be like a dinner without spuds." In fact the whole family liked dogs. Mr and Mrs Dodd preferred boxer dogs. I can remember when I first visited the house Mrs Dodd would be vacuuming round the house with a cute boxer pup called Nicky tucked under one arm.

Ken liked poodles. They are intelligent dogs. He bought his first *poodle, Touché, in Torquay, around 1960, not really thinking about how he was going to look after him while he was working away from home. It was never really a problem though, because all the dogs got on and there was always someone to feed them and let them out at 'Oak House'.*

In fact they could let themselves back into the house. I remember Mr Dodd being really confused as to how they were getting in and why the door would be left gaping open. It was ages before the mystery was solved. There were two poodles by that point and Nicky the boxer had grown up. The back door into the kitchen was an old latch barn door. What they discovered was happening was that the poodles would wait by the door while Nicky jumped up with one paw on the door frame and the other paw on the latch, which he'd learned to press down. His weight then sent the door flying open. The poodles would dash through before Nicky landed on top of them and they'd be in. They can be quite clever can dogs when they want something badly enough. He could even open the internal door into the living area, which had a round knob that he could turn with his mouth. The trouble is boxer dogs are rather slobbery and you'd put your hand on the doorknob and get covered in saliva. It was disgusting. So Mr Dodd swapped the round doorknob for one of those brass rings that you have to lift and twist. Of course it was only a matter of days before Nicky had learned how to bang against the door to make the ring bounce upwards, then catch it in his mouth and twist it. Very crafty he was. They couldn't train him to do anything, but he could learn what he wanted to learn. Apart from closing doors behind him of course.

Nicky the boxer attained a certain degree of national fame himself in 1966. Famed '60s pop portrait photographer David Farrell was commissioned by Columbia Records to take the sleeve photo for Ken's new vinyl L.P. release. He took Ken all over Liverpool snapping different photographs as contenders for the front cover. On their return to 'Oak House' Farrell spotted Nicky and got Ken to pose with him in the garden. That ended up being the chosen photograph for the front of Ken's album *Hits for Now and Always*.

There was one great sadness in Ken's triumphant decade. In May 1968 his beloved 'mini-mum', Sarah, died of cancer, aged just seventy-one. Anne remembers it was a very sad year:

I'd become a friend of the family by that time and I was very fond of both Mr and Mrs Dodd. It was terribly sad when she became ill. It upset Ken, but he was always able to compartmentalise himself, so he could carry on working as if nothing was wrong, but then he'd come home and lock himself away, grieving. Her death wasn't unexpected. We knew she was terminally ill, so you do a lot of your grieving in the last few months of their lives. It was very upsetting for both Ken and Mr Dodd, and of course Billy and June as well. I was upset too. She'd been like a second mum to me. Mr Dodd was from that generation where you didn't show your emotions, especially men, so he bottled up all his grief. They'd actually been a very devoted couple, but they weren't demonstrative about it. I only ever saw them kiss each other once. Mrs Dodd was going away for a few days with June and her family to the Isle of Man, and Mr Dodd gave her a peck as he saw them off, but Mrs Dodd shied away, saying, "Get off with you! Don't be so silly!" They were very close and devoted in other ways though. They had pet names for one another – 'Sal' and 'Arty' – but they definitely didn't go in for displays of affection.

The good thing was that Mrs Dodd lived long enough to see Ken get to the very top. He was so pleased that she came down to London to see him at the Palladium, and, later that same year, appearing before the Queen, by Royal Command. She was terribly proud of him.

Harriet Dodd, the grand matriarch, Ken's paternal grandmother

Watercolour painting of 'Oak House' in 1910

Arthur Dodd, Ken's father

Sarah Dodd, Ken's mother

Above: Older brother Billy & Ken

Above right: Billy, June & Ken

Right: Ken

Below: Ken's Knotty Ash primary
school photo, 1934

Ken with his mother and father at nephew
David's christening, 1956

Ken and his mini-mum

Ken & Billy, hiking in North Wales

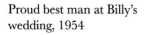

Proud best man at Billy's
wedding, 1954

Ken & Charlie Brown's first business card, circa 1935

The advert which started it all

Charlie Brown & Ken
helping Arthur make
props in the attic

EARLY PERFORMANCES...

An early performance at
The Oak Tree pub in Huyton

Professor Yaffle Chuckabutty

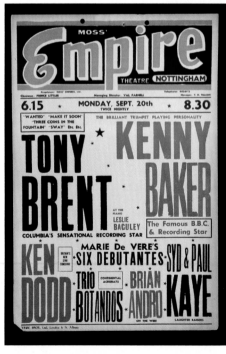

First week of professional life, 1954

KEN DODD

Above: The iconic 1960s Doddy image, as featured on the London Palladium Wall of Fame

Above right: Programme for local show, circa 1960, later inscribed with comments to comedian John Martin by Paul McCartney

With The Beatles again, during Beatlemania, circa 1963

KEN DODD
COLUMBIA RECORDS

Record cover with Nicky the boxer, 1966

Doddy's Here, London Palladium, 1965
& *Doddy's Here Again*, 1967

The great and the good all wanted to be there   Prime Minister Harold Wilson

STARS WHO CAME TO SEE KEN AT THE PALLADIUM...

Jack Benny

Bud Flanagan

Tony Bennett

ROYAL SHOWS...

Proud parents Sarah & Arthur Dodd
travel to London to see Ken's first Royal
Variety Performance, 8th November
1965, Ken's 38th birthday

Rehearsing their bow to the Royal Box

Royal Variety Performance, 2006

Above: Royal Gala Show, Liverpool 1971

Right: Royal Variety Performance 1999

Below: Royal Variety Performance, 1986

Ken with fiancée
Anita Boutin

Writer Eddie Braben,
Ken & BBC TV producer
Michael Hurll

Marathon joke-telling
Mirthquake,
Royal Court Theatre,
Liverpool, 1974

Ken as Malvolio in *Twelfth Night*, 1971

Ken with his 1970s straight man,
'Diddy' David Hamilton

Anne as a Bluebell Girl

Anne with her mother, Erika Jones

Anne (left) with her family, just before she became a Bluebell

Chapter 6:

HERE COME THE DIDDYMEN

During the 1960s, thanks to radio, television and his chart career, Ken Dodd had consolidated his success and established himself as one of the country's top entertainers. It can't be stressed strongly enough though how important the two staples of pantomime and seaside resort summer seasons were in those glory days of variety theatre. A good summer season, a lengthy panto run and, if you were lucky, a television series every year was more than enough for most successful performers. Both of those long-running lucrative theatre diary-fillers were of course very much family entertainment. Either families on holiday going to see a seaside show at the end of the pier, or parents taking their even younger kids to the pantomime, which was often a child's first experience of live theatre.

Ken knew that he had already developed enormous appeal to the parents, but he felt he didn't have as much to offer their children. He decided he needed something new in the act to appeal to 'the little people', as he called them.

With his love of surreal whimsy – remember his favourite book was *The Wind in the Willows* – he had already started inventing a population of gnome-like dwarfs for his hometown of Knotty Ash. Although Knotty Ash is completely real it does have a mythical, magical sound to its name. Ken started doodling sketches of these small imaginary inhabitants, who all seemed to come out looking like his Great Uncle Jack. Jack was a real local character, well-known to everybody around. He was unusually short-limbed, and therefore short in height. He enjoyed his pint, so he was quite round and had a bit of a tummy, plus he always wore a tall hat to give himself an extra couple of inches. I'm guessing by now you can see where this is leading.

In the Dodd household, right from Ken being a boy himself, the whole family used a local Merseyside word 'diddy' to describe anything that was small, cute, quaint or lovable, so it was a natural step for Ken to call his diminutive Great-Uncle-Jack-lookalike creations 'Diddymen'.

Ken took his rough sketches of the Diddymen, one of which he'd scrawled on a napkin in a posh restaurant, to a talented graphic artist in nearby Warrington, called John Geering. John turned Ken's doodles into polished drawings, which became the basis for all the stage Diddymen costumes, and later the TV puppets and kids' cartoon strip characters for the weekly *TV Comic* and *TV Comic Annual*. Sadly John Geering died young and another artist called Kevin Lavender took up the mantle. He did all the drawings for the Diddymen comics which Ken produced.

Ken soon let his ever-fertile imagination run riot and invented a whole Diddyman universe with specific characters who ran the jam butty mines, gravy wells, snuff quarries, moggy ranches and broken biscuit repair works. I feel sure these delicious sounding places of work were all an affectionate homage to Ken's other favourite whimsical book, written by Lewis Carroll, *Alice's Adventures in Wonderland*, where there was a wry reference at the Mad Hatter's tea-party to 'treacle wells'.

Ken started talking about the Diddymen onstage, but they first actually appeared, in their own right, on radio in the mid-'60s, where of course they couldn't be seen. Ken did all the voices himself, speeded up electronically to give them a higher pitch, which seemed to fit little diddy people. He gave them distinct accents so that they were distinguishable from one another – rough, tough Irishman 'Mick the Marmaliser'; Little Evan from Llantickleechlan in Wales; Harry Cott, the west country bumpkin; posh English gent, the

Honourable Nigel Ponsonby-Smallpiece; Wee Hamish McDiddy from Invercockyleekie in Scotland; and the most Doddy-like of all the Diddymen – Ken's 'mini-me', buck-toothed Dicky Mint. There were others over the years, but they were probably the most notable.

I'm not quite sure how Knotty Ash had become the regional melting pot and central hub for such diverse diddy men from all four corners of the United Kingdom, or how an all-male population wasn't destined for imminent extinction, but it doesn't pay to analyse children's characters too deeply.

Ken recorded 'The Song of the Diddymen' in 1965. It wasn't a big hit, but it became synonymous with his creations and in fact their signature tune when they starred in their own TV series a few years later.

By this time, including the second 1967 run at the Palladium, Ken was engaging various children's theatrical schools, local to the different theatres, to provide talented young kids who would dress up in padded rotund costumes, plus big hats, and dance and sing as 'Ken Dodd's Diddymen' onstage.

In the London area Ken would often use diddy kids from the Young Set Theatre School, run by the strict and very exacting Babette Langford, mother of entertainer and actor Bonnie Langford. After the opening night of a season in Wimbledon an irate mother came to the stage door, demanding to see Mr Dodd. It turned out she thought her daughter was going to be onstage as one of the Young Set Diddymen and she had bought tickets for the entire family to see her Diddy debut. The somewhat pushy mum was distraught when there was no sign of her offspring, and was demanding an explanation. Babette Langford intervened and said, "The opening night had to be perfect, and your daughter simply wasn't good enough for the first team…" And that, as they say, is showbusiness…

Closer to home Diddy kids were supplied for twenty-five years by the Russell Leite Theatre School in Manchester, run by Margaret Russell and Judy Leite; and, more recently, the Liverpool Theatre School, under the guidance of Norah Button.

In the very early days of the Diddymen, the Liverpool Theatre School was run by a remarkable old lady, a former dancer herself, known as 'Madam Vera'. Ken used to go along to audition kids, but found the deafening noise of all the excited children positively overwhelming. He once asked Madam Vera how she coped with all that ear-splitting racket, with the kids all shouting and screaming. The elderly lady tapped on a small box in her breast pocket and knowingly winked. It was an old-fashioned hearing-aid, which she could turn off when the noise became unbearable.

Naturally enough there were amusing moments working with children's theatre schools, although it wasn't always the children who created the drama, as Anne recalls:

During one performance at the Arcadia Theatre in Llandudno, Ken was getting ready to close the first half of the show. His perennial signal that he was going into the interval was to blow a kiss with both hands to the entire audience. That was my cue to tell the backstage staff to bring down the curtain. I knew the cue was about to come, so I looked around and realised there was no stage manager handy to take my instruction. However Judy Leite, one of the principals of the Diddymen's theatre school, happened to be standing in the wings. Judy was a diminutive figure – slight and petite – and she was getting on in years by this time. I quickly managed to figure out which rope was controlling which curtain, and found the rope for the 'house tabs', ready to bring the curtain down in front of Ken. We were getting closer and closer to Ken's cue, so I asked Judy to grab hold of the rope while I signalled to Ken to move back a little, so that the curtain didn't come down and land on his head. My intention, the moment Ken gave the kiss cue and stepped back, was to dash over to help Judy with the rope to bring the curtain down in front of him. However Judy must have released the safety catch, and she suddenly shot ten feet up in the air, clinging for dear life on to the rope. It was like something out of a Marx Brothers film! Of course the curtain had gone part way down, half covering Ken, who was looking confused onstage, and glaring off into the wings. I couldn't leave poor Judy dangling there however, so I grabbed her legs and pulled her back down, which of course meant the curtain shot back up, leaving Ken, who had now given the cue to bring the curtain down, looking exposed and rather embarrassed in front of the audience. My concern, just at the moment, was not the egg on Ken's face, but poor Judy. Fortunately she was fine and Ken had to walk off, in full view, wondering what on earth was going on backstage.

Another time, at a theatre in Mansfield, I had just done my singing spot in the show, and Neville King, the hilarious, anarchic ventriloquist, had gone on. I went to my dressing-room, where our little black poodle was patiently waiting, and took off my dress. Suddenly somebody opened the door and the dog shot out and ran straight on to the stage. The spotlight operators assumed it was part of Neville's act and focussed a 'follow spot' on the dog, who stood there, transfixed in this bright pool of light, panting. Of course Neville was clever enough to cope with the situation, and started giving the dog a voice, but I was panicking that I'd ruined his act. I'd wrapped an old dressing-gown round me for modesty, and had run into the wings, but I couldn't go onstage, so I spotted Margaret Russell in the wings on the opposite side of the stage, waiting to give the kids their cue for the upcoming Diddymen number. I was mouthing to Margaret and frantically pointing at the dog, who was getting big laughs, courtesy of Neville King's voice for him. Margaret wasn't dressed for the stage either, wearing comfy pom-pom slippers, but she was slightly more appropriately dressed than I was, so she marched onstage, picked up the dog under one arm, and marched off again, with Neville making funny noises to sound like her slippers squeaking and squelching, to a massive round of applause.

Ken liked to encourage the children in the show and he'd devise special costumed routines for the Diddymen, even letting the more talented kids sing and do quick impressions. Over the years there were Diddy wartime medleys, Diddy music hall tributes, Diddy circus routines, even a Diddy pantomime. A favourite Diddy routine of Ken's was 'comedy heads'. Prop maker Tony Stringfellow sculpted rubber heads of famous comedians, which the kids wore over the appropriate costume. Ken would sing the Stephen Sondheim classic, 'Comedy Tonight', and point out the different characters, with a spoken phrase for each one. Anne recalls there were some amusing moments approving new 'comedy heads' for the line-up:

Tony Stringfellow's model workshop was in the Midlands, so if he had a new 'head' to show Ken we would arrange to meet up in the car park at the Hilton Park service station on the M6, as we were passing through. This was usually after a show, so very late at night and in the pitch black. Tony would park his van in front of us and open the back doors so that we could shine our headlights on the new clay mould, for approval. Ken would inspect the life-size bust for accuracy and suggest improvements, always the perfectionist. We ended up with ten of those heads, so these night-time meetings became a regular occurrence, sometimes in the pouring rain. Other twilight travellers would approach to see what was going on. There could be quite a crowd, once they recognised Ken. I'm not sure what they made of it all – it must have seemed a very strange moonlit ritual...

The Diddy kids worked well as a novelty chorus line, and made a massive visual impact, but they didn't really allow Ken to interact with individual Diddymen characters, so their comedy potential was limited onstage and on television.

At that time there was a successful variety puppet act called The Roger Stevenson Marionettes. Roger Stevenson, a master puppeteer, had heard Ken's diddy characters on radio and also the Diddymen song. He lived in Southport, which isn't too far from Liverpool, so he arranged a meeting with Ken where he suggested making string puppets of the Diddymen, to really bring the characters to life. It was Ken's busy year, 1965, towards the end of the record-breaking

Palladium season, but Ken could see the potential and was interested enough to ask to see a prototype. The first puppet that Roger made was Dicky Mint, which is presumably why he was modelled on Ken himself. Roger took Dicky along to the theatre, where Ken was appearing that night. Ken liked the look of the puppet and said they should see what sort of a reaction he got from an audience, so that night they concocted a short routine where Ken spoke to Dicky, who just reacted and jumped around, operated of course by Roger. They hadn't had time to record a voice track for Dicky, so he wasn't able to speak, but he got a good enough reaction from the kids in the audience to warrant Ken giving Roger the go-ahead to make more of the Diddy characters into marionettes.

The first to be seen on television was Nigel Ponsonby-Smallpiece in 1966. As a supposed member of the aristocracy he was given a top hat, a monocle, a silver-topped cane, and a distinct lack of chin. Dicky Mint also made an appearance on the same show. Again the reaction was so good that the first group of Diddymen puppets became a regular fixture, featuring in their own short spot in all of Ken's TV shows, *Live from Blackpool*, in 1966. The early prototypes didn't have moving mouths, but, a year later, when the BBC said they would like to make a children's series based around Ken and his Diddymen, Roger set to work and made a whole new set of sophisticated puppets which were much more detailed and therefore more versatile for close-up shots and dialogue.

In 1967 a pilot was made by the BBC children's department in Manchester for the puppet series *Ken Dodd & the Diddymen*, which was filmed on a building site in Cheshire. The first series of ten-minute programmes was quickly commissioned, on the strength of this strong pilot show, so the BBC art department set about building the Knotty Ash diddy village, in a studio, which was in fact an old converted church in Dickenson Road. Coincidentally that same studio had been the first home of *Top of the Pops* in 1964. The diddy village was a fantastic lavish construction. The beautiful diddy houses were approaching five-feet high, and made in such a way that the puppeteers could lean over them to animate the figures outside. They even used a large platform on a forklift truck to elevate the puppeteers invisibly above the set for wide shots. Ken spent a lot of his time down on the studio floor, interacting with and talking to his diminutive diddy creations.

Once again Ken did all the Diddymen's voices, which were speeded up to give a higher pitch, in the same way they had been for radio. The dialogue was then edited together to fit the script. The puppeteers and Ken would work to this pre-recorded audio track to create the shows, with Ken adding his own lines in his normal voice as they went along.

Roger said Ken was always very professional and easy to work with, despite being extremely exacting about everything. However, as usual, the only problem was his punctuality. Or lack of it! In the end they developed a way of working where the puppeteers would come into the studio at around 10am and record all the Diddymen close-ups and any puppet action which didn't feature Ken, as he was still in bed at that time. Comedians have to work and travel into the wee small hours, so they tend to live to a different timetable to the rest of us. Around 2pm Ken would appear and they would then film his close-up shots and the scenes where Ken was interacting with the puppets.

Having taken to the idea of working with these ingenious talking puppets Ken cast his mind back to his early days of ventriloquism and, in 1969, commissioned Warwickshire-based master prop maker Peter Pullen to make him a ventriloquist doll, modelled on Roger Stevenson's puppet of Dicky Mint. Ken's hilarious second-half ventriloquist spot with Dicky was to become an iconic and much-loved part of the stage shows for the rest of his life.

Ken had always continued to admire stage ventriloquists, one of his favourites being an old friend from variety theatre days, Arthur Worsley, the vent' who coined the much-copied phrase, "Look at me son when I'm talking to you!" A more recent favourite was America's anarchic ventriloquist Jeff Dunham.

Anne says that Ken brought Dicky Mint to life so well that one day she actually told Ken to get Dicky closer to the microphone so that he could be heard properly. Ken found that very amusing.

It's rather nice that Ken had become a vent' again, as ventriloquism had provided his first forays into professional showbusiness.

Chapter 7:

ENJOYING LIFE AT THE TOP

As we rolled into the turbulent '70s Ken Dodd was at the top of his game and enjoying his continuing success, but he certainly wasn't one to rest on his laurels. Ken loved to work, but he also liked to stretch himself, so he relished an unusual opportunity which presented itself in 1971. Famed theatre director Antony Tuckey approached Ken and said he was mounting a new production of Shakespeare's *Twelfth Night* at the Liverpool Playhouse and wondered if Ken would consider playing a part in it. Ken was thrilled to be asked, but assumed he was being offered the minor comedy role of Feste the fool, the court jester. In fact Tuckey wanted Ken to play a leading part as Malvolio the steward, a much more complex and dour character – a puritan who despises fun and games and even disapproves of smiling – a character you would think very much at odds with the perception of Ken Dodd. It is a key role in the classic Shakespearian comedy however, which has been played over the years by dramatic heavyweights such as Sir Alec Guinness, Sir John Gielgud, Sir Michael Regrave and Sir Derek Jacobi.

Ken was quite offended when friends and colleagues said he'd never keep to the script and would start ad-libbing and clowning around. Of course he was a true professional and fully understood that if he took the part then he would have to do it properly, discipline himself and stick rigidly to the original text. Ken threw himself into serious preparation for this exciting new challenge. He was true to his word and his professionalism and did of course resist the temptation to go off-script, playing the part with conviction and depth. There was actually one small ad-lib during the run, which was almost forced upon Ken one night by an unfortunate incident with a prop. Anne was there in the audience:

As the pompous steward of the household the director wanted Ken to wear a gaudy chain of office round his neck. That particular night he held the chain in his hands and it broke. All the baubles bounced 'ping pong ping' all over the stage. There was an audible gasp from the audience, so Ken couldn't very well ignore it. Quick-thinking as ever he simply said to the Countess, "When I am with thee my lady, I have the strength of twenty men." The audience cheered his ingenuity, but he did look up to heaven and put praying hands together, saying, in a loud stage whisper, "Sorry, Willy!"

It has often been said that comedians make good actors. In fact great comedians are great actors. They spend their lives wringing laughs not just from the funny words they are saying, but, much more importantly, from the way they deliver them. Ken once said that a joke is like a little playlet, with a beginning, middle and end, where the comedian tells a complete story with an efficient use of words and often a dazzling array of emotions and characterisations. What's that if it's not acting?

Ken read up on his Shakespeare and learned the play diligently, making sure he fully understood every nuance. In fact he learnt the play in the back of the chauffeured car that drove him to and from his summer season in Blackpool that year.

As part of his preparations for appearing as Malvolio, Ken contacted a lady called Margaret Parsons at the Ackerley Studios of Speech, Drama & Public Speaking in Liverpool. She helped him with voice production and breath control techniques which was a great help because of his asthma. In fact he found the breathing techniques so helpful that he would visit Margaret occasionally, for a refresher, right the way through his later life and career. She also advised Ken on diction, although he had never really spoken with a strong Liverpudlian accent.

During rehearsals Ken kept asking Antony Tuckey why he had offered him the part of Malvolio, but Tuckey refused to tell him, promising he would disclose all after the production had ended. At the last-night party Ken once again asked why he had been cast in the role. Tuckey said, "Well I can tell you now. I saw the part of Malvolio as a jumped-up peasant with delusions of grandeur, far above his station…" Ken paused, and said, "Oh I see…" They then both dissolved into hysterical laughter.

An amusing postscript is that when Ken was the subject of *This Is Your Life* Antony Tuckey came along to tell that anecdote. Ken of course had no idea what had been planned by Michael Aspel and the team, so, the moment he saw Tuckey walk on, he was so pleased to see him he began reminiscing and told the whole casting story himself. Theatre directors are not used to being in front of television cameras, and are certainly unaccustomed to ad-libbing, so all Tuckey could say, with a somewhat sheepish grin, having been pre-empted by Ken, was: "That in fact was my script…"

The production of *Twelfth Night* was a triumph, and Ken got rave reviews from serious critics.

Michael Billington, theatre critic for *The Guardian* and Ken Dodd fan, recently said in a TV interview: "I saw him in the Liverpool Playhouse production of *Twelfth Night*. People were surprised at Ken Dodd playing Malvolio, not a funny part, a rather tragic part in many ways. He did it brilliantly, and he did it with absolute conviction and seriousness. Not playing for gags but still getting the right laughs from the character in the situation. He was very disciplined and restrained. I always thought Ken should have been persuaded to do more straight acting. I think he could have been very good in lots of plays."

In fact Ken never did do much more straight acting. He had a brief silent cameo role in Kenneth Branagh's film version of *Hamlet*, as Yorick the court jester. He played a small part in a 1999 all-star

Hollywood version of *Alice in Wonderland* as Mr Mouse. In 1987 Ken made a larger-than-life cameo appearance in *Dr Who*. He was a big sci-fi fan, so he was thrilled to be given this opportunity. However, as the garishly-dressed eccentric over-the-top Tollmaster, he was, in effect, playing himself, or at least his well-known stage persona. I think it was hard to bury a personality as big as Ken's.

Ken was justifiably proud of his successful three-week Shakespearian stint as Malvolio, and enjoyed the challenge enormously, but I think he was smart enough to realise that there is not much point in wasting time being pretty good at one thing, when you are the best at something else. His first love was clowning and holding court onstage, talking directly to an adoring audience.

Anne says there were occasional offers of long runs in plays, but Ken didn't want that kind of long-term commitment. The thought of sticking to the same script for literally months on end was anathema to him. He would have become bored. Not only that, but he would have missed starring in his own Ken Dodd stage shows, which was always where his heart really lay.

Of course there is another likely reason for Ken not choosing to do more straight acting. Actors in a stage play earn a fraction of the take-home-pay of a top comedian starring in his own show.

Ken was still keen though to take on new challenges and push himself to try different things. In 1973, having studied and read about comedy and comedians all his life, he decided to embark upon a one-man-show called *Ha-Ha*. This was very exciting as there would be no support acts, just Ken Dodd up there, speaking about a subject where his knowledge and experience was unsurpassed, and was the absolute passion of his life. It was initially intended to be a serious, in-depth, academic lecture, an exploration, dissection and celebration of humour. After a couple of try-outs of this three-hour comedy oration Ken was unnerved by the sound of silent attention. He was far too used to gales of laughter every time he performed. Although nobody complained he decided that people were perhaps more interested in actually laughing than understanding why they were laughing, so he re-worked the show to include a lot of great examples of all kinds of humour, including impressions and tributes to many of his own comic heroes. *Ha-Ha* was now hilarious. Of course, Ken being Ken, he didn't take much material out to make room for these funny new additions, so the show succumbed to the traditional Doddy tendency of over-running. Nevertheless *Guardian* critic Michael Billington said that when he saw *Ha-Ha* at the Liverpool Playhouse it was one of the funniest shows he had ever seen. In fact, in 2019, when Billington finally retired from his fifty-year career as *The Guardian*'s Chief Theatre Critic, they asked him to rank his favourite ten nights in a theatre. He had around ten thousand to choose from, but, at number one, no less, he selected: "Ken Dodd's marathon celebration of comedy, *Ha-Ha*, at the Liverpool Playhouse in 1973. One of many happy nights, stretching into the following day – watching a master at work."

During the 1970s there was a decline in the previously lucrative world of variety theatre. Summer season shows were suddenly threatened by the upsurge in cheap foreign package holidays, making top British seaside resorts like Blackpool, Bournemouth and Scarborough unfashionable and less popular. As audiences dwindled, ticket prices went up and production values went down, making holidaymakers less likely to return to these once lavishly extravagant shows. Pantomime seasons were getting shorter, and, worse still, theatres were beginning to lose hope and close as the downward spiral continued unabated. Massive inflation rates and a few greedy stars had made all theatre and club ticket prices less affordable at a time when mass-produced colour television sets were becoming much more affordable, so people stayed at home to enjoy their glitzy comedy and variety entertainment for free, without moving out of their favourite armchair.

Ken Dodd was always astute and on-the-ball, so he reacted quickly to these drastic changes in the business in two ways. Firstly he took the opportunity of producing his own shows. If the fat-cat impresarios were losing heart and investing less in variety shows then, with his assured fan following, he decided to mount his own productions, risking more, but also standing to gain more if his instincts were correct. Secondly, with his passion for theatres, he began a crusade to save a few iconic places of entertainment that were under threat of closure.

We will explore both those labour-intensive departures in future chapters.

It seems Ken's energy and work ethic knew no bounds at that time. He carried on with his sell-out theatre comedy spectaculars during the 1970s, but, ever the grafter, he kept making radio and television series as well. He found television extremely time-consuming, hard work and ultimately not very satisfying, as it was often a compromise. In those days though it was essential for a star comedian to be seen regularly on television, in order to maintain a high profile. Television comedy shows of that period could command regular audiences of between fifteen and twenty million. That national mass media recognition was the only thing that did still sell tickets in theatres and nightclubs, so television was a necessary evil. However Ken was always most at home onstage, in a live theatre.

In the late '60s Ken had been tempted over to 'the other side', making two series of *Doddy's Music Box* for ITV. On BBC TV Ken had been using a serious announcer called David Mahlowe as his regular straight man, but Mahlowe was under exclusive contract to the BBC, so Ken needed a replacement for his ITV shows. Living in the north-west he had spotted a fresh-faced, sparky onscreen announcer doing the local ITV links for the ABC studios in Manchester. He was called David Hamilton. As ABC TV was making *Doddy's Music Box* Ken suggested their young announcer as his new straight man. Hamilton was duly auditioned and got the job.

An onscreen announcer is of course only seen from the waist up, with nobody else around for comparison, so Ken hadn't realised that David Hamilton was quite short in stature. On set, during the first day's rehearsals, he started referring to Hamilton as 'Diddy David', which made the studio crew laugh every time he said it. At first the announcer was quite offended and quietly asked the producer if Mr Dodd would stop calling him 'Diddy'. Ken was obviously told that David wasn't too keen on his new nickname, because he approached his new sidekick and asked if it was okay to carry on calling him 'Diddy David', as it would be something that might catch on. He promised though that if it was causing offence he would stop saying it. Hamilton relented, realising that diddy was a Dodd word that was being used affectionately, and also he could see its value as a running gag. In fact his new moniker probably helped his career path enormously. He would for ever be known in showbusiness circles as 'Diddy' David Hamilton.

Doddy's Music Box was Hamilton's first ever series on national television, but Ken's agent Dave Forrester spotted his potential and signed him up, getting him work as a TV straight man for other comedians like Benny Hill and Tommy Cooper, as well as starring roles in major pantomimes. And of course 'Diddy David' became one of the names most synonymous with BBC pop music radio in the late 1960s and all through the 1970s.

Actors generally don't like being the straight man for comedians, because they are used to having a rigid script to learn and perform, but of course comedians like to ad-lib and drift off the script if they spot an opportunity for an extra laugh, and that terrifies straight actors. Hamilton however had already done free-wheeling chat during his early DJ work for the BBC Light Programme, and often had to make off-the-cuff changes to links live on television, so he could handle Ken's frequent temptations to go 'off-script', without getting flustered.

'Diddy David' was so successful as Ken's straight man that he started being invited along to personal appearances with Ken, almost like a double act. The first time they opened a supermarket together, in Oldham, the crowds were so huge that all the local traffic had to be stopped by the police. Hamilton found it positively overwhelming

– he'd never personally witnessed anything quite like the hysteria surrounding Ken's mass popularity. He himself commented: "To me this was a completely new experience. It was like being thrown to the lions! This was the first time I'd worked with a big star, and I thought it was incredible… When we were rehearsing the TV shows there would be constant interruptions from his agent, his publicist, even his tailor. I thought this is what it's like to be a real star."

Hamilton said Ken demanded a lot of editorial control over the television shows, and had an unusual way of working. They would record twice as much material as was actually needed, with some wild and wacky scripts written by Ken and Eddie Braben, some of which worked and some of which didn't. Most comedians will confirm that you only really know whether something new is funny or not when an audience gets to see it.

The shows were recorded on a Thursday evening, after which Ken would watch the tapes back with the producer, telling him which sketches they should keep and which they should discard. Sometimes Ken would say, "We can make that better, we'll do it again another time." The shows were then frantically edited together on the Friday for transmission on the Saturday evening.

Hamilton loved working with Ken and learned a lot from him. He always said though that, as the straight man, often playing the deadpan TV interviewer, the hardest part of his job was keeping a straight face, something which was essential to keep the sketch funny.

When David appeared in his first pantomime, as Buttons in *Cinderella* at the Alhambra Theatre in Bradford, Ken turned up unexpectedly to watch a matinee performance. Between shows Ken offered to take David out for dinner. Hamilton was flattered as Ken wasn't known for lavish gestures. He was somewhat deflated though when he followed Ken across the road to the local fish and chip shop, which had a dingy back room with a few Formica-topped tables and plastic chairs. Ken then ordered for them both: "Cod and chips twice love!" and, because the Bradford chippy was unlicensed, produced two bottles of lager from his inside coat pocket. However, whilst waiting for their fish supper, Ken proceeded to give David a masterclass in stage performance and the art of British pantomime. Hamilton said the meal might have been a little disappointing, but that kind of advice was worth its weight in gold – priceless actually. He concluded that he would much rather have had that invaluable lesson and fish and chips, than an inconsequential chat about football or summer holidays over a gourmet dinner at The Ritz. Ken could be very generous with his time and with his experience.

In 1972 Ken returned to ITV with another new series, *Funny You Should Say That*. The repertory company for the sketches included Diddy David Hamilton, once again playing his straight man, along with toothy Welsh actor Talfryn Thomas, lanky posh gent Jeremy Lloyd, and an attractive unknown flame-haired actress called Barbara Mullaney. It was a six-week series, but, with just one week left to go, Barbara received one of those life-changing phone calls. She was offered a small part in a major ITV drama series at Granada Television, but they needed her to start filming immediately. With great trepidation she had to approach Ken during rehearsals for the penultimate show and ask if he could possibly release her from her contract and find a replacement actress for the last episode of his series, as this was such a golden opportunity for her. He didn't say anything, just walked away, thinking. In fact he didn't speak to her at all for the rest of the day, which alarmed her. After the recording though he turned to her and generously said, "Don't you let me down in *Coronation Street* young lady!"

Ms Mullaney is now better known as Barbara Knox and that 'small part' grew and grew… and grew! She has been playing the much-loved feisty character of Rita in *Corrie* ever since – for almost half a century. Ken understood about opportunities that simply cannot be missed, even if it was a personal inconvenience. Barbara never forgot that generosity of spirit.

The format for *Funny You Should Say That* was a little contrived and it wasn't Ken's best work, but it kept him in the public consciousness. It must have been frustrating for Ken to have to keep making new series for television – a medium he didn't particularly enjoy – purely to maintain a high profile.

1974 saw Ken back on BBC1 with a new (and better) series called *World of Laughter*. It featured a different, but equally talented repertory company, including cartoonist Bill Tidy, comedy actors Windsor Davies, Vicki Michelle, Michael McClain and Miriam Margolyes, plus, in a much less politically-correct era, an often scantily-clad Faith Brown.

Anne told me a fascinating and quite scary insider story about a near disaster during the making of that series:

In one episode Faith Brown, in a daringly high-cut plunging leotard, was playing the ditzy magician's assistant to a real stage comedy illusionist, Terry Seabrooke. They were performing an updated version of the classic 'sawing the lady in half', using two electric hand saws, with Ken wearing a surgeon's gown and manning one of the saws, at Terry's side. The electric saws were demonstrated as being genuinely deadly, then Faith, as the simpering assistant, was laid on the 'operating table'. Two narrow wooden arches were positioned over Faith, to act as guides for the saw blades. Ken's arch was over her midriff, and Terry's was over her thighs. Of course there was a secret switch which made the real blades flip back out of the way, allowing the electric hand saws to appear to cut through the wooden guiding arch, and Faith's midriff and legs, whilst actually leaving her perfectly safe and unharmed. The trick blades would then snap back into position as the saws emerged out of the other side of the two arches, completing the illusion of 'sawing through the lady'. Faith was hamming it up, acting terrified and making cod comic squeals as the electric blades started to saw at high speed and were pushed into the guiding arches. Her squeals would have been a lot louder and more realistic had she realised the truth of the situation. As Terry and Ken started to push the saws through the arches Ken noticed a puff of sawdust as the rapidly moving steel teeth of his saw started to pass through the wooden arch, only inches now from Faith's belly. He realised that Terry had forgotten to flip the safety switch on the second saw, so the fast-moving blade hadn't flipped back out of harm's way, and was really cutting through the wooden arch, and was heading rapidly towards Faith. Quick-thinking and even faster-acting Ken managed to stop sawing and flip the switch himself, just in the nick of time. Presumably the studio audience were totally oblivious to the fact that they had been seconds away from seeing Faith Brown really get sawn in half!

During the 1970s Ken Dodd was consolidating on his fame, embracing his many achievements and was of course reaping the rewards of his massive success. While Arthur Dodd was still alive Ken had never actually left the family home of his childhood, so, in the early 1970s, when his career was doing well and income was plentiful, he decided to invest in a house of his own. He sent Anne along to an auction to buy one for him:

It was a big house, bigger than 'Oak House' actually, in a beautiful little village called Tattenhall in Cheshire. Ken was taken with the place, but he was working away so he asked me if I would go along to the auction and bid for it, on his behalf. I was nervous about spending such a lot of somebody else's money, so I asked how much I could go up to. He didn't really give me a limit, but when the bidding got up to £25,000 I daren't go any higher, so I lost my nerve and stopped, which meant he didn't get the house, obviously. But £25,000 was a huge amount of money in those days.

Instead Ken bought a large house in the country, near Whitchurch in Shropshire, which he really fell in love with. Anne says he always kept promising to "make it nice", with a view to living in it, but he never got round to it. He paid a local man called Stan Chesters to visit the house every day and keep an eye on it. Stan, who was a builder by trade, looked after the place and maintained it for many years, by which time he was in his eighties. Ken even bought a few bits of second-hand furniture, to make the house look more homely, but nobody ever actually lived there.

When Arthur Dodd died in 1979 he, quite naturally, left 'Oak House' to the three siblings. Billy and June were settled in family homes of their own by then, so it was mutually agreed that Ken should get the Dodd family home valued, in order that he could buy his brother and sister's shares from them, as he was keen to remain in the home of his childhood, rather than the house he'd bought in Shropshire.

While I was interviewing Anne for this book she was in the process of selling the Whitchurch house and, because it is in the country, standing alone in five acres of land, away from the usual services, namely sewers, she was being asked questions like, "Does the septic tank comply to current building standards and regulations?" Of course the answer was 'no', because nothing like that had been needed, used or modernised for over forty years.

I was surprised to learn that she and Ken hadn't even used the impressively large detached country house as a weekend retreat. Nobody ever stayed there, even for a single night, in all the time they owned it.

Ken and Anne would visit the house occasionally, to remind themselves how beautiful it was, and what great potential it had. I suppose Ken was thinking it was for their retirement, but he had made it very clear on many occasions that he had no intention of retiring, and of course he never did. However, whilst in hospital, towards the end of his life, Ken did ask Anne to get on with making the house habitable, so that they could spend some time away from it all, whilst he was convalescing.

Apart from the complications in his personal life things couldn't have been better for Ken Dodd in the early 1970s. They had all learned to live with those complications. It was never spoken about but Anne says everybody understood that by far the most important thing was Ken's career, and nothing had to rock that delicate but vitally important boat.

We have to remember at that somewhat hypocritical time there was still moral indignation from the public and the press if there was the slightest whiff of scandal surrounding a celebrity. Comedian Max Wall had his career blighted by damning press reports of 'scandals' in his private life, all of which would seem tame by today's anything-goes standards. Back then sex outside marriage, and, worse still, co-habiting, was still regarded by many as an outrageous cardinal sin. Even divorce was considered a moral stigma in those days. Oh how times have changed!

Ken was still engaged to Anita Boutin and he still felt loyal to the way she had always supported him in his early days, but marriage didn't appear to be on the agenda. Twenty years on Ken didn't want the upset, bad feeling and negative publicity that would have come from a definite break-up, and he genuinely didn't want to let Anita down after all this time, or be the one to end their relationship. Like a lot of men Ken avoided confrontation when it came to matters of the heart. Meanwhile Anne had become a friend of the Dodd family and would visit Ken at 'Oak House' from time to time, when airline work commitments permitted.

Anne has kept a note she received from Ken during that period, while she was away on a holiday break with some of her BEA colleagues. It says, "Please come home safely soon, because I need you. I really need you." There then follows row upon row of kisses.

Ken had always promised Anne that he would never let her down, and, in fairness, he never did. Inevitably there were occasional moments of jealousy on both sides, but they all knew better than to upset the equilibrium.

Events however were about to take a most tragic turn, which was undoubtedly heart-breaking for all concerned. In 1976 Anita fell seriously ill and was diagnosed with a brain tumour. A major operation bought her a little more time, but sadly she died in 1977, aged just forty-eight.

Ken was visibly shattered by the news of Anita's fatal condition and was extremely attentive during her illness, visiting her as often as inescapable contractual obligations allowed. He would regularly go to the hospital late at night after a show and stay until the next morning, holding her hand.

In her last few days it seems an emotional Ken may have made Anita a somewhat rash promise, which he perhaps later regretted. Only they know exactly what was said, but the informed supposition is that they talked about having never married, and Ken, overcome by the tragic situation, probably vowed that he would never marry anybody else. Perhaps this explains why he felt he couldn't marry Anne, until he was on his own deathbed. It always seemed surprising that a man with such firmly held Christian values lived with Anne, the love of his life, for over forty years before he finally married her. Perhaps this also explains why he refused to talk to journalists about his private life, especially regarding personal matters to do with marriage and relationships. It was complicated and he felt no obligation whatsoever to explain himself.

Unfortunately there was more sadness to follow for Ken. By the mid-1970s Ken's beloved father Arthur was failing. He'd suffered with asthma and emphysema all his adult life, probably as a result of breathing toxic coal dust for over forty years on his delivery round. Anne says he would get frustrated with his breathing problems, but he still had a twinkle in his eye, enjoying telling his funny stories or sharing a joke with Ken and Billy.

By the end of the decade Arthur Dodd was critically ill and Ken, as he had done with Anita, would try to get back to Knotty Ash after a show, to visit his dying father. There were odd lighter moments, as Anne recalls:

In 1978, when Ken's father was terminally ill, Ken would try to get home as often as possible, even though he was headlining in summer season in Bridlington, over on the east coast. I was still working for BEA at the time, but, using flexi-time, I could get away from

Manchester Airport a bit early and go over there to drive Ken back to Knotty Ash. One night Ken was in his dressing-room, winding down after the show, and everybody else had gone back to their digs, so the theatre was empty, or so we thought. I'd had an early start at work so I was just having forty winks in a neighbouring smaller dressing-room. After Ken had done everything he needed to do he called out and said he was ready to go, so I just said I'd use the theatre's backstage communal ladies' bathroom before we hit the road for the long drive home, literally cross-country, east to west.

There I was in the Ladies, thinking there was only Ken and I left in the whole theatre. It was an old-fashioned sort of bathroom with a flimsy five-foot wooden partition separating the loo from the bath, creating a sort of cubicle which didn't go all the way to the ceiling. The partition had a frosted glass panel halfway up. Suddenly there was a thud of something or somebody heavy hurling themselves against the partition, with a blood-curdling loud roar. I just about leapt out of my skin, and I was obviously feeling pretty vulnerable sitting there on the loo. There was another thud and a loud roar and a ferocious-looking furry face appeared at the frosted glass window next to me. It was a leopard! Yes, a real live leopard! Its paws, with very sharp claws, were scrabbling at the big gap between the top of the wooden panel and the ceiling. I screamed and managed to make myself decent remarkably quickly! Somehow, while it was still trying to climb over the top of the partition, I pushed the door open and fled for my life.

The leopard was part of one of the other acts. Magician Johnny Hart used it in an illusion. It turned out that particular night he'd been invited to an after-show party and didn't have time to take his leopard back to his digs at a local farm, so he risked leaving it in the backstage ladies' bathroom, thinking he'd be first back in there next morning.

It's bad enough when another person bangs on the loo door, wanting you to hurry up, but it's very scary when a leopard's trying to join you in there!

I'm sure, if he was well enough, fun-loving Arthur Dodd enjoyed that story when they finally arrived home.

Sadly Arthur died in 1979, aged eighty-two. Ken was heartbroken, but out of respect for his father, he carried on working, because he knew that's what his dad would have wanted and expected. It was difficult though. In a 1995 television interview with Jeremy Isaacs, Ken said the first time he went onstage after his father's death was terribly hard. He used his old trick of compartmentalising to get through it: "It's like two people. Ken Dodd the private person, before he goes onstage, might feel quite down and sometimes you don't feel like being the comedian at all. But once the music starts and you're onstage something happens, you become another person..."

During that difficult end to the decade Ken had, for the first time, let his politics come to the fore. Despite his grandmother, Harriet Dodd, having been one of the early leading lights of the local Labour party, Ken always seemed to be true blue. He was insistent that he was a Conservative though, not an over-privileged land-owning Tory. The Dodd family of course had always managed to make their own way in the world, so Ken wasn't particularly at odds with the controversial 'every man for himself' / 'survival of the fittest' aspects of Thatcherism. Also, like a lot of people in Britain at that time, Ken was despairing of the ostensibly all-powerful Trade Union movement, and disliked the way they could, and frequently did, bring the whole country to its knees to make their point. Out of control inflation and seemingly endless strikes, culminating in the so-called 'winter of discontent', had effectively toppled Prime Minister James Callaghan's Labour government. It's not too surprising therefore that Ken was a fan of Margaret Thatcher, who became Prime Minister in 1979, vowing to take on the unions and emasculate their immense power. Ken was photographed on several occasions with Maggie, who claimed to be a fan of his. It's hard to imagine that they shared the same sense of humour, but who knows? Ken even went so far as to attend a rally in Bolton for Mrs Thatcher and her party in the run-up to her election victory in 1979. Of course this fleeting allegiance didn't go down too well with the ordinary people of Liverpool, a traditional Labour stronghold. They blamed previous Conservative governments for the decimation of local industry, especially the docks, and the consequent mass unemployment, poverty and despair in the city. Thatcher, from all she was promising and espousing, was only going to make matters worse. One is reminded of Alan Bleasdale's powerful drama *Boys from the Blackstuff*, which reflected the real tragedy of unemployment in Liverpool at that time.

It appeared, on the surface at least, that Maggie's regard for Liverpool was as low as their regard for her. In 1981, following the violent Toxteth Riots, her extreme right-wing colleagues seriously discussed a 'managed decline' of Liverpool, believing that it was a waste of public money to pump resources into the troubled city. In fact she didn't agree with her advisors and sent Michael Heseltine to plan a regeneration of Liverpool, but Thatcher's politics were still at odds with the city and she was universally hated there. Despite her reputation she did genuinely seem to want to rescue Liverpool. One of the first times she met Ken she asked what she could do to ease the apparent rift between her and the city. Ken told her to listen to the people and then do something concrete to help. I have seen a letter from her to Ken where she basically says that's easier said than done, but she will try.

In the end her government did help, and, in 2012, Michael Heseltine somewhat belatedly received the Freedom of the City of Liverpool for his sterling regeneration work.

Nevertheless Ken's apparent support for Maggie was bound to create waves. This was the first time, and I think the only time, that his faithful Liverpudlian followers questioned his actions. He began to realise that perhaps it was better to keep his politics to himself. Later in life he refused to be drawn on the subject by the *Liverpool Echo*, and said that there are two subjects that a comedian has to tread very carefully around – religion and politics. There are times when we perhaps all wish more entertainers would heed those wise words...

The 1970s went down in history as a turbulent decade both nationally and globally. The latter half of the '70s was also a turbulent time for Ken Dodd. There was a lot of sadness and some aching holes left in Ken's life as he approached the next decade, but it meant that he could eventually have a fresh start and begin a new life offstage. He had bought June and Billy's inherited equal shares of 'Oak House', so now Ken owned his happy childhood home. It also meant that Anne Jones could emerge from the shadows at long last, to visibly be Ken's partner in life. It must have been hugely liberating for Anne, although she is understandably a little uncomfortable talking about it, as the circumstances leading up to that new beginning were so tragic.

Ken and Anne must have been very sensitive and respectful to Anita's memory however, because they maintained a good relationship with most of the Boutin family, long after Anita's death. Her brother, Billy Boutin, had always been good friends with Ken and, in fact, after Anita's passing, he was hired to drive the car to and from gigs for Ken and Anne for quite a long period, and consequently he remained a close friend.

Ken employed various drivers over the years because, wherever possible, he would get home after a show, however late that may be. He often played long seasons in Blackpool, but he nearly always went home after the second house. He had to be driven, after having performed two long shows, but he could be home within an hour, thanks to quieter late night traffic. Ken didn't particularly like hotel rules, and they didn't particularly like his dogs, or the way he wanted to stay in bed most of the morning. More importantly though, deep down, Ken was a home-bird and much preferred to wake up in 'Oak House'.

Chapter 8:

MASTER OF HIS OWN DESTINY

In 1977, when Anita was terminally ill, Ken had decided not to take on a pantomime commitment, or any other theatre run for that Christmas season, so that he would be free to be at her bedside. Sadly she died that July, so, after an inevitable period of grieving, he felt he needed to get back to work. It was, by then, too short notice to offer himself up to the panto bookers or theatre impresarios. Instead he decided to hire a theatre; book the support acts, dancers and musicians; organise the scenery and costumes; sort out the publicity and ticket sales; and produce a last-minute Christmas show of his own. Ken had heard that the Manchester Palace Theatre was 'dark' (not in use) and threatened with closure, so that became the venue. We will explore more about the fact that this actually saved the iconic theatre in a later chapter.

It was all hands to the pump and Anne had to help him with all the many administrative tasks and creative decisions, which were part of staging a major theatre production. The show was a huge success, both critically and financially, and heralded the beginning of what was to become Ken's preferred way of working. It gave him a newfound freedom – he was his own boss. This must have been extremely liberating for a man who didn't much like doing as he was told.

The self-produced Manchester Palace 'Christmas' show was so successful it sold out every night and kept running right up to March. It only closed then because Ken had a contracted commitment to re-launch the newly refurbished Theatre Royal in Nottingham.

Anne can't have ever stopped working at that time. As well as holding down an important and sometimes stressful job with BEA she was helping Ken behind the scenes, and even appearing in his shows, whenever she possibly could. As Anne herself says, "You can do all that when you're young, fit and able, and you don't think anything about it…"

Despite having been promoted to a senior role in personnel management at Manchester Airport, Anne's heart was always really in showbusiness. She'd even been offered a further tempting job promotion as Cabin Crew Manager for the exciting, brand new transatlantic British Airways Boeing 747 'jumbo jet' fleet at Heathrow Airport, but of course that would have meant moving to London. Naturally enough Ken didn't like that idea and Anne didn't want an enforced separation from the love of her life now that they were properly together as a couple. Anne says Ken did actually ask her not to go.

Towards the end of the 1970s she'd taken leave from work to travel overseas with Ken to entertain troops in concert parties with the CSE, Combined Services Entertainment, the successor to the renowned wartime military entertainment unit, ENSA. Anne had really enjoyed supporting him in those shows, so, with her newfound freedom to be seen at Ken's side 24/7, she decided to stop working for the airline in the summer of 1980, after nearly twenty years, so that she could go on the road with Ken and become his regular support act, as well as helping him to produce his own shows.

Anne did have a little nudge to help her take that life-changing step. Her decision was spurred on by the fact that she was all too aware, from her job in personnel management, that top-heavy nationalised airline BEA had been rationalising resources, tightening their belts and cutting staff during a lengthy protracted merger with state-owned BOAC to become a privately run, more streamlined and efficient concern – British Airways. She declined the top cabin crew management job with BA in London and resigned. Despite BEA closing down their operations in three regional northern airports,

Anne had prided herself in keeping redundancies to an absolute minimum, relocating and redeploying staff wherever possible, but she was exhausted by all the re-organisation and felt her heart was no longer in it. This momentous turning-point of BEA becoming part of the new British Airways seemed like the perfect opportunity to make a clean break. The big party her colleagues threw on Anne's departure from Manchester Airport shows the esteem in which she was held.

Ken would still accept major summer season bookings when they were offered, for instance he played the prestigious Blackpool Opera House in the summer of 1981, but those kind of lengthy runs were becoming unsustainable, and therefore more scarce, as British holidaymakers abandoned the traditional seaside resorts in favour of cheap foreign package deals. The big companies who had staged all the major touring theatre shows and summer seasons were disappearing or diversifying. Undeterred, Ken started doing single nights or short runs of his self-produced show, touring it all around the British Isles. Although this was harder work and involved more travelling, both Ken and Anne seemed to love the life. They could choose who they worked with, and made sure they were all people they liked. Ken was his own boss, which meant nobody was telling him when to end the show – allowing him to start doing the marathon performances he became famous/notorious for in later years. They also reaped the financial rewards. Ken always maintained a loyal following, and would attract new younger fans, so he could always fill theatres, long after mainstream entertainment became less fashionable and therefore less commercially viable.

Many lesser 'old school' entertainers of Ken's generation were forced to share the billing (and earnings) in packaged shows where several previously big names were grouped together on the same bill, in order to sell tickets; or nostalgia shows where the tour promoters played on the fact that people were coming along to see 'the good old days' of entertainment. Other mainstream entertainers had to resort to doing late-night adult 'blue' shows. Ken never had to do any of that. He almost had a unique place in showbusiness, where he'd managed to stay at the top, on his own terms. The touring *Happiness* shows were a major event in any theatre and would often outsell the supposedly more current comedy names.

A former professional dancer called Keith McAndrews had been successful staging a live version of television's popular gameshow *Mr & Mrs*. The original host Derek Batey would take the game to theatres up and down the country, all booked and set up by McAndrews. Keith and Ken developed a friendship, and a successful working relationship, whereby Keith would help book the theatres for Ken's shows as well.

Ken hadn't broken ties with his first agent Dave Forrester, but Dave was in his eighties by this point, and didn't want to bother with the everyday hassle of booking theatres, although he would often supply the support acts for Ken's stage shows.

It was hard work to maintain the quality and keep the show going, much harder than the easy ways out taken by some of his contemporaries, but hard work was something that neither Ken nor Anne were ever afraid of.

Of course they couldn't do it alone, but they were keen to enjoy life on the road, so they surrounded themselves with people whose company they enjoyed. Ken employed a couple he and Anne had known for many years – Di Brooks and Roy Boardman. They would all muck in and do anything, but Roy's main job was to drive to and from the venues.

Roy must have been a good safe driver, because Ken was a slightly nervous passenger and didn't like any reckless behaviour on the road. Anne says Roy did have a very brief successor:

After Roy stopped through ill-health Ken tried employing an ex-police driver, thinking that with all his advanced driving skills he would be a good safe pair of hands. Unfortunately emergency driving and high-speed car chases had made him somewhat blasé, so, when he was driving at normal speeds, he only used one of those 'safe' hands to steer, resting his left arm on the back of the passenger seat, whilst he casually chatted away, gesticulating with his left hand from time to time. A somewhat alarmed Ken had to tell him to keep both hands on the wheel for the rest of that first journey, and then said he'd changed his mind about having a driver.

I said afterwards that he must have been a safe driver, having learned advanced skills at the police driving school, but Ken said that with all those hand gestures he thought he must have gone to the Marcel Marceau Driving School.

Anyway, that was the end of the shortest job in living history, and, from then on, I did all the driving.

Di Brooks' main job was to set up and run the merchandising stand in the theatre foyers – selling souvenir programmes, tickling-sticks, CDs, tapes, and so on.

Anne fondly remembers the fun times they all had together on the road:

Both Roy and Di would help with the 'get in' and the 'get out' at each theatre, but Ken would co-opt them into playing bit parts onstage as well. It came quite naturally to Di, who had always been keen on the theatre, and is now an accomplished actor, but even her partner Roy, who was much more reticent about appearing in public, would make brief appearances onstage as Ken's fictional manservant, 'Knockers'. Ostensibly his job was to carry off the floor-length, red, moggy-skin coat and other items of costume and props at the end of routines, but Ken would have a bit of fun with him while he was onstage, even giving him the odd line to perform. Just after the tax trial Roy would come on wearing a medieval torturer's mask and carrying a whip, and Ken would introduce him as his accountant, to great roars of approval from the crowd.

That butler/manservant/'Knockers' role evolved over the years. One of our longest-standing drummers was Kenny Adams. His wife

Pam would come along with him, so Ken got her to come on dressed as a deadpan, mute French maid. Gradually Ken started giving her lines, and it became quite a novel routine in the show, as Ken was usually a solo performer. When Kenny became ill, and Pam was no longer around, I took over as the French maid, and it became an even more crazy sketch, with Ken ad-libbing so much we'd both lose track of where we were. I loved doing it. In later years he would give me new lines to say, just before we went on, but then he'd give me the wrong cue, so I'd have to prompt him. He was quite deaf in his left ear by then, which was the side I was on, so I'd have to prompt him quite loudly, which always got big laughs from him and the audience. It became quite a feature, with a running gag of, "Are you trying to give me my lines?" and then him getting me to repeat them.

Over the years we had different musicians supporting Ken onstage. Our regular keyboard players were Stan Clarke, Kevin Speight, Nigel Hogg, and, latterly, David Carter and Terry Bell. Because I can play piano and keyboard, people often ask me if I ever accompanied Ken onstage. I only ever did it once. It was a demanding job and I didn't want to let Ken down, so I left it to the more experienced session players. Ken was a strict taskmaster when it came to his music. It had to be right. But this one night in the early 1980s we were doing a big charity gig and Ken had forgotten to book a keyboard player. He rang round a few he knew that morning, but none of them were available, so he turned to me and said, "You can play the piano. You'll have to do it!" Of course I protested, but I could see that we didn't have much choice. I was terribly nervous about it, so I quickly got out all the sheet music. There was the Diddymen music for his Dicky Mint spot, 'Happiness' of course, and a song he was doing at the time called 'Hold My Hand'. Then there were some 'dots' for his play-on music, which was complicated because it had been composed in D flat, so it was actually quite hard to read and play for somebody who wasn't used to it. By the time it came to the show I was absolutely petrified. In the first half I did a couple of false *starts, but Ken made a joke out of that, then 'Hold My Hand' went well, so I started to relax a bit. In the second half I played him on with Dicky Mint to 'The Song of the Diddymen', which was fine, but I'd forgotten there was a different tune to play him off at the end of the vent' spot. Kenny Adams the drummer prompted me, urgently telling me to play them off, but I couldn't think what to play, so I panicked. I don't know why I didn't just reprise the Diddymen theme, but, for some reason, the only tune I could think of was one of my old piano exam pieces – Dave Brubeck's famous jazz riff 'Take Five', so I played that, which was the most inappropriate piece of music you could imagine. Drummer Kenny burst out laughing, Ken turned round, looking at me as though I'd gone barmy, and Dicky Mint looked over Ken's shoulder and said, "What the… ??! That's not my play-off music!"*

Despite all my multi-tasking on the road – that's one job I only ever did once!

CHAPTER 9:

LIFE ON THE ROAD

The one-night gigs went on for years, so obviously a fixed routine evolved for getting everything done as efficiently as possible. In their busiest times Ken estimated that they travelled around 100,000 miles every year touring round Britain. I was curious to know what 'life on the road' was like. Anne admits she was a bit bossy, but I think she had to be. I feel she often does herself a disservice and plays down her importance in the whole touring 'circus'. Without her none of it would have happened. Ken was lucky to have somebody so well organised, diligent and industrious at his side. She also had to be very understanding, although she is always at pains to insist that she loved every minute of it. There's no doubt though that Anne was very much in charge and they all stuck to what became almost a ritual. As a fan of the live Ken Dodd shows I find Anne's recollections of the minutiae fascinating:

Ken and I would arrive at the theatre and, whilst I was unloading the props and the costumes from the car, with the help of our support team, Ken would go off to sign autographs, and do 'selfies', chatting to the people outside the theatre, who had arrived early to meet the star of the show. I would then have to try to pry Ken away from the fans to get him in to do his soundcheck. He could never be rude though and would chat perhaps a little longer than he should, with me having to nag him to come in. Quite often the curtain would go up a few minutes late because of this delay, but nobody seemed to mind.

Eventually I'd get him in to do his soundcheck, then he'd like half an hour in solitude to think and prepare himself for the show. People would ask to see Ken, but this quiet time was sacrosanct, so I had to say no. Often someone would say, "Oh I'm an old friend – he'll see me!", but I had to insist that he didn't see anybody in that thirty-minute build-up to the show. I was the only one who was allowed in the dressing-room during that time, but even I didn't talk to him. He rarely ate anything before a show, but I'd make him a cup of tea and check that he'd got everything, all in complete silence. During that crucial thirty minutes he had a set procedure. He'd get out his old wooden stage make-up box, which he'd had since his first fully professional shows in the 1950s. It was rather dilapidated latterly, but it was a theatrical tradition and you didn't throw things like that away. He'd lay out all his 'pancake' (theatrical foundation make-up) and greasepaint in a particular way, then start putting it on, thinking all the time, and planning what he was going to say in his opening spot. There was an old theatrical trick he'd learned when he was young of putting a red dot in the inner corner of each eye. It was to stop it looking as though he was squinting in the lights. Close up it looked quite strange, but, from the audience, it made his eyes look vibrant and alive. Then he'd pause to think again, and slowly darken his eyebrows. When his make-up was done he'd put on a bow tie for his first spot. He would just sit there looking at the tie in his hands for a couple of minutes before he put it on. I think he was saying a quiet prayer to himself at that point, lost in thought. It was an important moment of contemplation for him. Just before he went on he'd check his ever-present notebooks and scribble little reminders of the new jokes he was going to try out, just a few key words, written on the backs of his hands with a ballpoint pen. He liked to try quite a few new jokes every single night.

The last part of the pre-show ritual was in the wings, just before he went on. He gave me a kiss. Even if we'd 'had words', or argued about something, he always gave me a kiss, then he'd walk out onstage.

While he was onstage doing his first spot, which could be an hour and a half, Di Brooks and I would go to his dressing-room and lay out all his clothes for his second spot. The Union Jack hat, the big red fur coat and the bright yellow suit, which went underneath the coat – the one he used to say he got by sending away the tops off twelve Birds' custard packets.

Ken never drank alcohol before a show, but he'd have a can of lager in the interval. Never more than that – always just one can. He was quite particular about what he liked, so I'd bring the lager to the theatre, rather than rely on what they might have. He actually had a drink spiked at one theatre in Jersey, which made him ill, so we played safe after that. He was fussy about his tea too, which was rarely provided by theatres anyway, so I'd take along a kettle, teabags and milk. Quite often I'd have to go into the corridor to find a plug socket, squatting down on the floor to boil a kettle for him. Oh, the glamour of showbusiness! Even in television studios we'd take our own kettle to make tea.

During the interval, while he was drinking his lager, I'd make him a bowl of soup, which meant finding a microwave oven. Sometimes that was a long way from his dressing-room, but I usually managed to find one. Tinned Baxter's asparagus soup was his favourite.

Of course more people would try to get to see him during the interval, often saying they couldn't stay right to the end of the night, but I'd have to say no. It was his only break, and his only real chance to catch his breath and re-group for the second half, including yet another costume change. In later years I started opening the second half with a musical spot to extend his break and give him a bit longer before he started again. He was in his eighties by then, and still doing five-hour shows.

As well as the kettle, teabags, milk, cans of lager and tins of soup, I'd have a box of provisions with me at every theatre. It was a long night and he hadn't eaten before he went on, so I'd lay out cheese and crackers, or sandwiches – tasty snacks that he could grab between spots.

The one break with tradition was if we were on the east coast I would get fish and chips for us both in the dressing-room during the interval. Ken and I thought the east coast, especially Scarborough, had the best fish and chips ever. That was a little treat when we were in that part of the country.

After the show Ken would head straight back to the dressing-room to write notes. This was before he'd even changed out of costume. He'd be scribbling notes about how the new material had gone, or writing down any ad-libs that had gone down well. When Kenny Adams was our drummer they had a system where Kenny would make a note of any ad-libs as they happened. Musicians often take a break and leave the stage when comedians do long spots without music, but Kenny never minded staying there the whole time. So, if Ken came up with a new line or ad-libbed about something, he'd nod towards Kenny, who would write it down on a pad, which would be given to Ken after the show. Every night there would be a page or so of new ad-libs. I keep coming across Kenny's notepads and lots of his notes, which make fascinating reading, and are further evidence of Ken's seemingly never-ending creativity.

The ventriloquist spot with Dicky Mint always seemed to spawn lots of ad-libs. It was a peculiar thing really. Dicky would say something and Ken would laugh, because he'd never heard it before. That sounds almost supernatural, like those spooky films about ventriloquist's dolls who come alive, but it wasn't like that of course. The simple fact was that Ken knew the Dicky Mint character so well that he could literally be writing dialogue for the two of them as he went along. The vent' spot was never quite the same two nights running.

In the 1980s and even into the 1990s Ken would slip on a dressing-gown as soon as he'd finished making his after-show notes, and go off to talk to the people who wanted to see him. Don't forget this could be anywhere between midnight and one in the morning. Sometimes there were as many as fifty people waiting, so it was often an hour and a half before he came back to his dressing-room to *properly remove his make-up and get changed. It was anything up to three o'clock in the morning before we finally got away. As he got older I managed to streamline things a bit. I began insisting that he take off his make-up and change into his travelling clothes before he went out to meet his fans. While he was changing I'd gather up any autograph books from the stage door, so that he could sign those quickly in his dressing-room. The stage doorkeeper would then hand them out to those people who needed to leave before Ken came out to say 'hello' in person. To streamline things even more I would load up the gear while he was chatting with friends and supporters, so that, as soon as they had gone, we could get straight into the car and go. It also saved on exorbitant overtime payments at the theatres, as they would charge overtime right up to the moment we finally left and the staff could lock up the theatre.*

Sometimes though I'd find it difficult loading up the car, even with the help of the stagehands, because of the crowd gathered at the stage door. I'd have to keep asking them to make way for us to get through. It could be after one o'clock in the morning, and sometimes it was a bit of a struggle with arms full of props and costumes, especially in bad weather. If there were no stagehands available, I'd have to manage on my own. An all-too familiar, but well-meaning cry was, "I'll bet you wish you had the Diddymen to help you!" Of course I had to smile as though I'd never heard it before.

People waiting to talk to Ken were very kind and did offer to help, but, truthfully, I preferred to load up myself, because I had a check-list and a set way of loading everything into the car. If anybody else tried to help me I couldn't be certain that we'd got everything, and it would all be in the wrong place when we got to the next venue.

After one show in St Albans, while I was loading up, somebody pointed to a man running across the car park with a small case of ours and said, "He's just nicked that out of your boot!" Nobody had tried to stop him, so I hared off after him. I recognised the case – it was the one containing the iconic Union Jack hat. Ken would have been lost at the next gig without it, and it wasn't the kind of thing you could pop into a local shop and buy. I was so mad I somehow managed to catch up with the man and grabbed at his coat, accidentally pushing him over in the process. I panicked then, wondering if I'd killed him, but he was fine – a bit breathless and shocked, but not hurt. Cheeky devil, in an almost offended tone, said, "I only wanted it as a souvenir!", as though that made it alright.

I did have my own moments with fans after the show as well. One night in Whitley Bay there was a man left waiting all on his own at the stage door, so I asked if I could help. He said he'd been coming to the show regularly over many years, and was in love with Sybie Jones. He told me he'd only just plucked up the courage to ask if he could meet her, in person. He was looking right at me as I truthfully replied, "Erm, well... she's not in her room I'm afraid, but I'll let her know when I see her..." Pam, the wife of Kenny our drummer, was killing herself laughing, safely out of sight nearby, enjoying my predicament. I was trying to keep a straight face, be polite and not embarrass the poor fellow, praying he wouldn't twig that he was actually talking to Sybie Jones.

On another occasion in Llandudno I had to get something for Ken from the merchandise desk at the end of the show, when I heard a last-minute lady customer asking if there was a CD of Sybie Jones playing the piano. I said, "Oh there isn't one, but that's nice of you to ask." Once again, as the woman was looking straight at me, with obviously no recognition, I said, "I'll tell her. She'll be pleased you enjoyed her music." The woman then asked me politely, "Are you her mother?" In my defence I should add that I had taken off my make-up and was in my roadie comfort zone!

However, the most disconcerting incident of all was when, some years ago, a famous theatrical producer was in Ken's dressing-room and asked if he could meet the girl singer to book her for a summer season. I was standing three feet away from him when Ken said, "Ask her yourself." His face was a picture and Ken assured him that, "She scrubs up well for the stage..."

There was another amusing incident when we were getting out of the theatre late at night. We'd had a lovely woman called Joan Hinde supporting us. She was a superb trumpet player. Joan was quite broad-shouldered and had strong arms, essential qualities for somebody playing a brass instrument, and she also had a short cropped hairstyle. After the show her husband was carrying her glittering sequinned dresses out to their car and John Pye, Ken's writer pal, heard a woman in the car park say to her friend, "See! I told you it was a fella!"

Joan had a great sense of humour and subsequently would tell this story herself, onstage, during her performances. Offstage she and Ken would share wonderful memories and anecdotes about their long careers in variety, and it would be a joy for me to see Ken relaxing and roaring with laughter. As they say in the business – two real old pros together.

John Pye was a great observer of real people and he loved hearing those kind of funny things. Another time there were two little old ladies, who were on holiday in Eastbourne, and were looking at a big poster for Ken's summer show, outside the Congress Theatre. John Pye happened to be standing right behind them, so he could hear every word the old ladies were saying. One said, "Ooh, I don't know if I like this Ken Dodd," and her friend thought for a moment, then said, "Never mind – it'll be a sit down..."

Ken loved that when John told him after the show.

Ken never liked getting to venues too early so we'd ask any support acts to get there before us to set up and do their soundchecks. That way we could come in, unload, get ready, and go straight on. We would plan to arrive an hour and a half before 'curtain up', as a comfortable time to get in and get ready. Of course if the traffic was bad we'd arrive later than that. Sometimes the theatres would be panicking when the audience were starting to arrive before we'd even got there. Before mobile phones we'd sometimes have to stop to make a quick call from a pub or a service station to reassure the theatre that we really were on our way.

There were odd dramas on the way to theatres. I remember one time when we were nearly at a theatre in Wisbech, which is quite a long way from Liverpool, and I looked over at the clothes rail across the back of our vehicle and realised I'd left all my costumes at home. Inwardly I said, "Oh my goodness!", not wanting to alarm Ken, when suddenly he shouted "Oh my goodness!" himself. He couldn't have realised about my costumes so I quickly asked him what the matter was. He said, "The dog's just been sick in my hat!"

A few years ago I was driving the car and there was heavy traffic on the motorway over a big viaduct. I'd got a huge articulated lorry right on my tail in the middle lane. He was trying to push me on and make me go faster, driving as close to our back bumper as he could. Ken was asleep in the passenger seat, and I didn't want to go any faster or change lanes, so the truck driver kept tailgating me for quite a distance. Eventually I was able to safely pull in to the inside lane, so I stuck my right arm out of the window to impatiently wave him past. The lorry passed us, giving a long piercing blast on a painfully loud klaxon horn at me as he overtook. I was so mad I stuck my right hand back out of the window to shake my fist at him. But I must have touched the electric window switch as I was sticking my hand out, because the window whirred up and trapped my right arm outside the car, at the elbow. So now I'm driving with just my left hand, and my right arm is trapped outside the car, waving around like crazy. I panicked and screamed at Ken to wake up. He then panicked at being woken up by me yelling, and yelled back, "What's the matter?" I shouted, "Take the wheel!!" He was in a daze as he'd only just woken up and didn't know what was going on. I was yelling, "My arm's stuck out of the window!", which must have been even more confusing for him, but he did take the wheel just long enough for me to use my left hand to reach across and push the electric window switch to 'down'. Phew!!

One time we were doing a corporate gig in a posh hotel in Harrogate. Ken had an audience participation joke he'd do at those type of functions which involved inviting on to the stage "any lady who is off men". After a bit of banter he would present her with a rubber hot water bottle as a daft prize. This particular day I'd been having trouble with my back, so I'd filled the hot water bottle and used it to ease my lower back pain during the drive. Just as Ken was about to go on to do his spot I remembered I'd left it on the car seat. I told Ken not to panic – I would go and get it and have it ready in time for the gag. I dashed out to the car and got the hot water bottle, but of course it was full and it had to be empty for Ken to lift between finger and thumb. Thinking quickly, and not noticing anybody around, I squatted down beside the car and noisily poured this large volume of water out on to the sloping car park, with it running out the other side of the car. I suddenly spotted this elegant-looking woman, two cars down, who could obviously see the water running past her feet and my head crouching down next to our car and she yelled out, "I think that is absolutely disgusting!" I had no time to explain, so I ran off, waving the offending item over my head, shouting, as one does, "Well that's my hot water bottle emptied!"

Lots of people in the business have their personal affectionate Ken Dodd stories. Jeremy Hicks, an agent friend of mine, was an assistant stage manager when he first left school, and was working on a pantomime with Ken in Manchester. As usual Ken didn't like arriving until the very last minute, so they worked out a system whereby somebody would stand on the theatre fire escape looking out for Ken's car as it approached the theatre. His driver would flash his lights as he drove round the corner, then a signal would be passed to the stage manager to indicate that Ken was about to enter the building, so he could cue the pantomime orchestra to start the overture. By the time the overture and the opening chorus number had finished Ken would have leapt out of the car, thrown on his first costume and would bound on to the stage, just in the nick of time. Of course the inevitable happened one day – another driver happened to flash his lights just outside the theatre. The signal was wrongly passed to the stage manager who cued the orchestra and the panto started with no Ken anywhere to be seen…

Lots of the stories about Ken Dodd on the road and in theatres, not too surprisingly, revolve around his unique relationship with time. Anne recalls a theatre where the show got extended even further, as though it wasn't long enough to start with:

We were playing a little place in the Midlands called Corby where there was a big Scottish population. During the interval a handful of men appeared on the stage, setting up trestle tables. Some of them started moving the keyboard and drums. I had a fit. Musicians hate other people interfering with their instruments, so I tried to stop them, saying, "What on earth are you doing? The show isn't over yet! I know it's after ten o'clock, but it's only the interval. We've got the whole second half of the show to do yet! In any case you can't touch the equipment! Leave everything alone!" I was shouting at them, but they completely ignored me and carried on setting up these four trestle tables with white damask cloths. Then I spotted somebody wearing a BBC T-shirt, so I dashed off indignantly to Ken's dressing-room. I ranted at Ken: "You're not going to believe this! There are people onstage moving all our equipment – they're probably breaking everything! They're setting up tables with white tablecloths! I tried to stop them, but they took no notice! It's absolutely unbelievable!" He looked slightly embarrassed and said, "Oh yes, sorry, I forgot to tell you. The booking agent said the theatre is holding the World Haggis Eating Championship during the interval…" Forty minutes of sizable sturdy Scotsmen guzzling down massive mountains of haggis, and not a napkin in sight! A strange form of interval entertainment. Ken could have warned me!

Latterly Ken would refer to himself as a 'gigster'. I asked Anne if he ever got fed up touring, just to do the odd night here, and the odd night there:

He never tired of the performing – he absolutely loved it – but, in the last few years, he would be completely exhausted after the show and finding hotels and checking in with the dog in the wee small hours of the morning did become a strain, but he didn't want to stop.

He never talked seriously about retiring, but, in later years, we'd take January off for a complete break and a short holiday abroad somewhere. The only snag with that was that four weeks was a long time to take a break from speaking for so long, so I'd have to remind him to do vocal exercises about a week before we started again. He'd also start writing out parts of the act, just to get his brain back in gear for performing. To help him out I got hold of an audio recording of a complete show, and transcribed the whole lot on to paper and put it in a big purple ring-binder for him. I told you shorthand and typing was the most useful thing I ever learned! He called it 'the purple book'. He did find it particularly useful in the last three or four years. Funnily enough he mainly used the first few pages as a reference guide, just to get him back into it, then the rest would come flooding back.

In those last few years we'd cut back on the number of shows we did a year, and we did no more than two or three a week. He'd discovered that the Dicky Mint spot worked equally well if he sat on a high stool, which meant less time on his feet each night. But, even when he was in hospital, just before he died, he was still planning new shows. He said that he'd cut back his time on the stage and put more support acts in the show, but he didn't ever think about stopping completely. The first show he was going to do, when he was well enough, was a free show for the Lord Mayor of Liverpool, as a thank you for the wonderful 90th birthday celebrations the city had laid on for him. Sadly he never recovered sufficiently to do it, but the spirit was certainly willing.

CHAPTER 10:

TELEVISION –
A BLESSING AND A CURSE

B ack in the 1980s Ken's self-produced life on the road as a 'gigster' had proved a highly enjoyable and profitable lifeline, at a time when other mainstream entertainers were struggling.

Provincial theatres were closing at an alarming rate, seaside summer seasons were rapidly becoming a thing of the past, and even pantomimes had been usurped by Australian soap stars, DJs and television-created 'personalities' and were doing considerably shorter runs. This meant that there were less and less guaranteed theatre bookings for the variety stars of the golden age – apart from the ever-popular Ken Dodd of course, who had shrewdly found a way of generating his own work.

There was another major factor which all mainstream comedians had to contend with in the mid- to late-1980s. Comedy, on television at least, was undergoing a seismic shift. University-educated, left-leaning, angry young men, like Ben Elton, Rik Mayall and Alexei Sayle were doing for comedy what 'punk rock' had done for melodic pop music a decade earlier. So-called 'alternative comedy' was born. Television executives were quick to jump on the bandwagon and in-your-face anarchic shows like *The Young Ones* and *Saturday Live* blasted from our screens.

I always think it was unfortunate that part of the alternative comedy ethos was to mock and deride the previous generation of 'old school' comedians. In some cases they maybe had a point about sexism, racism, homophobia and misogynism having played too big a part in 1960s and '70s 'club' comedy, but that criticism was hugely unfair when levelled at the greats – Ken Dodd, Tommy Cooper, Mike Yarwood, Morecambe & Wise, Tony Hancock, Dave Allen, Larry Grayson, Bruce Forsyth and countless other top variety comedians – who had never found it necessary to plumb those depths.

Even more unfortunately the TV executives listened to these unfair accusations and mainstream entertainers suddenly became persona non grata on television. Instead they clamoured to sign up all the youngsters making a name for themselves in the new emerging comedy club circuit.

In fairness, many great stars, some of whom are ironically now the new comedy 'mainstream', were discovered during that period – the likes of Paul Merton, Dawn French, Stephen Fry, Julian Clary, Ade Edmondson, Jennifer Saunders, Harry Enfield, Rory Bremner, Jo Brand, to name but a few. However it was extremely ungracious and dishonourable of the powers-that-be in television to turn their backs on the guys who had been so successful for them in the previous two decades, and shun them. Surely the sensible and fair attitude would have been to make room for both kinds of comedy, thus appealing to all age groups. In the end of course many of the older comedians survived this shameful slump and were eventually welcomed back on to television as 'national treasures' – Bruce Forsyth, Bob Monkhouse, Ronnie Corbett, Frankie Howerd, Dave Allen and Ken himself, to name a few honourable examples.

Many 'old school' comedians became very bitter during that period, and some careers were destroyed by it. Ken, ever sanguine and pragmatic, just accepted that's the way things were and carried on doing his own thing. Thanks to the success of his touring live show he could almost ignore what was going on around him. He'd never particularly enjoyed making television programmes anyway. His popularity with his massive hardcore following was certainly untainted by 'the new wave'.

Having been a student of humour all his life, Ken took a great interest in this change in comedy, however. He didn't approve of the excesses of bad language and crudeness, and the darker aggressive side of a lot of the humour, but he could admire the cleverness of some of the new performers, even if he didn't agree with their politics! He had always been interested in changes in comedy, and, let's not forget, he had been the new 'young pretender' himself, back in the day. Consciously, or not, Ken did appear to introduce more observational material into his own act during the late 1980s, which helped him keep fresh and attract new, younger audiences. He had this shrewd theory that comedians need to reinvent themselves every ten years or so, or run the risk of being left behind.

I can personally vouch for how quickly things were changing in the world of television. I worked as an Assistant Producer in the Entertainment Department at the BBC in Manchester during the 1980s. In 1987 my mentor and producer Alan Walsh had the simple but clever idea of taking the BBC brand created by *A Question of Sport* and producing a showbiz version called *A Question of Entertainment*, with teams of showbusiness personalities answering questions on TV, film, radio and stage. Alan got the go-ahead to make a 'pilot' episode, and asked me for suggestions for the chairman and the two regular team captains. They all had to be big names from the world of entertainment with a wealth of knowledge and experience in the business, and the ability to be competitive, likable and funny. The next day I came back with my dream team of comedian Tom O'Connor (then king of the gameshow) in the chair, with team captains Larry Grayson and Ken Dodd. Alan thought they were all great ideas, but wondered if I was maybe being a little over-ambitious to get such big stars to share equal billing, but he said I could take each of them out to lunch to try to convince them. It was all very thrilling for me, because I was fairly new to television production, so I thoroughly enjoyed my three lunches with these giants of comedy – all people I greatly admired. I was even more delighted when all three of them said they would love to take part in *A Question of Entertainment*. Alan Walsh was very pleased with me too.

On a side note I took Ken to lunch at his favourite meeting place, the Adelphi Hotel in central Liverpool. Despite his reputation, and much to my surprise, he turned up exactly on time! I remember that lunch as quite intense. No jokes, which surprised me. Ken was very business-like and wanted to know every single detail before he would commit himself. At that time I hadn't realised just how suspicious he was of television, and that it wasn't his favourite medium. In the end I think Ken really enjoyed *A Question of Entertainment*. He was in a high profile captain's role for several months on prime-time television, surrounded by showbiz friends and colleagues he liked and admired, and there was no pressure on him to be responsible for hours of scripted material. Not only that, but Ken was pretty competitive, so I don't think it did any harm that he and his team usually beat laid-back Larry Grayson's team.

To cut a long story short we made a successful 'pilot' and were duly commissioned to make a series of eighteen shows for Sunday evenings on BBC1 – a fantastic slot. We got a regular following of over five million viewers, and the list of our guest team members still reads like a Who's Who of twentieth-century showbusiness. However, in the relatively short space of time it took to get the shows on air (in the spring and summer of 1988), things had changed so much in television entertainment that the top BBC executives in London decided our casting was old-fashioned, and the whole show was to be taken away from us and revamped as *That's Showbusiness,* with three younger protagonists in the key roles.

It was simply a question of right people, wrong time. Five years earlier it would have been seen as a real coup to gather such major showbusiness players together in one programme. Ten years later it would have been regarded as a real event to see so many 'national treasures' sitting side by side. Unfortunately, just at that moment, mainstream variety stars were unfairly deemed as unwanted and untouchable on television.

A Question of Entertainment was to be both Larry Grayson and Ken Dodd's last ever television series, although Ken had his best individual television programmes still to come – his two specials for ITV, under their *An Audience with...* banner.

Television was both a blessing and a curse to the world of entertainment back in the 1970s, a period often referred to as 'the golden age' of the small screen. For the public it was mainly a blessing. Whole families could sit at home and watch all the big stars in quality, big budget, lavish entertainment programmes without having to buy a single ticket, or even having to move out of their own front room. This was a curse though to showbusiness because it meant far less people were parting with their hard-earned cash to go to theatres. This self-destructive downward spiral actually created a peculiar Catch-22 dilemma, because the only stars who could still sell tickets at the box office were the big names from television.

For the entertainers themselves TV was both a blessing and a curse. A blessing because a television series guaranteed instant national fame and acclaim, thus making you a top earner in what was left of the live circuit – summer seasons, pantos, theatres, holiday camps and cabaret clubs. It was also a blessing because, in those days, television stars were paid exceptionally well. However, TV was a curse because it was rapidly killing off that lucrative live circuit, the very lifeblood of variety entertainment.

A television appearance was also a particular curse to comedians because it gobbled up material at an alarming rate.

In the pre-TV days of variety theatre a good comedy act could last an entertainer a lifetime. There were enough theatres that they could keep doing pretty much the same material night after night, moving on to somewhere new where they hadn't seen the act, so it appeared fresh. Television was different. Instead of a few hundred people hearing your jokes each night in one tiny corner of the British Isles, a TV appearance meant that just about every comedy fan in the country heard them all in one evening, and would feel cheated if you tried to use the same jokes again. There were only three TV channels back then, so as many as twenty million viewers had seen and heard that material, and didn't want to hear it again. That would be equivalent to using that material at 20,000 average-sized theatres – a lifetime's touring.

Many comedians got wise to this and wouldn't use their stage act on TV, instead relying on teams of writers for new throw-away comedy scripts, allowing them to preserve their precious 'best' material for live shows. Perversely this meant that very often they weren't as funny on TV as they were when you went to see them live. This, in itself, was another double-edged sword. People might still pay to see them in a theatre or a club, because comedians were often 'better live', but they wouldn't risk buying an expensive ticket if the comic wasn't any good at all on television. It was a balancing act – trying to do the best you possibly could on TV, without giving away your funniest material.

Ken Dodd was one of the more intelligent performers and understood this dilemma. Ken had always had a bit of a love-hate relationship with television anyway. He completely understood that it was a necessary evil as a tool for promotion, PR, and maintaining a high profile, but, as an art form, it didn't float his boat as much as "slaving over a hot audience", as he used to call his legendary live work.

He didn't like all the cameras and technical paraphernalia in a television studio. He thought they created a barrier of "scrap iron" between him and his beloved audience. He wanted to look straight out into the whites of their eyes. He didn't have much time for television producers either. He often said, "The trouble with producers is – they will produce!" What he meant was that sometimes producers (and directors) appeared more interested in the look of the show, and the glossiness of the overall package, often at the expense of the comedy material, thus interfering adversely with Ken's tried and tested skills at raising laughter. A director would tell him to stand on a particular mark on the studio floor, and Ken would question it, saying his comedy instincts were to stand somewhere else. The director would say it gave a better camera angle, but that wasn't a satisfactory answer as far as Ken was concerned. Ken never liked doing as he was told, so it was a battle of wills between producers, who had the ultimate say on TV matters, and the star who felt he should have the ultimate say.

Ken also knew that it was a compromise over the quality of television material. A series was at least six shows, and that was a lot of jokes at the speed he worked. There never seemed to be enough preparation time. He could try odd new jokes out onstage, but not enough to fill a whole TV series. He knew that the best comedy material had to be honed and sweated over, but that just couldn't be done for television, so the quality was inevitably much more hit and miss. His TV shows often filled the airtime with sketches, but Ken's personality was so huge that it was hard to bury himself in character comedy. Sketch comedy wasn't really his forte.

Ken would insist on a good degree of editorial control over his TV series, because he understood the importance of editing a show together – not least what to leave in, and, crucially, what material to discard and leave out. Unfortunately of course he simply didn't have the time to spend days on end in a video editing suite, so, again, it was a compromise.

Anne recalls the pressures of making TV:

I know it has been said that Ken's television shows didn't always match up to his stage shows, but he did work very hard at television. The problem always was the quantity of material that was needed to fill a series. His enthusiasm and professionalism meant he wanted to try all sorts of different things, but, with his busy 'live' diary, there wasn't always the time to road-test every new idea, something he could do for the theatre shows. Due to the fast turn-round of mass-produced television, you can find yourself having to settle for second best, but there was always a huge amount of invention and innovation in those series. His producers didn't always meet him halfway, however, so he could find television frustrating.

You can actually see that frustration at times. When you look back at recordings of those old shows Ken occasionally looks tense and ill-at-ease, whereas, when you saw him in his element, performing his joyously funny stage shows, his enjoyment was palpable and infectious.

The truth is most comedians struggle to fill television programmes with material of the same quality as their stage shows, and Ken's stage show had set the bar very high indeed.

Even his friend and fellow Liverpudlian Jimmy Tarbuck, who described Ken as the greatest stage comedian this country has ever produced, admits that television didn't always serve Ken well. Somehow it didn't do him justice. Jimmy is quick to add one rider to that statement however: "A lot of his television work didn't reach true Dodd heights, but his greatest TV show, in my opinion, was when he did *An Audience with Ken Dodd*. That was superb!"

CHAPTER 11:

THE PRICE OF FAME

It seems these days that some people are hungry for fame for fame's sake. Our television screens are filled with people who don't have any particular talent, but who are willing to let their lives unravel in front of us all on reality shows, purely with one goal in mind – fame.

When we think of fame I suppose we think of all the attractive things that go with becoming a 'celebrity' – wealth, adulation, recognition, self-worth. However there can be a dark side to fame.

Unlike the 'reality show' stars, Ken Dodd earned his fame through hard work and talent. He enjoyed being successful and was proud of what he had achieved, but there was an aspect of his fame that he didn't enjoy. Something most of us don't really think much about with regard to the price of celebrity – stalkers. Anne shocked me with some of her stories of crazed obsessive fans:

I always helped Ken with his fan mail and anything that came to the house. Wherever possible we would respond. In the early 1980s there was a lady who kept sending an unusually high number of quite obsessive love letters, which could be quite sinister in tone. Then the envelopes started to contain various items – bits of jewellery and that sort of thing, along with yet another barbed love letter. We wanted to send the stuff back but we couldn't because she never gave an address, so we just had to ignore the letters and keep the gift items on one side. For months we'd been having a series of phone messages, which we realised were from her as well, often quite a few at a time, where she wouldn't say much, but she wouldn't hang up either, which was irritating because then we couldn't use the telephone. The line would still be open to her phone, and there were no mobiles at that time, as a back-up.

After a while we got a request through her local vicar to send the gifts back, which we of course did, still not being able to identify her, as this was all done through the vicar.

We thought that was the last we'd hear from her, but then she contacted the News of the World *newspaper and said that something terrible was going to happen to Ken while he was onstage that night, warning of a serious threat to his life. Thankfully the* News of the World *did the right thing and called the police, and also the theatre where we were appearing in summer season. It was all very alarming as you can imagine, but the police put guards on every door. We had her name, so, through the box office, we could identify which seat number she had booked for the show. When she arrived at the theatre and presented the ticket for that seat the policeman at that particular door refused to let her in, so she started kicking him and causing quite a scene. Ken asked the police what she wanted and what could be done about her. They said she just wants to say 'hello' to you, so Ken agreed, providing they escorted her to his dressing-room. There were a few of us from the show there as well, just in case she got physical. Strangely she just stood there and said nothing, and then went quietly away.*

A little while later though she threatened a total stranger in a café near the theatre. Poor woman was minding her own business, having a cup of coffee, and Ken's stalker picked up a knife and threatened to stab her if she didn't take a letter for Ken to the theatre on her behalf. That time she was sectioned and diagnosed with serious mental health issues. We thought well that's twenty-eight days of peace at least, but, when we got home, there was another phone message from her.

Unfortunately the whole thing went to court. We felt sorry for her when we realised she was mentally ill. Of course she had no money so Ken paid her legal costs for her. The irony of that kind gesture was that she then sent us her phone bills to pay, for all the huge number of long calls she had made to our number. Understandably we drew the line at those.

Ken never much liked the word 'fan' because it's short for fanatic. He always preferred to call them 'supporters'. There were a lot of those who used to regularly come to the shows and send nice letters. They were no trouble at all and some of them became close friends. Ken loved chatting to them at the theatres.

Another problematic one started in the early 2000s, however. I opened a fan letter from a woman which was highly sexually suggestive, and she'd enclosed some extremely sordid explicit photographs of herself, that really didn't look very nice at all, so I showed it all to Ken. "Oh," he said, "I've had others like that from her – throw it in the bin!", but I thought we should keep them, as potential evidence, if it was becoming a regular thing. Sure enough more followed with equally unpleasant lewd photos. They'd be there in Ken's dressing-room, posted a few days before to the theatres where we were due to appear, but we still didn't know who she was. Then she started sending T-shirts with obscene words or crude phrases written on them, and things like that.

A while later we discovered that a theatre in Southport had received a massive parcel for Ken, to be given to him. It turns out they'd had it months and hadn't told us. When I opened it I discovered it was a huge embroidered picture of Ken in a very expensive wood and glass frame, and it had the name and address of the embroiderer on the back. It was very good actually, a lovely picture done with really neat dainty cross-stitch, and a good likeness of Ken, so I wrote to the woman named on the back and thanked her, telling her how clever she was, how much we liked the tapestry, and how impressed we were at all the work she'd obviously put into creating it. I even said that we were appearing at a theatre near her soon and we'd be delighted to give her a couple of complimentary tickets so that we could meet her after the show and thank her properly, in person.

She did come along and we met her at the stage door at the end of the night. I told her again how much I liked the picture and admired her talent, and then she started talking to Ken, saying she'd like a private word, which wasn't really possible. Before long she turned up at another theatre saying she'd brought a stack of vintage 78 rpm comedy records for Ken – Max Miller and people like that. I think Ken had said he might be interested in buying them when he heard about her collection. By now I was beginning to get a bit suspicious about her. She always seemed rather intense and kept insisting on having a private word with Ken. She'd say, "I MUST see him on my own!", so I said to Ken that I thought she was trouble. She was behaving quite strangely this time and she was becoming quite stroppy, demanding to see Ken alone to give him the records. From the way she spoke to him at the stage door he agreed that she was behaving like a stalker, so he was keen to jump into the car and make a quick get-away from the theatre, never mind the records. I remember him saying to the driver, "Move quick! Drive! That woman could have anything in her handbag – a knife or a gun!"

The very next night we were at a small theatre nearby and she turned up again, accosting one of our helpers and demanding to see Ken in person to give him the records she had promised to sell him. I went out to intercept her and asked how much she wanted for the records. I paid her what she wanted, in cash, just to get rid of her. She still wanted to see Ken, but we managed to persuade her to leave the theatre.

When Ken and I got home we decided we should return the framed tapestry picture, with a letter saying how good it was, but she should have it back to use as an exhibit and a lovely example of her work to show to other people. I packed it really well when I sent it back, but apparently the glass got broken in transit. We didn't know that at the time, but she later said that the breakage had annoyed her and was responsible for sending her over the edge.

Some time later a box arrived in the post for me. Inside was a neatly gift-wrapped package with an envelope on top, which I opened *first. It was a well set-out, intelligently and neatly hand-written letter saying what a marvellous job I did of looking after Mr Dodd, so I then opened the package which was wrapped in silver gift wrap and ribbons. Inside that was the biggest dead rat you have ever seen. The smell was awful. Of course I screamed, which brought Ken running. It was only then that we started studying the handwriting on all these things – bear in mind we used to get lots of letters, most of them perfectly harmless. To our horror we realised that the embroiderer was the same woman who had been sending the sexy letters and disgusting photographs, under a different name, and now had sent me the dead rat, so we went to the police. They weren't terribly interested at first, but they said they might arrest her for sending 'illegal content' in the mail.*

One policeman studied the letters with me and he found coded messages hidden in them which could be interpreted as things like, "Kill... Anne... Jones..." In the meantime, before they got round to arresting her, we were still working and she kept showing up at every theatre, sitting on the front row in the shortest tight skirts and lots of make-up, obviously trying to look alluring. When Ken was onstage she would be staring adoringly at him, and when I was on she'd be looking daggers at me. I couldn't look at her, it was scary.

When the police had gathered enough evidence they said they would apprehend her before our next show, which happened to be at a theatre in New Brighton. Detectives, in plain clothes, did indeed take her away that night.

During various statements I had to give to the police they asked if any other threats had ever been made against me, or whether anything odd had happened. I said, "Not really, although somebody did set fire to the guest cottage at the back of our house a couple of years ago. They never did catch who did it." A couple of days later they phoned me to say that they thought it was the same embroidery woman who had set fire to the cottage. They had raided her house and confiscated twenty-seven black bags full of evidence, including notes and diaries talking about the best way to commit arson. There were even train tickets and a hotel receipt which put her in our area on the date of the fire. She had put burning rags through the letterbox, in the dead of night, believing that's where I lived. Fortunately the cottage was empty that night, which she claimed in court she knew, but there's no way she could possibly have known that. My brothers used to use it when they visited, and my name was on the electoral roll at that address, so she obviously thought it was my home.

Some newspaper reports said we were away and not in danger when the fire happened. That's not true. There was nobody actually staying in the cottage, but we were right next door, asleep in the main house, and the fire brigade came knocking on our door warning us of the close proximity of the blaze. It could easily have spread.

We didn't want her to be punished particularly, we just thought she needed treatment, but arson is arson, which is a serious crime. In the end, during the course of the trial, she said she would plead guilty if Ken agreed to speak to her one last time, in person. The cheek of the woman! Ken really didn't want to come face to face with her, but the lawyers said it would make life easier and there would be glass between them, plus police guards all round, so he reluctantly agreed to go and talk to her. She had the audacity to tell Ken that we brought it all on ourselves by sending her embroidered picture back with the glass broken.

She did plead guilty to arson and was sent away to a secure psychiatric unit for an unspecified time. She was released after two or three years, but we were told with conditional restrictions on coming anywhere near us. That didn't seem to help much. I'd heard that she'd been released and, within days, I spotted her in the audience of a show we were doing in Weymouth. She was in disguise, wearing a grey wig in a bun, and dowdy clothes, but it was unmistakably her. Of course a shiver went down my spine. She didn't cause any problems, but we discovered that she'd booked ahead for lots of other shows, so I checked with the police what her conditions of release were. She'd been told that she couldn't come anywhere near me or our home, and couldn't attend the theatres where Ken *was performing, so she was clearly in breach of those terms. The next show there were plain clothes police all round and unmarked cars outside, ready to pounce, but she didn't show up. She'd obviously been warned. Thankfully that's the last we ever heard from her.*

Anne tells these stories with disarming candour and takes the events in her stride as though they are all part of life's rich tapestry, but of course, thankfully, most of us will never be in the position where we think we are being stalked by a deranged individual, or could even be murdered.

One tends to think that these strange unfortunate people will never really do anything terrible, that they just make attention-grabbing hollow threats, but Anne sent a shiver down my spine when she pointed out that one of their stalker episodes was going on just about the time that television presenter and journalist Jill Dando was shot dead on her own doorstep.

What I think is particularly frightening is that you never really know whether a stalker episode is over. These people are still out there.

CHAPTER 12:

THE UPSIDE OF FAME

O f course there were plus sides to fame for Ken as well. For example he never minded being recognised in the street, and he positively enjoyed chatting to people who stopped him for an autograph or a 'selfie'. If they showed him respect he would return it in spades. Anne says a short walk in a busy area could easily end up taking a couple of hours, because he enjoyed chatting to fans who stopped him in the street. Some famous people hate that, but Ken genuinely relished it. As Anne puts it:

Ken liked people. He'd chat to anybody, and he could talk about anything, not just showbusiness. He enjoyed meeting people at the theatres before and after shows. If we arrived a bit late I'd be trying to hurry him up to go in and do his soundcheck, but he'd say, "No – they have been waiting for me – I'll just have a quick word." He knew that they were the people who had put him where he was. He'd say, "They are very important these people."

Latterly, after the rise of auction websites like eBay, I'd get a bit irritated because there would be groups of people waiting to get a pile of memorabilia signed – records, posters, programmes, things like that. They'd probably found them in a car boot sale the week before. I knew they weren't fans particularly, they just wanted to get his autograph to add value to these items so that they could re-sell them online, at a profit. Ken never minded though, and he'd always oblige. He used to say to me, "I've been very lucky in my life, and if this gives them a bit of a break, then good luck to them."

It's perhaps surprising that Ken was so happy talking to strangers in the street as he was such an intensely private person offstage. However I think the secret lay once again in his Englishman's castle, 'Oak House'. As soon as he was home he could pull up the drawbridge and be the other Ken Dodd he so often spoke about – the thinker, the reader, the quiet man of faith, the caring modest family man, the lover. This gave him the freedom when he was out and about to be a bit larger-than-life, Ken the performer, and enjoy the adulation and friendship of his admirers, knowing he could escape back to peace and sanity at the end of the day. He really did like people though, and he really did enjoy talking to them. He was also smart enough to know that they were the people who had bought his records and theatre tickets, and had given him the career and privileged lifestyle he so enjoyed. He hated other performers dismissively referring to audiences as "that lot", or belittling them. These were real hard-working human beings to Ken, who had paid him the honour of giving up their time, and handing over their hard-earned cash, to be entertained. He appreciated and worshipped his audiences just as much as they appreciated and worshipped him. He often insisted in interviews, "You can't make somebody laugh – you give them laughter", which was an important distinction to somebody who respected his audience.

His nephew John Lewis told me that it was almost impossible to walk around Liverpool with his Uncle Ken, because they'd be stopped every few yards by people just wanting to say hello, or get an autograph. He says he never once saw Ken refuse to talk to anybody or even say he was in a hurry. He'd always stop and chat. On a side note it's probably also why Ken was always late for everything…

One day Ken phoned John and said he had found a new kind of pen that he liked in a local stationery shop and he was going to take John there to buy him one. They arrived in the shop in the centre of

Liverpool and Ken started having a laugh with the people serving behind the counter. Within a few moments John could hear people outside saying, "Ken Dodd's in there!", so the shop started to fill up with fans, eager to meet their local hero. In no time the shop was so full John found himself being pushed out of the door into the street where he had to wait for forty minutes for Uncle Ken to re-emerge. John told me, "I never did get that pen!"

An interesting flipside to that aspect of Ken is that John also told me that at family gatherings Uncle Ken was never the performer. He would arrive with Anne and quietly behave like any normal family member, far more interested in the rest of the family and what they were doing, rather than boasting about his own successes, or cracking jokes and trying to upstage everybody.

John was clearly extremely fond of his Uncle Ken, and learnt a lot from him, admiring his respect for other people, despite his fame. He said Ken had this instinctive and highly agreeable knack of making you feel like you were the most important person in the room, not him. He'd give you his undivided attention, and was never looking over your shoulder to see who he could talk to next. John says that's the way he was with fans as well, which is why he was so well-loved in Liverpool.

Ken prided himself in showing respect for his fans. Some of the regular followers of his shows would become friends, spending a lot of time with Ken and Anne, before and after stage performances. This did lead to one embarrassing incident, as Anne recalls:

Back in the 1970s there was a couple, Syd and Pearl, who came along to the shows so often they became good friends. They were nice people and did like to come into Ken's dressing room after the shows for a long chat, which was normally fine. However, while I was still working for BEA, I was studying for a Certificate in Industrial Relations one day a week at Manchester Polytechnic, which was very interesting, but quite intensive and academic. At the end of the course I had a single day to finish a long thesis entitled

'Reorganisations within BEA' for the final assessment, but we'd got a show to do that evening, so I was going to have to stay up all night, after we got home, to finish my written dissertation. Ken was very understanding and said that we'd get away from the theatre as quickly as possible, for once not hanging around to chat to people, and he'd drive home so that I could have a nap and be fresh enough to work through the night, writing my thesis. The only problem was that we knew Syd and Pearl had front row seats that evening and would expect to see us after the show. Now, at that particular theatre, there was a rather serious and intense little chap called Alan from Bolton. He was semi-retired, but he liked to help Ken as a dresser and general factotum whenever we were there. The funny thing was he would always insist on referring to himself as Ken's manager.

Ken and I had a word with Alan before this particular performance and asked him to make an announcement at the stage door after the show that Mr Dodd had to leave the theatre immediately, and unfortunately would not have time, for once, to sign autographs, or invite people into his dressing-room. I pointed out Syd and Pearl, who were sitting on the front row – she had flame red hair and so was very distinctive looking – and I said that they would probably expect to come backstage, but he must make sure they didn't, on this one occasion. I told him to explain to them, as tactfully as possible, that we had to get away promptly, for personal reasons and that we'd see them next time. So, after the show, Alan, feeling very self-important, walked to the stage door, where the usual crowd of fans and autograph-hunters had gathered, including Syd & Pearl, and said, in his broad Bolton accent, "Right! Good evening ladies and gentlemen. I am Ken Dodd's spokesman and his personal manager while he's at this theatre, and I have a very important announcement to make. I have to tell every one of you, if you will please pay attention, that Mr Dodd will not be speaking to anybody after the show – especially that woman there with the red hair!"

Of course poor Pearl nearly fainted. The theatre manager came running to Ken's dressing-room to say he'd got a near riot on his hands at the stage door, so we had to invite Syd and Pearl backstage, after all, to explain and apologise. I think we ended up being later than normal...

Another plus side to fame for Ken was the opportunity it gave him to meet his own heroes. People perhaps don't realise that stars get just as star-struck as the rest of us mere mortals. I remember, in my earliest days of television production, standing in a BBC green room after a show recording, having a glass of wine with all the celebrities, hardly able to believe that I was there and feeling slightly overawed. I found myself in a small group, chatting to Barbara Windsor and famed sitcom actor John Inman. I was pinching myself at this privileged opportunity, when they started talking enthusiastically about how thrilled they'd been earlier that week to meet legendary Hollywood horror movie actor Vincent Price. They were like a couple of excited giggling fans themselves. I had a sudden moment of realisation, which put it all into perspective for me – fame is relative. And, of course, they are only human. Famous people still get awestruck by other famous people. It was an interesting lesson for me, and made meeting stars much less daunting from that point on.

Ken Dodd was no different. John Fisher, one of his TV producers, recalled at Ken's funeral that it could take an hour to achieve a ten-minute walk through the labyrinthine corridors of BBC Television Centre with Ken, because he'd be stopping constantly to pay homage to the people he admired. One day he bumped into Ronnie Barker, by chance, in a BBC corridor, and almost bowed, as though in the presence of royalty. Ken meant it too. As far as he was concerned Ronnie was showbiz royalty.

Ken loved it even more when famous people paid him the great honour of coming to see his theatre show, especially if they came backstage to his dressing-room afterwards to say hello. Anne fondly remembers a few of those memorable evenings:

One of the most surprising was legendary film actor and 1960s heart-throb, Lawrence of Arabia himself, Peter O'Toole. It was one night in the early 2000s, so Peter would have been in his eighties by then. We were appearing at the Pavilion Theatre on Worthing Pier. It's a funny picture really. Kevin and Irving, our very down-to-earth keyboard player and drummer, were sitting outside the stage door, puffing on their pipes and chatting before the show, and one of them said, "See that old chap over there, walking up the pier? He looks the spitting image of Peter O'Toole!", and the other said, "Can't be! What would he be doing here?" Anyway, sure enough, after the show, a rather flustered theatre manager came into Ken's dressing-room and said, "There's Peter O'Toole, the famous actor, outside. He'd like to have a word. Is it alright if I bring him in?" Ken said, "Of course it is! Just give me two minutes to get my make-up off…"

Well, what a gentleman. It turns out he was a big variety fan and he'd seen the show advertised, caught a train down from London, bought his own ticket, watched the show and then had politely asked if he could say hello to Ken afterwards, because he'd enjoyed it so much. They chatted for ages – probably an hour or more. To break the ice, when Peter first came in, Ken had complimented him on his smart, dapper attire, and had particularly admired a very natty, expensive-looking tie he was wearing. As Peter got up to leave he slipped off his tie and said, "I'd love you to have this dear boy! I've had such a good night tonight, please take it as a keepsake of our meeting." I thought that was lovely.

Another unexpected one who made a special journey to see the show was Barry Humphries, creator of his infamous alter-ego, Dame Edna Everage. Coincidentally it was another time when we happened to be in Worthing. I suppose it's because it's not too far from London. Barry apparently had just flown in to Gatwick Airport and got a taxi all the way down to the south coast. Again he came round to the dressing-room afterwards and was extremely gracious, charming and generous with his praise. I think Ken thought Dame Edna's humour was a bit more acerbic than his, so he wondered if they'd get on, but they hit it off surprisingly well, chatting happily for ages.

Barry even helped Ken play a practical joke on Di Brooks, who travelled with us, helping on the show. Ken knew that Di had a bit of a phobia of Barry's other alter-ego, Sir Les Patterson, the repulsive, slobbering, lecherous Australian 'diplomat' he sometimes plays. She couldn't bear to watch him when he was portraying that character. So Ken got me to go and get Di to come to the dressing-room, under some false pretext, and, as she walked in, Barry somehow miraculously transformed into Sir Les Patterson. His whole body seemed to hunch over and change shape, his face contorting into his deliberately offensive character. It was quite amazing to watch actually. Barry, or rather Sir Les, leered at Di and said, "Hello my dear!" Well that was all it took. Poor Di shrieked and ran off.

Another night I was in the foyer of the King's Theatre in Southsea, selling programmes, and I realised my next customer was Stephanie Cole, the great comedy actress. I refused to take her money, but she kept insisting, not realising who I was. I told her that Ken was a great admirer of her work, and that he'd never forgive me if I took money from her. It turns out she was a big fan of variety comedians, especially Ken. She'd seen him work several times before. So I asked if she'd like to come back to his dressing-room after the show. At first she said she didn't want to bother him, but I assured her that he'd be disappointed if he found out she'd been there and he hadn't had the opportunity to meet her. So she and her friend Ariel Bruce came to see us after the show and we chatted for ages, striking up long-lasting friendships. I still see Steph and Ariel whenever I possibly can.

Stephanie Cole told me that Ken was so refreshing because there was no obvious ego. She echoed the observation others have made that Ken always seemed to be more interested in the person he was talking to, rather than in talking about himself – something she says is extremely rare in showbusiness. Because she works a lot in comedy roles she said Ken loved to discuss and try to analyse what makes things funny, particularly in things she had done. She also stressed what many others who knew Ken said about him, that he could talk about anything and everything, and be knowledgeable about so many things. She went so far as to describe him as a polymath. In summing up, Stephanie said she felt incredibly lucky to have known him, and to learn from him.

Another chance meeting was Irish comedian Dara O'Briain. Ken was appearing at the City Varieties Theatre in Leeds, former home of BBC TV's *The Good Old Days,* when Dara just happened to be in the city. Dara had heard the Dodd reputation for long shows, but said Ken never played Ireland, so he didn't really know too much about his act. Despite (unfounded) fears that Ken might be one of the 'old school' who resorted to sexist or racist humour, he decided to go and see Ken's show, almost as a comedy pilgrimage – something every comedian should do at some point in their life. The City Varieties was perhaps the perfect venue to see somebody like Ken, so, with some trepidation about a five-hour show that he might not even enjoy, Dara bought a ticket and went off to have a meal before the show. He didn't think Ken would even know who he was, so he was very surprised when he got a message in the restaurant saying Ken would love to say hello before curtain-up. Student of comedy Ken of course knew exactly who Dara was, having seen *Mock the Week* many times, and was flattered when he was told that Dara had popped in to buy a ticket. They chatted for a few minutes, with Ken surprising Dara with his extensive knowledge of current comedy and comedians. They agreed to meet again in Ken's dressing-room after the performance, if Dara managed to survive the full five hours.

Super-intelligent Irishman Dara loved the never-ending cascade of joke after joke, impressed that there were no 'Irish jokes', nothing politically incorrect at all in fact. He was surprised to find that Ken's act didn't feel old-fashioned in any way, and was hilarious, with appeal to all age groups. He said Ken's obvious enjoyment of being onstage was infectious, and reminded him of why he got into comedy in the first place – "the sheer joy of performance and making people laugh." After the show, over a beer, they had a wonderful hour or more discussing the history of comedy, tracing their origins right back from vaudeville and music hall, through Charlie Chaplin and early silent comedians, to *Mock the Week* and the current wave. Dara told me, "It was genuinely one of the most gorgeous hours I've ever spent in this industry…"

Ken, because of his lifelong love of whimsy, was a huge fan of *The Muppet Show*. In 1988 he was thrilled to get the chance to meet Kermit the Frog and *Muppets* creator Jim Henson. They were appearing together at the Victoria Palace Theatre in London, on that year's Children's Royal Variety Performance, in the presence of HRH Princess Margaret. Anne picks up the story:

During the afternoon rehearsals Ken and I were sitting in the audience seating, with the ever-present dog on my lap. It was Doodle the poodle, at that time. Jim Henson, with his arm inside Kermit the Frog, came over to introduce himself. He was American of course, so he didn't know too much about Ken's work, but he was very charming.

"Mr Dodd – the great comedian – I have heard so much about you…"

Ken was thrilled and told Jim what a big fan he was of The Muppets, *so Jim brought Kermit closer to Ken, bringing the famous green Muppet to life. No sooner had Kermit started animating and said, "Hello Doddy!" than Doodle started growling fiercely and, with one bound, leapt up from my lap, biting Kermit firmly on the nose, and refusing to let go. Poor Ken was mortified. So was I! Thankfully, other than a little poodle saliva, Kermit's nose (and Jim Henson's hand!) survived unscathed, but I really did think Doodle was going to pull Kermit's nose right off, just before his important Royal appearance.*

Ken always had a lot of time for other laughter-makers. One of Ken's friends in the business was Yorkshire comedian Charlie Williams. Charlie had risen to fame thanks to his regular appearances on Granada TV's *The Comedians*, alongside other club comics, like Frank Carson, Roy Walker, Bernard Manning and Jim Bowen. Some of those comedians broke through as game show hosts, and, in the early 1970s, Charlie was given the opportunity of hosting the popular game show *The Golden Shot*. It was a complicated, fast-moving show, which was transmitted live, so there was no room for mistakes. It had been made popular by one of the great game show kings – Bob Monkhouse, who was always sharp as a tack. Poor Charlie found himself out of his comfort zone and struggled, receiving a mauling from the critics. He only survived for one series, before being unceremoniously dropped by ITV. Ken kindly phoned Charlie to commiserate and point out that it wasn't his fault, that it just hadn't been the right vehicle for his talents. Charlie was philosophical about the crushing experience and just said, "You know Doddy – my old man used to say, 'The man who never made a mistake, never made anything'..." Ken was so impressed by that profound and optimistic maxim that he had it mounted and framed.

Chapter 13:

THE ROAR OF THE CROWD

Ken Dodd simply loved theatres. Why wouldn't he? They are magical places which have no other purpose than to give people pleasure and happiness. They had also provided him with a wonderful career.

He often said to journalists, and on chat shows, in later life, that he had made a pact with himself to attempt to play every theatre in the British Isles. It was a publicity stunt really, as it was pretty much an impossible task. So much depends on how you define 'a theatre'. If you include every arts centre, village hall, leisure centre and church annexe that has a stage then the number is phenomenal. Nevertheless it prompted Ken to play some unlikely venues, and to spread his wings literally to all four corners of the British Isles, from Shetland in the extreme north, to small theatres in the far south-west of Cornwall and the Channel Islands, and from west Wales and the Isle Of Man, to the furthest extremes of East Anglia and Kent.

Here's Anne's take on Ken's self-inflicted challenge:

He soon discovered that there were hundreds more theatres than he ever knew existed. He regularly received letters from tiny theatres in remote places he'd never heard of, saying "come and do your show here". Some were so small and so far away it just wasn't economically viable to go there. Having said that it could be quite gratifying to do shows in small venues. They were so grateful. I remember we did a little village hall in Ystradgynlais in south-west Wales. It was

just Ken and I, plus our backing duo, to keep the costs down. I was
selling the programmes that night, because we had no backup team
with us. This sweet little old lady came up to me before the show and
said, in her gentle lilting Welsh accent: "Oh, I do hope we're good
enough for you." I said, "Well I hope we're good enough for you!",
but I thought that was very touching.

In the end he couldn't possibly do everywhere that called itself a theatre. However, it is probably fair to say that Ken Dodd did play more British theatres than any other comedian, which I guess was his real goal in later life.

Ken's love of theatres stemmed from his first childhood visits with his family to the Shakespeare Theatre in Liverpool, often known in those days as the Shakespeare Theatre of Varieties, or 'The Shakey' for short. At that time it was home to the great variety stars of the day and was where Ken first fell in love with "the rosy cosy glow of a theatre and the rumpty-tumpty sounds of a theatre orchestra."

In the 1970s Ken was therefore horrified to see so many theatres closing or being turned into bingo halls or supermarkets. He began a crusade to save some of the better-known theatres, all of which had meant a lot to him on the way up. Ken didn't like to think of it as an official crusade. He was just keen to keep as many theatres open as possible, so he'd help where he could. It was the press who dubbed it a crusade, which actually seems fair enough to me, in view of his sterling efforts in some quite bloody battles.

The first battle started in 1974, and was right on his doorstep. Ken heard that the Royal Court Theatre in Liverpool was in trouble and under threat of closure. They desperately needed publicity and public awareness of their plight. There had been a theatre on that site since 1826. The original building had been completely destroyed by fire in 1933 and rebuilt in the art deco style of the period. The sumptuously appointed new theatre re-opened in 1938. It was a venue Ken had visited often and played many times, a place dear to his heart. He wasn't going to stand by and watch a theatre closure so close to home. Not without a fight at any rate.

Buoyed by the thrill of performing completely solo the year before in his *Ha-Ha* show at the Playhouse Theatre, Ken decided one way to drum up publicity for the campaign to save the Royal Court was to use it as the venue to stage an attempt to get into the *Guinness Book of World Records*, with the longest ever joke-telling session. He called this event the *Marathon Mirthquake*, and, as planned, it attracted a lot of press attention. Determined and single-minded as ever Ken did of course create a world record, and, in the process, raised enough money and public awareness to get the Royal Court a stay of execution.

Ken's astonishing feat is often misquoted, but this is the correct version, transcribed directly from the *Guinness Book of World Records 1974*. The entry appeared in the Human Achievements chapter, in the section on Endurance & Endeavour, under the subheading *Joke Cracking*:

"Ken Dodd, at the Royal Court Theatre, Liverpool, on 4th June 1974, told jokes to a paying audience, unremittingly, for 3 hours 7 minutes and 30 seconds."

If Ken kept up his usual target of seven TPM (Titters Per Minute) then that was over 1,300 different jokes, non-stop.

Fellow comedian Russ Abbott was there as one of that paying audience at the *Marathon Mirthquake*. This is what Russ told me about that day:

"Oh you had to go and see it. First and foremost it was for such a worthy cause, and it was wonderful for Ken to get into the record books in his hometown of Liverpool. It really was quite special. Miraculous to be on for so long without repeating a line. I can't believe anybody else would have had the gall, or the bottle to do it, only Ken. He knew he could pull it off though. He wanted the challenge, and he did it. Bless his heart."

The Royal Court at that time was still owned by the entertainment group Howard & Wyndham, but they were winding down their theatre interests and investing in film production and television (specifically

ITV). They were losing money on their theatres so they were trying to sell them off to the various local councils. A cash-strapped Liverpool Council didn't exactly snap their hands off, so, despite Ken's best efforts in 1974, there was a brief closure of the Royal Court, as Howard & Wyndham's financial problems worsened. However Ken came to the rescue again. He was part of a consortium, the Royal Court Theatre & Art Trust, who bought the theatre temporarily, and he put on a Christmas show in 1978, spearheading its re-opening. He even sat in the box office on the first day, selling tickets, much to the delight of Liverpudlian theatre-goers.

At the time he told a BBC journalist, "I think (the Royal Court) has a very good future. Every theatre in Britain has a good future, providing they are run properly, marketed properly, and if their policy is right. This theatre closed because it was being run from a desk in London. Now it's being run from the heart of Merseyside, and it will reflect the tastes of the people of the north-west."

Ken's words were prophetic and all his efforts paid off. The success of his Christmas show relaunched the Royal Court as a popular entertainment venue in Liverpool. It was eventually taken over by Merseyside County Council. In the 1980s it became well known for big name rock concerts, one of the first being local hero Paul McCartney, launching his UK 'Wings' tour there in 1979. Next it became a major comedy club, and it is now home to contemporary plays, comedies and musical shows, all with a Liverpudlian slant, produced by local talent.

A heart-warming postscript to this story is that in 2018, on the eightieth anniversary of the re-opening of the Royal Court, Anne unveiled a brass plaque in the foyer, honouring the memory of Sir Ken Dodd, OBE as a Liverpool legend, and entertainer extraordinaire, who played an integral role in saving the theatre. On the second anniversary of Ken's passing, Anne was invited back to unveil two large murals of Ken and the Diddymen, painted by local artist Paul Curtis, on the wall outside the stage door, right next to a plaque Ken had himself commissioned to celebrate his own local comedy heroes from bygone years. She was thrilled to be told that 'Doddy Day' is to become an annual event in the city's cultural calendar, and the Royal Court will lead the celebrations each year, on Ken's birthday.

His theatre-saving crusade continued almost by accident when Ken heard that the Manchester Palace Theatre was closing in 1977 and was being put on the market for re-development as a hotel or office complex. This happened to coincide with his need to find a gig for Christmas of that year. As we have already learned he had deliberately kept that period free in case he needed to be at fiancée Anita's bedside during her dying days, so he had declined offers of pantomime. Sadly Anita died that summer, so suddenly there was a huge hole in Ken's normally packed diary. This gave him the impetus to take the reins and produce a long run of his own show. This is how Anne remembers that time:

We'd heard that the Manchester Palace was 'dark', so Ken thought he could perhaps do a few weeks there. The Palace at that time belonged to Moss Empires, which had been bought by the Grade family. Audiences had been declining, so it was sitting there empty, waiting for a buyer. Ken phoned the Moss Empires' head office in London and asked if he could put a Christmas season on there. They initially said no, because they had closed the theatre and there was no longer an infrastructure in place, but Ken pointed out that the building and the stage were still there. In the end they said the only way it could possibly be done would be as a 'four wall contract'. Ken asked what that meant, and he was told it meant Moss Empires would provide nothing but the building, and Ken would have to employ staff to run the place and pay for everything – right down to the toilet rolls in the loos. Ken thought about it and agreed to do just that. It was a nice theatre, which Ken liked very much. He had happy memories of pantomimes at this venue, so he hoped putting on a successful show for a lengthy Christmas season might just save it from permanent closure. Moss Empires weren't too keen, because they were hoping to sell the place, but it was a Grade II listed building so it couldn't easily be re-developed for a different use, which meant they weren't exactly inundated with offers. Grudgingly they agreed to let Ken hire the place on this 'four wall' basis. Of course it turned out to be a lot more complicated than it sounded.

I was still working for BEA, and it was my really busy time there in personnel management, so I couldn't help too much, but I did what I could to take the pressure off Ken. Nancy George from the Forrester-George office helped quite a lot on the business side of things, and Dave Forrester provided some of the support acts, but a lot of it was down to Ken himself.

The first thing Ken had to do was staff the place, so he rang the former manager, Paul Goldsworthy, who contacted all the original staff from the box office, plus the front-of-house and backstage teams and re-engaged any of them who were still available.

It was hard work. I remember we were still working flat-out, right up to the opening night. We were at the theatre all day getting ready for the first show, knowing it had to be just right, because all the press had been invited. That afternoon, totally unexpectedly, this massive silver salver arrived with a huge mountain of sandwiches on it, from the pub across the road. We thought how kind of them and we all tucked in. Now Ken had a naughty habit of lifting the tops off sandwiches to inspect the fillings, and then not replacing the tops if he didn't like what he saw, so, although we hadn't eaten the whole great mountain, it was looking quite bedraggled by the time we'd all picked at what we fancied. Suddenly this press officer chap arrived and said, "Has anybody seen my sandwiches?" It turned out he'd ordered them from the pub for the gentlemen of the press that evening. We panicked and started trying to reassemble what was left of the sandwiches to make them look respectable again.

Ken even had to market the show himself. I remember him hiring lorries and open-topped buses, to take him round Manchester, literally banging a big bass drum and shouting into a megaphone to advertise the show. He did say though that the local Manchester press, and both BBC North West and Granada (ITV) got on board the 'Save Manchester Palace Campaign' to rescue this iconic theatre. Of course that helped enormously with media coverage, publicity stunts and photo opportunities. The whole city seemed to get behind the campaign in fact.

I remember we were rehearsing one bit where Ken was in a Mickey Mouse costume. Dave Forrester, his agent, had come up from London to see the show, and there was this lovely image of the two of them standing on the stage, in deep earnest conversation about business, with Dave in a suit and tie, and Ken in little red shorts, big boots, braces and Mickey Mouse ears.

Ken must have already started to get a reputation for long shows by then, because he had this lovely idea of starting with the finale, for those in the audience who couldn't stay right to the end. All the cast walked down in crazy costumes and took a bow, before the show had even started.

The result was a resounding success. Ken's show sold out twice-nightly, virtually every night for three months. He only closed it then because he had a prior commitment which he couldn't postpone. He was due to re-open yet another venue – the Theatre Royal in Nottingham. The good thing was he'd done enough to save the Palace, by proving it still could make money and put bums on seats. It was then bought by the Manchester Palace Theatre Trust, who got hold of some land at the back and actually extended the stage. It was also extensively refurbished and improved, before being relaunched properly in 1981. It's now run by the Ambassador Theatre Group, and is still very popular to this day – all thanks to Ken.

The Blackpool Grand Theatre is an exquisite example of the genius of the matchless Frank Matcham. He designed and built some of the finest British theatres during Victorian times, including the world-renowned London Palladium. Matcham was commissioned to create 'the prettiest theatre in the country' in Blackpool. The resulting beautifully-appointed Grand Theatre was a favourite of many northern artists, including Ken Dodd. In fact Ken was a patron and honorary member of the Frank Matcham Society, who are dedicated to 'the appreciation and enjoyment of great theatres'.

From 1968 onwards the Blackpool Grand was owned by the EMI Group, but sadly it had fallen into disrepair and it lost its theatre licence in 1972, on safety grounds, and had to close. EMI scheduled it for demolition in 1973, to make way for a new development of shops. However, thanks to the foresight and quick-thinking of 'The Victorian Society', who had managed to get the Grand registered as a Grade II listed building when the theatre closed, EMI's demolition plans had to be shelved.

Ken was an early member of a group called 'The Friends of the Grand', who formed in 1973 to save the theatre. They literally rolled up their sleeves and were hands-on, doing minor cosmetic repairs and decorating, but major costly structural repairs and renovation were needed before it could re-open. EMI asked the Blackpool council for financial help, but that was declined, so, in 1974, a campaign was launched called 'Save the Grand', again supported by Ken Dodd. Unfortunately they still couldn't raise sufficient funds.

The sadly decaying theatre remained unused and 'dark' for three years, until EMI proposed turning it into a bingo hall. This heresy was initially opposed by 'The Friends of the Grand', but at least it meant that the building wouldn't fall into further disrepair. It also meant that EMI would have to pay for all the costly but essential repair work, to make it pass safety standards and current fire regulations for a public building. Not only that, because of its new Grade II listed status, any changes would be closely monitored, and EMI wouldn't be allowed to decimate the beautiful aesthetics of the place as a sumptuous theatre. On that basis the change of use was reluctantly allowed to go ahead. As part of the deal the Friends were permitted by EMI to use the Grand for monthly 'midnight matinees', to keep the spirit of the theatre alive in there. Ken did several of these. The midnight shows were extremely successful, unlike the bingo hall, which, fortunately for 'The Friends of the Grand', never really took off.

EMI closed it as a bingo hall, after three unprofitable years, and agreed to sell the building at the knockdown price of £350,000 to 'The Blackpool Grand Theatre Trust' in 1980. To help them raise the necessary deposit Ken staged a show at the Grand, and gave his support to lots of other fundraising events to help swell the coffers. The remainder of the cash was raised from foreign investors.

Further refurbishment was undertaken to restore the Grand to Matcham's former glory and, in 1981, it re-opened as a proper theatre again. It is now recognised as one of the most beautifully ornate theatres in the country. Ken returned there many times, often doing Sunday night concerts, so he was thrilled in 2006 when the actors' union Equity awarded the Blackpool Grand the title: The United Kingdom's National Theatre of Variety.

At the time of writing this 'The Friends of the Grand' are planning to install a prominent bronze statue of Sir Ken with Dicky Mint, in honour of his major part in saving 'the prettiest theatre in the country'.

There were other theatres which were helped by Ken, as Anne recalls:

He did various fundraisers for the Liverpool Playhouse over the years, and he'd often offer to put on a show at a special cut-price rate at different theatres and halls who needed financial support, so that they could make more money for themselves.

The Plaza in Stockport was one we helped in the 1990s. It belonged to the Rank Leisure Group who had reluctantly decided to close it, because it had got a bit run down. They'd tried various things – it had been a cinema and a bingo hall, but it wasn't making money. There was an amazing voluntary group called 'The Friends of the Plaza', who worked really hard to save the theatre, successfully stopping the closure and threatened demolition. Ken gave them lots of encouragement and help. Ken would play there when other companies refused to put on shows. We did three nights there with buckets on the stage, because the roof was leaking. One night there was a power cut, because the electrics were faulty. The whole place went into total darkness while Ken was onstage. Rather than risk a panicky exodus in the dark, Ken took a torch that was being offered to him from the wings, shone it under his chin, up at his face, and carried on performing until they managed to get the power back on.

The campaign was successful and, in March 2000, Rank Leisure sold the theatre to 'The Stockport Plaza Trust', and it's still going strong to this day, having been restored to its former art deco glory.

Ken loved the traditions of theatre. Showbiz agent Laurie Mansfield thinks that's why Ken was so keen on pantomimes, even though they imposed scripted restrictions upon him. Pantos are part of our Great British theatrical heritage, they keep theatres alive, they give children an interest in theatre, and, in Ken's day, they were an important staple to fill diaries for variety performers. Pantomime was a tradition to embrace, even if it did mean (loosely!) sticking to a script.

Ken loved all theatres, but he had nostalgic reasons for loving some even more than others. The London Palladium obviously held very fond memories, as did the City Varieties in Leeds, where he'd appeared so many times on *The Good Old Days*. He was often asked if he had a favourite theatre, to which he always replied, "The theatre I'm playing tomorrow night." That was partly a diplomatic ploy, so as not to offend anybody, but I think it was also true, because he could never get enough of the roar of the crowd...

Chapter 14:

TIME MATTERS NOT ONE JOT

It has often been said that Ken Dodd had a peculiar relationship with time. He was notoriously late for everything, and he appeared to have no concept of time when it came to the duration of his later shows. Right up to the end, beyond his 90th birthday, Ken was still touring his *Happiness* shows, which usually ran for at least five hours. There was an interval of course, and there were a couple of short support acts, including Anne's own musical spot, but the rest was Ken. I would estimate that was approximately four hours of Ken holding court, up there on the stage on his own. Nobody else, in the history of entertainment, has performed that amount of solo material on a regular nightly basis. I have thought about it long and hard, and discussed it with other showbusiness professionals, but not one of us can think of another precedent for doing such marathon performances. It is quite surprising actually that Ken Dodd was unique in that regard.

Ken's friend and fellow Liverpudlian, comedy actor Ricky Tomlinson, tells a lovely story. He says there was an old couple walking out of a theatre where they had been watching Ken. They looked at their watches and said, "Well that really was good value for money. What a great show. We should be just in time for the last bus home." Ricky says he tapped them on the shoulder and said indignantly, "Excuse me! Where are you going? This is only the interval!"

Dara O'Briain says that contemporary comedians start with perhaps five or ten minutes of material as a try-out spot, then they develop and start doing maybe thirty minutes when they get proper comedy club bookings. An hour is the next step, say for the Edinburgh Fringe Festival, then, if you become a top headlining act in big theatres and arenas you might do a full two-hour show, with an interval, and that's really where it stops. Dara points out that Ken had already done two hours of material in the first half!

In Ken's days of variety theatre that evolution of performance actually followed a very similar pattern. Lesser-known comedians would do a ten- or twelve-minute spot 'front of cloth' in the first half. As they became better known they might do twenty minutes to close the first half. The top of the bill would do thirty to forty minutes. For working men's clubs a comedian needed three twenty-minute spots, and for the big cabaret-style 'theatre clubs' the headline act would do an hour, plus perhaps a short encore.

What should be noted is that in those days of variety the managements were extremely strict. The company manager would put a stop-watch on the acts and report anybody who exceeded their allotted time. They would then be disciplined. There were a lot of acts in those shows and if they all over-ran, even by just a couple of minutes, the whole schedule would become unmanageable and costly. So Ken could keep to time when he knew he had to. He was trained in the business at a time when there really was no choice. You kept to time or you didn't work again. This of course means that his later lack of discipline about time was a conscious choice.

There have been all sorts of theories about why Ken chose to perform such long shows, but personally I don't think there has ever been one specific reason. I believe there were many factors at play. If you pinned me down and made me choose one, I'd say, "because he wanted to."

There have been outlandish theories, such as it was a form of control – a macho bullying of the audience. Ken, quite rightly, emphatically denied such allegations. He always pointed out that, despite jokes to the contrary, the theatre doors weren't locked. Anybody was free to leave whenever they chose to do so. In fact most people wanted to stay to the bitter end, unless they really did have a last bus or train to catch, or a weary babysitter to relieve at a specific time. Eric Sykes said that Ken's audiences who had to leave would slowly walk out backwards, to avoid missing any more than absolutely necessary. The truth is Ken, perhaps more than most other comedians, adored his audiences. He considered them as friends. Why would he want to bully them?

As a fan of Ken Dodd myself I used to go every couple of years to do the whole marathon *Happiness* show experience with Matt, my younger son and fellow Ken Dodd fan, when Ken was in the south of England. We can clearly remember one particular Easter show in Bournemouth, after five and a half hours of Ken and company (mainly Ken!), Matt and I, along with the entire audience, were all on our feet crying out for "More!" as Ken was trying to wind up the show and cue the final curtain. The show had started at 7.30, and, unbelievably, it was one o'clock the next morning when we were all still begging Ken for more. If anything we were bullying him. Hadn't he done enough for us already?

Michael Billington, the *Guardian* theatre critic, described that phenomenon as almost like an orgy of mutual love between Ken and his audiences.

Friends have said to me that I must have been mad going to such long shows, but I just felt they were mad for not going.

It is probably worth recounting one other personal memory from as far back as 1979. Ken was starring for the summer season at the Opera House in Scarborough, performing twice-nightly. My wife and I had tickets for the second house one night, which was due to start at 8.45. At nine o'clock hundreds of us were waiting patiently, lined along the length of St Thomas Street, waiting to get in, because Ken was still onstage, having over-run massively during the first house. Thankfully it wasn't raining.

That was just the beginning though of the marathon shows which were still to come. As we have seen, due to radical changes in showbusiness, the once lucrative variety theatre circuit was almost dead, so Ken, ably assisted by Anne, had started producing his own touring show, which meant he was his own boss. No longer was there a company manager breathing down his neck and telling him he couldn't over-run. That is when the shows really started to grow in length.

Rumours abounded that theatres dreaded Ken appearing there, but when I asked theatre owner and impresario Nick Thomas about Ken's long shows he told me that the staff loved Ken and he was always charming with them. "The over-running was no surprise. They knew in advance that it was going to be a long evening, so we'd lay on refreshments for them all. Nobody minded. It was always a special night when Ken was around."

Ken used to defend his long shows by saying he was giving value for money. It had a kind of logic to it, but I don't think that was the reason he stayed onstage so long. If he'd hated being up there I'm sure he would have terminated the show at a normal time, and he would have still said he'd given value for money, just the same as any other entertainer.

The bottom line is Ken loved to be onstage. It was his domain. He wanted to be up there all night.

Ken's close showbusiness friend Roy Hudd once asked Ken why he stayed on so long and he said, "I won't come off because I love it on there." To which Roy replied, "Well I love it on there as well Ken, but I want to get home!"

Dara O'Briain asked a similar question and Ken just said, "Why break up a good party?"

The simple fact is Ken wanted to be on that stage as long as possible. It's where he had the most fun in his life, and, so long as the audiences were having fun as well, then why not just keep going? As I have said earlier in this book Ken didn't like discarding old material which still guaranteed him big laughs, but he also liked to add new material all the time, so the act just grew and grew.

Of course the one person who must have known better than anybody why Ken stayed onstage so long, because she had to wait for him every night, was Anne:

I never minded, but I did start to get worried about it when Ken got into his eighties. I tried telling him that he was killing himself. I used to say, "Shorter show, longer life. You must take it a bit more easy. You don't need to do so long!", but he just used to dismiss my warnings by saying that he was enjoying himself. He'd say it wasn't stressful because he was just standing there chatting to old friends. There is no doubt the stage was Ken's natural environment.

It was funny really – the regulars in the audience would bring flasks of tea or coffee and sandwiches because they knew it was going to be a long evening.

They talk about 'Doctor Showbusiness' magically healing sick or tired performers before they go onstage, but it really was like that with Ken. If he wasn't feeling so well or even just as he got older, he would walk onstage and you could see the years literally fall off him. It was amazing.

After a show we did at St George's Hall in Bradford, Vee Sweeney was packing up the merchandising in the foyer. She was one half of a musical support act who often toured with us, 'Andante'. She overheard a couple complaining that they had been ripped off, as they had been watching a Ken Dodd lookalike perform the second half of the show. Vee tried to reassure them it really was Ken, but they said that was impossible as the Doddy 'double' in the second half looked a lot younger than the real Ken who came on at the beginning of the show.

Once he was on there and the adrenaline kicked in, he really did look younger, so it probably prolonged his life doing the live shows, rather than shortened it. Sometimes, by the end of a show, people in the audience looked more exhausted than he did.

And of course it didn't stop when he came offstage. That wasn't the end of the night for us. He'd need time to wind down. He'd get changed, have a quick drink and scribble down any new jokes, or ad-libs. He'd also make notes about how any new material had gone down. He never stopped with that forensic approach to the work. Then there would be people wanting to see him – fans, friends and colleagues. I'd keep them waiting until he was ready for them. He always found time for people though, no matter how tired he was. Then of course we had to load up the car. It could be three o'clock in the morning before we actually left a theatre.

The funny thing is he could cut the show down if he needed to. If there was going to be a massive overtime bill at a particular theatre, then he managed to shorten the show alright. Some theatres would let us start as early as 7pm, but they insisted he had to be off by one minute before midnight, which he was. Other theatres would insist on the interval being at a specific time so that they knew when to serve drinks and coffee, and he could keep to that promise. He wasn't nearly as ill-disciplined as people make out. He could tailor the show if he needed to, but, if he was given free rein, he'd stay on as long as possible. He really did love it. That's the real reason he did long shows.

Every comedian who knew Ken Dodd had their apocryphal stories about his long shows. Jimmy Tarbuck said that a woman went to the police one morning, very upset, to report her elderly mother as missing. The desk sergeant asked if her mum had gone to see the Ken Dodd show the previous night by any chance. The woman said, "Yes, actually she did." "Oh, that explains it!" said the policeman. "He's still on!"

That was obviously a Tarby joke, but comedian Joe Pasquale told me a true personal anecdote about Ken's long shows. Joe was starring in summer season at the Blackpool Grand Theatre, back in the 1990s. The tradition was that summer season shows would play from Monday to Saturday, allowing the theatre to put a different star in for a weekly 'Sunday concert'. That freed up the weekly star to either have a day's rest with the family, or go off and do a Sunday concert in a different seaside town. That particular summer Ken was taking over the Grand from Joe on Sunday nights, while Joe was driving off to do Sunday concerts in Skegness, over on the east coast. Of course it meant that for one day each week Ken was using Joe's star dressing-room. Every Sunday Joe would go to the Grand to pick up his props and costumes, and drive to Skegness, right from west coast to east coast. His and Ken's shows would start at about the same time at opposite sides of the country. Joe would finish his two-hour show in Skegness, pack up his car, and drive two hundred miles back to the Blackpool Grand to drop his stuff back into his dressing-room there – and he'd still have time to catch the last few minutes of Ken, who was still onstage.

In the business Ken was known as the patron saint of taxi drivers, because vast numbers of his audience would miss their last buses and trains home.

Of course it became part of Doddy mythology and a conspiracy between Ken and the audience in the end. He'd extend the show even further by doing material about how long the show was going to be... and of course the audiences lapped it up. After a few hours he'd shout "Give in?" and the happy crowd would shout back "No!" He would say, "It's no good trying to leave early – I'll follow you home and shout jokes through your letterbox!"

Ken would get audiences chanting a little ditty about "Time matters not one jot!", then he'd say, "I'll remind you of that in a couple of hours' time..."

The longer the shows became the more new jokes he'd come up with on the subject: "It's like a long-haul flight this show – by rights you should all be wearing special socks!"... and, "By the end of tonight you'll all know what a hostage situation is really like...", and, "I've seen children grow out of their trousers while I'm on..."

I think Ken, with his disdain for rules and doing as he was told, really couldn't help himself, and never stopped to think about the consequences of over-running. Anne told me that one year he was honoured to be invited to lead the traditional singing of the famous hymn 'Abide with Me' before the prestigious Rugby League Challenge Cup Final at Wembley Stadium. The rousing chorus went so well that Ken, instead of taking a bow and leaving, said, "That was marvellous – let's do it again!", and repeated the whole hymn. Of course the officials were having canary fits because it delayed the critically-timed start of the televised match.

Chapter 15:

IT'S ALL IN THE MIND

When you talk to people who knew Ken well the one recurring theme which they all refer to is his intellect. In many ways this is surprising. Partly because mainstream comedians aren't particularly renowned for their impressive brain power; partly because the public usually only ever got to see Ken as the crazy wise-cracking buffoon he played onstage; and partly because Ken abruptly terminated his full-time formal education at the age of just fourteen. However that didn't mean he stopped learning. Far from it in fact. I think, because he kicked against authority and obeying the rules, and because he didn't much like his grammar school, perversely he started to learn a whole lot more the moment he left school. His parents had always impressed upon him the great importance of reading and books, so he would visit the library, and all the Liverpool bookshops, and read constantly. If ever there was a living embodiment of a self-educated man it was Ken Dodd.

He was also interested in just about everything, and enjoyed discussing just about anything. He was particularly interested in other people. That is again surprising in a celebrity, because they are generally far more interested in themselves, often at the expense of all else. However we must remind ourselves once again of something that Ken himself readily admitted – that there were two Ken Dodds – and the other Ken Dodd, the private offstage home-bird, wasn't a celebrity. When he met people he was interested in their story, far more so than telling them his own story. And it wasn't feigned interest, it was absolutely genuine.

Anne told me:

I hate to admit this, but I didn't realise just how clever Ken was until after he died. I discovered the sheer depth of his intellect when I started to look in his personal notebooks. I'd never dreamed of looking in them while he was alive, because they were private, and I respected that. I was open-mouthed when I did look at them for the first time. I was absolutely amazed at the creativity and the profound nature of some of his private thoughts. I suppose I hadn't given him the credit because he left school so young, but of course life gives you the greatest education. He never did like doing as he was told, so that was always going to be a problem for him at senior school. And, although he didn't particularly enjoy grammar school life, finding the teachers cold and aloof, he did often quote his headmaster telling them that they were there to have their minds opened. That maxim really resonated with him.

In Ken's notebooks you sense a surprising lack of confidence in himself. A feeling that he could have done better, even though he achieved so much. Somebody once told me that most high achievers are never totally satisfied with themselves. The notes Ken made are often self-critical, and he obviously understood his problem with time. There are lots of notes to himself about cutting down the length of the shows, tightening up long-winded routines, and generally being more disciplined regarding time and self-editing. He had always been in awe of his comedy heroes Ted Ray and Arthur Askey who could walk onstage and leave a lasting impression in just ten or twenty minutes. Ken felt he had to slave for much longer to get that same level of approbation.

Some of his notes are soul-searching, deeply personal regarding his emotions, and often quite philosophical. Of course, because these were his personal books for getting all his thoughts down as they came to him, the deep meaningful jottings are interspersed with new jokes, and funny ideas for the shows. They're not diaries, although some pages are dated. But it's possible to date some of the books by what he is talking about in them. When he was due to do something important and out of his normal comfort zone, like a speech, or a radio or television interview, he would make copious notes in preparation for those things.

He always had a notepad with him wherever he went, just in case an idea came to him, or in case he wanted to jot something important down. He lived in fear of having a great idea and then forgetting what it was.

He'd also have a different notebook on the go, where he made a list of the ideas he wanted his scriptwriters to work on. He called it his 'turkey order book', because it was in triplicate, like an old butcher's pad. I'd hear him on the phone, firing off all these clever funny concepts for jokes. Sometimes I'd say to him that he didn't need the writers, he could work the ideas up himself, but he liked to get a new perspective and get somebody he trusted to put a different slant on things. In any case he had so many ideas he needed other people to work on them, because he simply didn't have the time.

Books to read and books to write in were Ken's life when he wasn't onstage. When we loaded up the car to go to a gig there would always be three or four large carrier bags full of reading books and notebooks to take with us. Quite often we'd only be away for one night and I'd say, "You won't have time to look at all this lot!", but he wanted to have them with him. When we got home he'd line the bags up in the hall, then add to them and take the odd thing out to make room for the new additions, but they went with us everywhere we went. I have no idea how he knew which books he needed, but he had his system.

Before I had the big library constructed from one of the old outhouses, all Ken's thousands of reference books, comedy books and novels would go up in the attic, where I'd assembled numerous six-shelf bookcases over the years. Sometimes I'd worry about all that weight up there. If they had brought the ceiling down into our bedroom they would have killed us. It got to the point where I didn't know what to do with all his books, but still he'd go out and buy more every week. If we were in London he loved going to Foyles, one of the biggest bookshops in the world, and he'd always buy literally dozens of new volumes. It was his one self-indulgence. Ken always had a great thirst for knowledge, and a constant yearning to feed his creativity.

When we were at a gig people would give him books, because they knew he loved them so much, but I'd despair about where we were going to put them all. Ken's main scriptwriter in later years was a very nice chap from the Midlands, called Barry Reeves. They spoke on the phone almost every night. Barry loved reading nearly as much as Ken did, and he volunteered in a charity bookshop, so he'd keep an eye out for books that would appeal to Ken. If Barry came along to a gig he'd often bring along a whole stack of hardbacks and paperbacks, but they'd try to do the hand-over secretly, so that I didn't see them. I think they forgot that I loaded up the car afterwards and would want to know where all the extra books had come from.

The other thing about Ken's intellect is that long car journeys were never boring. Obviously we were together in the car a lot, travelling from town to town. Sometimes he'd be tired and want to sit in silence, or sleep; sometimes he'd be working and making notes; but a lot of the time we'd talk. He liked to discuss politics and current affairs, but we'd sometimes have quite deep philosophical conversations. He used to say that because I was the daughter of a lawyer I always had to play the devil's advocate, and found it impossible to just agree with him. But I think he actually liked the fact that I had my own opinions and didn't just say "Yes dear" to everything.

I was never bored in his company. He always had something interesting to say. I don't know whether I talked too much about inconsequential things, but he never complained. I do talk a lot. My mother, who was always very loving, but somewhat direct, once told me I talked too much. I said that I must take after my aunt, who used to do public-speaking, to which my mother replied, "Yes, but she was interesting!"

I adored my mother and will always be grateful to her for introducing me to classical music, especially the German composers, but she could be a constructive critic when necessary. I remember once she was having a meal at 'Oak House' with Ken and I, and the soup wasn't hot enough. Her culinary advice, in her strong German accent, which never did diminish, despite seventy years in England, was: "Sree sings should always be hot – coffee, soup... and... vimmin..." Ken loved that, but, shocked, I said, "Mother! Really!" Ladies of her generation could be quite prudish – but not always.

Ken was always so busy he hadn't holidayed much when I first lived with him, so gradually I introduced him to the delights of foreign travel, for pleasure, not just for work. He began to enjoy taking time off and seeing the world. We could never go away for long periods, because of leaving the dog, but holidays abroad certainly broadened his horizons regarding food. He'd always stuck to a traditional meat and two veg sort of diet, but he started to try different foods when we travelled. He never did acquire a taste for garlic, that was his pet hate, but he found he really enjoyed all sorts of foreign cuisine, especially Italian food.

We'd take two different sorts of holiday. A holiday to rest the brain when we'd been busy and just needed to relax, in somewhere like Tenerife, but other times we'd have a holiday to stimulate the brain, where we'd visit a foreign city and soak up the culture and the history. That comes back to Ken's intellect. He was like a sponge when it came to learning about new places and broadening his mind. We liked Prague, Venice, Paris and Ken found Berlin particularly fascinating. We were intrigued to see the former Gestapo headquarters where my mother had gone to get permission to marry my father. It is now an international museum – the Topography of Terror. We visited Germany quite a few times over the years, including a lovely river cruise down the Rhine. Ken also enjoyed delving into ancient history on trips to Pompeii, Rome and Egypt.

As well as his surprisingly broad intellect, Ken had a phenomenal memory. It's something that has never really been explored before, but when you think of the speed he worked as a comedian, combined with the marathon length of his shows, there were literally thousands of jokes coming out every night when he was onstage. He always said he aimed for six or seven TPM (Titters Per Minute), so, as the Americans say, 'do the math'. And Ken didn't just learn this incredible four-hour monologue parrot-fashion, because he was always adding new material, and he proudly boasted that he never did the same show twice – consciously changing the order of things, dropping bits, adding bits and shifting the material around, to suit each individual audience. He was also well aware that a lot of his audience were fans who came to see him 'live' on a regular basis, so he didn't want them to see the same old show every time. An admirable sentiment. Of course it stopped Ken getting bored himself, and I'm sure he positively enjoyed the challenge of shaking things up every night, with odd 'aides-memoire' scribbled in ink on the backs of his hands.

Showbusiness supremo Laurie Mansfield fondly recalls that when Ken got on a roll of quickfire jokes you would still be laughing at the last gag, while he was starting to tell the next one, they came so fast: "It had an ongoing rhythm, like a song, and sometimes you'd find yourself thinking, 'Stop! I can't take any more!', because you were begging for a breather."

In the many times I saw him onstage I think very occasionally, and totally forgivably, he used a throw-away funny line twice in the same show (possibly two or three hours apart!). Other than that he never seemed to have any problem with remembering what he'd already said, and what was coming next. That is quite some skill. Laurie Mansfield observes that there is a form of genius just in that memory feat alone.

Like all good comedians Ken had a useful little trick to give himself some thinking time if he ever did get a fleeting mental block.

He would ask the audience, "Has anybody seen my show before?", which always got a huge cheer from his regular followers, then he'd say, "Good – can you tell me what I do next?" This of course would get a big laugh, which gave him all the thinking time he needed, and he'd be off again. In fairness though you can only use that ruse once a night, which is not bad when you are performing four hours of stand-up comedy. I think it's fair to say his memory was second to none. He had a massive, almost encyclopaedic, bank of jokes tucked away in his extraordinary mind.

Ken was justifiably proud of his keen intellect, but didn't often get chance to showcase it to the general public. That is possibly why, in 1987, he took the arguably misguided step of agreeing to an appearance on the BBC Radio 4 programme *In the Psychiatrist's Chair*. This was a revealing radio series where the late eminent Irish psychiatrist and broadcaster Anthony Clare invited prominent well-known personalities, from different walks of life, to be probed and psychoanalysed on air, laying bare their innermost thoughts, fears and emotions. The reason I say it was possibly a mistake on Ken's behalf to agree to this lengthy in-depth grilling was that it inevitably invaded the intense privacy he held so dear.

Clare, in his book, which transcribed some of those legendary interviews, commented: "Ken Dodd in the studio was not a relaxed man, although he exuded a cheery bonhomie and was both genuine and amusing." Clare also said that there was an element of control about Ken and, when he repeatedly tried to raise the subjects of Ken's marital status, and his attitudes towards family and marriage, Ken "used his considerable *(comic)* abilities to distract me." Clare summed up the experience by saying that Ken was not easy to interview, as it was a struggle to get anything out of him about his personal life, which was really the essential essence of the programme. He concluded in his book: "… right away I sensed a battle within the studio for control of the subject matter – a battle I lost."

Ken even struggled with the minor personal revelations required by broadcaster Sue Lawley for what is regarded as a relatively soft interview on *Desert Island Discs*. He appeared on the iconic radio show in 1990, harmlessly naming the eight records he would choose to take if he was stranded on the BBC's imaginary desert island. During the interview segments, between his favourite tunes, Ken amiably talked about his happy childhood, his parents and his career. He even mentioned the fact that there are two very different Ken Dodds, but the moment Sue Lawley asked about the private Ken Dodd in his house in Knotty Ash he prickled and said, "Ahh, that's the journalist coming out!" He quoted his friend and comedy hero Arthur Askey, who had once told him, "When confronted with a journalist, close the front door... and keep it closed." Ken of course didn't answer the question. When pushed he did admit to the existence of a great love of his life, but declined to name Anne.

I should perhaps mention that Ken did appear on a much earlier episode of *Desert Island Discs*, in 1963, at a time when it was still being hosted by its creator, the genial, avuncular Roy Plomley, and they had a very amiable chat, with no clashes of personality whatsoever. It was the hardnosed journalist in Sue Lawley which made Ken bristle.

Ken had a bit of a problem with most journalists. The trouble was they would insist on asking him questions which he didn't want to answer. Personally I think that he didn't do himself any favours, although it was of course his prerogative to only answer certain questions. The problem is that when a journalist, rightly or wrongly, perceives somebody as 'secretive', then the cynical assumption is that there is something to hide, which, in Ken's case, wasn't true.

The ultimate car crash interview came in 2010 when journalist Stephen Smith interviewed Ken for BBC2's *Newsnight*. Once again I'm not quite sure why he agreed to the interview in the first place, because he bristled straight away that Smith hadn't introduced him properly, and then testily asked what his "opening gambit" was going to be. A couple of minutes into the interview Ken accuses Smith of asking "a typical journalist's question", and then he irritably threatens him with "a slap round the ear'ole" for attempting to ask about the infamous tax trial. The interview finally goes off the rails when Smith asks Ken about retirement. Eighty-two-year-old Ken gets quite prickly about the subject, and dislikes the suggestion that he should ever retire, suggesting though that perhaps, after this interview, Mr Smith should consider retiring himself – to an allotment, raising chickens.

There were a few favoured journalists who Ken would happily speak to, presumably because they knew and respected the taboo and off-limit subject areas. His favourite journalist was Paddy Shennan from the *Liverpool Echo*, who was always keen to promote Merseyside's favourite son, writing positive stories, without giving Ken a hard time or asking awkward or impertinent questions.

In fairness to Ken he happily gave long and in-depth interviews to people like Michael Parkinson, Terry Wogan, Carol Smillie, Melvyn Bragg and John Stapleton, where he could dictate pretty much the safe parameters of the chat, but he was always wary of anybody who might ask personal questions about his private life.

Laurie Mansfield made an interesting observation regarding Ken's intellect. He told me that talking to Ken was like having a discussion with a highly successful businessman: "This was somebody who knew exactly what he was doing, and understood completely what he had to offer the world… You had to listen to what he said, because it was always worth hearing, but the joy of Ken was that he'd also listen to you." Laurie says however that Ken was very much his own man and it was virtually impossible to persuade him to do anything that went against his highly-tuned instincts.

Ken's intellect gave him a need for mental stimuli and good conversation. He had plenty of showbiz pals, but one of his closest friends, Peter Rogan, had nothing whatsoever to do with showbusiness – he was a university-educated head teacher. They met when Peter was organising a charity event in the Merseyside area and plucked up the courage to phone the great Ken Dodd to see if he would help. He said it was the easiest 'begging call' he ever made in his life, because Ken said yes right away. They got on well and struck up a friendship which lasted forty-two years, right up to Ken's death. In fact Peter was best man at Ken and Anne's eleventh-hour wedding.

Peter described Ken as a friend this way: "He was a super friend, he was loyal, and he was compassionate. If you were in trouble, or if you had a problem, then Ken was your man. If you needed someone boxing for you in your corner, it was Ken you would turn to. He was a super, super friend."

Peter, in his very moving eulogy at Ken's funeral, referred to the almost daily, late-night, long phone conversations he had with Ken about religion, philosophy, literature, theatre, television, sport, current affairs and politics – especially after BBC's *Question Time*, which they would both enjoy dissecting and analysing. Ken liked to keep himself well-informed with what was going on in the world, but of course he and Labour Party supporter Peter didn't always agree on every political point, so their discussions could become quite 'lively'. They were both deeply religious men, but they didn't even agree on everything in that regard either, as Ken was Church of England, and Peter is a staunch Roman Catholic. However Peter says they would often agree to disagree and then say goodnight with a joke and always end on a laugh.

Chapter 16:

A MAN OF FAITH

K en Dodd's religious beliefs and his devout Christian Church of England faith defined him as a human being. They also defined his comedy, as we will see.

Ken said that his mother was the religious one, and, as a family, they all attended St John's Church, just round the corner from 'Oak House'. His father was also a churchgoer, but Ken said that Arthur became slightly more cynical and sceptical as he dealt with life's blows in later life. I think it's fair to assume that his wife Sarah's premature death in 1968 dented his faith.

Like most kids Ken was slightly reluctant about going to church as a small boy, because it meant less time for fun and games. However, as a St John's choirboy, he soon found he enjoyed the hymns and he took a great interest in the stories from the Bible. In later life he realised, like most of us, that many of the Old Testament Bible stories had been invented, exaggerated or elaborated upon over the ages, but they were well-crafted yarns which served as useful allegories and morality lessons regarding right and wrong, good and evil.

As we have already established Ken's devout beliefs seemed to stem from the fact that he believed he cheated death as a toddler thanks to the prayers of a Christian Scientist neighbour. From the moment he was old enough to understand the enormity of what had happened he believed he had been blessed by God. In interviews throughout his life, when talking about his extraordinary career, he would say, "I used to think I was lucky, but now I believe I have been blessed…" Anne thinks that is why he always carried around with him that small print of *The Light of the World*, painted by William Holman Hunt, showing Jesus standing at a door with a brightly shining lamp.

Ken certainly believed that his gift for comedy was a blessing from God, and gave him his God-given purpose in life. Personally I think making people happy and erasing their sadnesses, even if it's just for a few hours, is a very worthwhile purpose in life.

He never drew much public attention to his faith, however. In fact I was surprised to find just how religious Ken was when I started researching the BBC2 documentary. It was hiding in plain sight however. He'd made high-profile guest appearances on things like BBC TV's *Songs of Praise*, *The Heaven & Earth Show* and *Summer Praise*, as well as ITV's *My Favourite Hymns*. I'm actually surprised, looking back now, how often he did mention his faith in other more general interviews as well. Ken never shied away from talking about his faith, but he never laboured the point or tub-thumped about it either. He certainly didn't try to mix preaching with entertainment, which other religious showbusiness stars have done – sometimes to the point of being sanctimonious. It was very much a part of the offstage Ken Dodd, but not something to take with him on to the stage – even though he did believe that his God helped his career and boosted his confidence onstage.

Ken's faith also informed his style of comedy. He was always proud of the fact that his humour was positive, and never cruel or mean-spirited. He didn't much care for satire, dark humour or jokes which targeted somebody in an unkind way. His jokes could be silly, but they were always upbeat and life-affirming. It's no coincidence that one of his recurring springboards for jokes was his catchphrase, "What a beautiful day…" Many comedians derive humour from telling the audience what a terrible day they have had, but not Ken Dodd.

Ken was a great believer in the power of prayer, which he considered to be a conversation with his maker, up there in 'head office'. He said he prayed every night, and before every show he ever performed. Anne says those prayers were not ostentatious displays, just quiet moments when he just looked as though he was thinking about something. When he habitually said grace before a meal, it was just a fleeting silent word to himself. People around wouldn't even be aware he'd said grace.

Ken liked to attend church all through his life, but of course he wasn't a morning person. Bear in mind most Saturdays he would have had a late night doing a show, so he was still in bed when Sunday morning services were starting. For that reason he preferred evensong. He also liked the fact that these services had a greater emphasis on choral singing and music. There have been times when his local church didn't do evening or afternoon services, so then he and Anne would drive into Liverpool to attend evensong at the gargantuan gothic Liverpool Anglican Cathedral.

Reverend Julia Jesson, the vicar at the Church of St John the Evangelist in Knotty Ash, to give it its correct name, described Ken to me as "a deeply spiritual man who worshipped regularly." She said though that he didn't expect special treatment, or want to have attention drawn to him. He was merely an ordinary member of the congregation, who had come to worship, just like everybody else. Naturally enough, however, she was proud to have him as a parishioner, and she said how well-loved and respected he was in the local community, because he used his fame to help people, but never for personal glory.

I asked Julia Jesson how she will remember Ken Dodd. Without hesitation she said, "With a smile!" Then she went on, "It was a privilege to have known him. I'll always remember the twinkle in his eye, and the deeply spiritual conversations that we had. Not just about his life, but about life in general. It's always a privilege to talk to someone on that level, because, whilst he was so funny on one side, he was so serious and full of depth on the other. I was aware, all the time I was talking to him, that I was talking to someone who could outstrip me intellectually any day. I was sitting, listening and learning myself. A deep, deeply thoughtful man..."

Anne is a keen church-goer too, although she says she believed Ken's faith was even stronger than hers. She now plays the church organ for St John's Church, where she is a prominent figure, patron and organiser, sitting on the Parochial Church Council. She has become a close friend of the vicar, Julia Jesson.

Of course Ken had a few wobbles with his faith – especially during the bleak period when he lost his beloved mother, then Anita, and soon after that his father. The cruel losses made him question his faith at the time, but he always returned to his core beliefs. Although he did reveal, in his interview with Anthony Clare, that he briefly lost faith when his prayers for help went unanswered during Anita's fatal illness: "… if you knock at a door and nobody answers, you tend to think nobody's home…"

Whilst attending the Anglican Cathedral he befriended the then Bishop of Liverpool, the Right Reverend James Jones, KBE. Actually they first met in 1998 when the newly appointed Bishop was conducting a service at a church in nearby Woolton, part of his new Liverpudlian diocese. Ken arrived at the church that night to hear James' sermon. He must have been having a troublesome time, because he knelt when he arrived and inwardly cried out from his heart for God to speak to him. During the sermon James used the words: "… if you've come here tonight to hear the new Bishop, you may go away very disappointed, but if tonight you've come to this service, because you want God to speak to you, then that could just happen…" Ken was overwhelmed. He believed it was the sign he'd come looking for. After the service Ken and Anne hovered in the shadows, hoping to get a private word with their new Bishop. When an appropriate moment presented itself Ken grabbed both the Bishop's hands and thanked him profusely for what he perceived as a personal message from God, through his words. Ken never did tell James what he needed to speak to God about that night, but he did believe that God had come and answered him. James says what that revealed to him was that Ken was a man of great faith and somebody who deeply wanted God to be real to him.

Bishop Jones invited Ken and Anne to lunch at his family home, and their friendship blossomed. At the end of a four-hour lunch, with Ken on form telling endless hilarious stories, Ken told James he should never hesitate to ask if there was ever anything he could do to help. As it happened, as part of his new job as Bishop of Liverpool, James was helping to organise an occasional Church of England conference. It was a major event, held every few years, and was attended for several days by a large number of people from the British clergy. James wondered if Ken might entertain the conference on the last evening. Of course he readily agreed, despite it being a slightly daunting prospect.

Anne recalls:

I was the support act that night, but, as I discovered, the clergy don't know much about the practicalities and logistics of putting on a show. I was in my dressing-room, tuning my guitar, when Kevin Speight, our musical director, came running in to tell me that somebody in a dog collar had just introduced me, without checking whether I was in the wings, ready to go on – which of course I wasn't... The audience were all watching an empty stage. Somewhat flustered I ran on and promptly tripped over my guitar lead, which got a huge laugh. They all thought it was part of my act...

James says he was surprised how nervous Ken was before he went on that night, and said it took him quite a few minutes to get into his stride. He felt Ken was worried about offending somebody, or saying the wrong thing. In fairness a sea of clergy is a tough crowd for a comedian. Ken needn't have worried however because he soon relaxed and got a huge reaction. He didn't really have any cause for worry about offending anybody either, because, as James himself says, "Ken didn't talk publicly about his faith, but I think his faith shines through the fact that he was not a cruel comedian. I think his own belief in God's goodness, was that he shouldn't make fun of other people's misfortunes in an unkind way. Certainly, like all comedians, he points out the incongruities that we all face in our lives, but it was never with a cruel edge, he never wanted to put people down. He wanted only to tell stories, that made people laugh, and made them happy."

He also said, "Ken was a compassionate and kind person, who genuinely believed that laughter was a gift from God. He felt that God blessed us through humour, through laughter, and that was, if you like, our pathway to happiness."

I found Bishop Jones' insights into Ken and the links between his faith and his humour fascinating.

In 2008, because Liverpool was the European City of Culture that year, James was hosting an annual gathering of Christian church leaders from Belfast, Glasgow and Liverpool – all cities with perennial tensions between Catholics and Protestants. Clergy from both faiths met every year to discuss ways to bridge the nineteenth- and twenty-first centuries, trying to find a more harmonious way into the future. Again James asked Ken if he would address this select gathering of around twenty senior clerical figures, which included a Roman Catholic Cardinal and several Anglican Bishops. Another tough crowd!

Ken began by talking about a concept dear to his heart – 'the rainbow of laughter'. This was something he felt strongly about. Ken often told interviewers, "The most beautiful sound in the world is the sound of laughter."

His metaphorical rainbow had white light at one end of the spectrum, representing the complete innocence of an infant's laughter and the joyous happy sounds of children at play; then yellow, the whimsical happy laughter of clowns and jesters; followed by the slightly cheeky warm colours of red and orange, representing double entendre and ribaldry; passing by naughty blue jokes; to the darker violets and purples of ridicule, insult, sarcasm, cynicism and satire, to the inky blackness of sick and cruel humour, which of course Ken detested.

Next Ken surprised them all by drawing a direct link between being a comedian and being a priest. James says they all sat up and listened attentively at this. Ken explained his intriguing hypothesis by saying that both comedians and priests are natural observers of life, and both are trying to use the right words to get their message across. Then he took them aback by adding that both jobs are lonely callings. Anne, who was sitting at the back of the Dean's Room in Liverpool Cathedral, giving moral support, says you could have heard a pin drop.

James was stunned at Ken's profound observation, saying, "That's so true, certainly for a priest, because you take things upon yourself. People share things with you that are bound to remain confidential, and there is a loneliness to carrying somebody else's burden. But for Ken, if I can use a religious word, there is a joyous moment of extraordinary communion between the audience and the comedian, and then they all go, and then you're left, and you're on your own. And I think Ken felt that aloneness as a comedian, and as a performer."

I find Ken's admission of loneliness to be astonishing. I don't think 'the other Ken Dodd', the quiet offstage home-bird, was lonely. He had friends, family, and Anne, the love of his life, constantly at his side, but presumably it was the onstage showman Ken Dodd who felt loneliness. Could this be another reason he did such long shows?

Any performer will tell you that, when things are going well onstage, there is no feeling like it. The adrenaline rush and the release of pleasure-giving dopamine into the brain creates a natural high like no other. For comedians especially there is tangible and immediate gratification when a huge laugh comes back from the audience. It's like a wave of love and approval. Bishop Jones recalled: "I remember Ken saying there is nothing quite like standing on a stage, and seeing one thousand heads thrown back in laughter."

Ken even admitted he got withdrawal symptoms and became uptight if he went too long without that rush he got from performing. Like any 'high' it is addictive, but also like any high there is a 'crash' afterwards, a period of coming back down, which is not so pleasurable. Perhaps Ken didn't want that high to end and stayed onstage as long as he possibly could, in order to remain on that high.

The Bishop's observation that at some point the audience go and then the performer is left all alone is a revealing insight into the psyche of a comedian. Fellow Liverpudlian, humourist and performance poet Roger McGough picked up on the same theme when talking about Ken doing long shows: "I suppose it's like why you don't get out of the sauna when it's cold outside, so you stay in there. Or when you're in the pub and you're having a nice time. Why leave when you can stay a bit longer? Ken enjoyed what he did. He enjoyed the love he was getting back from the audience, and I suppose, once the lights went out and he went back to his dressing-room, it was a come-down. A lot of artists say this after a show – It's dark out there…"

Bishop James Jones added, regarding the similarities of their callings: "Life is about the joys as well as the troubles that you bear. That was really important to Ken, because for him happiness wasn't just something that happened, it was a gift. If you could laugh, then you could find happiness, so, in that way, comedy was something of a calling for Ken. He had been given this gift of laughter by God, and he thought it was his responsibility to use this gift to spread happiness in the world. I think he really believed that."

Ken used to quite rightly point out that humans are the only species who laugh: "When did you last hear your tomcat say, 'By Jove that was a good un!'?" He believed God gave humans the gift of laughter to release tension and calm our minds; as a balm to heal our pain and suffering; as a defence mechanism; and as a means to make even the most heated arguments seem ridiculous.

Of course it wasn't the performer Ken Dodd who went to church and prayed, it was 'the other Ken Dodd'. James spotted that right away: "Ken was a traditional Christian churchgoer. He loved just to be part of the liturgy. He didn't want to perform if he was in church, he wanted to participate in it as any other worshipper and as somebody who said their prayers. I think that just being a faithful member of the congregation was important to him."

Of course Anne, as his closest confidante, knows more about Ken's faith than anybody:

When I started going through the private jottings in his notebooks and Ken's papers, after his passing, I began to realise just how vitally important his faith was to him. I'd always known it was significant to him, but perhaps I hadn't realised just how important. It was quite moving to see, for instance, that papers and copious notes that he'd made at the time of the tax trial were all covered in religious crosses he'd drawn. I know he often asked for God's help during that difficult time, and he felt he received it. He was a great believer in prayer. Although he never forced his religion on anybody, he would extol the virtues of prayer, because he believed that having a conversation with God really works. He always said a quiet 'grace' to himself before a meal, which I never did. I'm afraid I'd have already started eating.

Once, when we were on a cruise down the Rhine, we shared a dining table with four chatty Americans, who noticed Ken saying grace before his meal. They suggested sharing grace with us before future meals, which we did – all taking it in turn to say a few words. The only thing was the Americans didn't quite understand the concept of 'a few words'. Their well-meaning, but rambling grace went on and on, until the food was in danger of going stone cold. I couldn't look at Ken because I knew I would have got the giggles.

We'd always try to get to a service at either the church or the cathedral every Sunday, if it was humanly possible. It could be difficult if we were working away on the Saturday night, but we'd try to get to evensong.

It was true though that Ken didn't want to be the centre of attention when we went to a church service. I remember when Julia, our current vicar, was inaugurated into St John's church. I'd gone ahead to robe up for my role that night in the church choir, and I told Ken to make sure he wasn't late. In fairness he wasn't, but the moment he arrived two old ladies pounced on him and started taking him to the front of the church. He protested and said he just wanted to sit in the family pew, about half way down on the left, but they insisted he had to go right to the front pew, saying, "But Sir Ken you are our guest of honour!" He looked uncomfortable because he really didn't want that preferential treatment. He didn't like to draw attention to himself in church. At a normal service we'd just slide in quietly to the family pew, say a prayer, and keep a low profile.

Because this was an important occasion the Bishop was there, who introduced the Archdeacon to formally install Julia into her new parish. The first thing the Archdeacon said was: "Reverend Julia Jesson – how tickled I am to welcome you to Knotty Ash!" Well Ken nearly died! From my seat in the choir stalls I could see him put his head in his hands. He was worried everybody would think that it was his fault that they'd brought him into the ceremony, which was something he didn't want. He had no desire whatsoever to upstage the new vicar, or steal her thunder. Actually it worked very well because it broke the ice for Julia, who had obviously been a bit nervous up to that point, but poor Ken was mortified.

Far from feeling upstaged Julia remembers that occasion fondly. She obviously knew she was going to have a famous parishioner before she even got to Knotty Ash. Her first sighting of Ken was on that front pew when she came down the aisle of the church to be 'licenced', to give her inauguration the correct terminology. She was delighted to formally 'exchange the peace' with him, and then have a proper chat after the service: "He introduced me to Anne. They were obviously very much in love and very much a couple, and he wanted me to know how important she was to him. So that was lovely on my special evening to meet them both like that."

I asked Julia what the other parishioners made of having Ken as part of the congregation: "I think there was a huge amount of pride over having Ken still living within the community. He was very much a Knotty Ash boy, known by the locals. There was pride, not only in his achievements as a comedian, but also in the fact that he'd remained in Knotty Ash, so there was that sense of him always being present. He was always an exceptionally personable person, not the big celebrity 'look at me', but a genuine man who just enjoyed meeting people and chatting with them in the street. For somebody used to being in the spotlight all the time he was a surprisingly good listener."

Ken himself once said, "I go to church whenever I can, because I think going to church recharges your batteries. It's like making a phone call to head office. I'm not being flippant, because going to church, or to the cathedral, is like going to a place where you can communicate with God. You can do it outside church as well, but the act of going in there, getting down on your knees, closing your eyes and fervently praying to God – knowing he's listening – that's when your faith is strengthened. There have been times during my life when I've been very very sad, when I've been bereaved. There have been times in my life when I've been under tremendous stress and pressure. But when you feel you need help in a particular situation, and you pray – you do get help."

In another interview he said, "I believe that life is a quest, and you're searching for communication with your creator. I think we're all looking for God, and we all hope to find him, and, at different times of your life, you feel that you really are in the presence of God. I pray all the time, every day. They're not always very articulate prayers, but I believe they are heard, and many times when I've been feeling down and I've prayed – I have been lifted up."

Ken's attitude to religion was quite modern and forward-thinking. He said his conversations with God were in contemporary colloquial words, the words we use in our daily lives to our friends and family. Interestingly he thought that some of the language of religion was a bit medieval, and he struggled to find the more ancient aspects of church services relevant to a modern world. In that respect he didn't always approve of the way some services were conducted. He felt the message could be lost because the way it was delivered, using old-fashioned language, wasn't attractive to a modern-day congregation. He said, "Religion has to be relevant in changing times. When you go to church it should be because you want to go. It shouldn't be a penance or a duty. You should look forward to going to church."

If anybody ever questioned the existence of God he would just tell them to go outside and look properly at a flower or a tree, or to think about the miraculous complexities of the human body. That was all the proof he needed of an omnipotent creator and supreme being.

Anne rather movingly remembers how much Ken enjoyed going to the Anglican Cathedral, even though services there are perhaps a little 'high church' and rather too ritually formal and traditional for her personal tastes:

We did sit near the front at the cathedral, but that was more because Ken was getting a little deaf in later years and it was the only way he could hear everything properly. He loved the choral music during evensong and he thought they had good preachers who had something worthwhile and relevant to say about the modern world. Every Christmas he would spend time preparing several funny but appropriate short readings to deliver himself from the cathedral pulpit at the annual NHS Choir Carol Concert. He looked forward to that. I do still go to the cathedral at least a couple of times a month, but I don't really like being there on my own. I do miss him terribly. When I go for communion, in the Lady Chapel, I always sit where we used to sit, but I put my handbag in his place, because I don't want anybody else sitting there…

Anne summed up Ken's faith in this way:

It was extremely important to him, but he was never self-righteous about it. He never ever tried to ram his faith down other people's throats. But, if somebody came to him with a problem, he would encourage them to pray. Even then he wouldn't impose prayer on them, but he would suggest they sit quietly and say a few words to articulate the problem, even if it was just to clarify their innermost thoughts to themselves, not necessarily talking to God.

I think he knew his faith was stronger than mine. He once asked me, when I came back in after playing the church organ for a service, whether I did it because I enjoyed the performance aspect of playing the music, or whether I went because I enjoyed the worship. It was an interesting question. The truth was both. I did enjoy playing the organ, performing if you like, but I also enjoyed taking part in the service and worshipping. I still enjoy both aspects to this day. There's no doubt though that the depth of Ken's faith has given me strength since his passing.

He was very good at comforting people when they'd been bereaved, because he understood what they were going through, as he'd taken his own bereavements quite hard. People would often come up to him when they'd lost a loved one. He'd put his hand on their shoulder and say, "Keep them with you... Talk to them..."

I know from personal experience how sensitive and comforting Ken could be in times of sickness and bereavement. In 2008 Elizabeth, my younger sister, who had emigrated to South Africa, sadly died after fighting breast cancer for fourteen years. We had been out there to see her some time earlier and, as always, Ken had been a great comforter and gave me strength. Her passing was a difficult time for me. Lizzie's grieving husband Tom called me and said there wasn't going to be a funeral service, he just couldn't face it, only a 'wake' the night before her cremation. Ken took me to Liverpool Cathedral to ask if there was a way we could share some prayers on the day of Lizzie's cremation. We were kindly seen by Justin Welby, then Dean of Liverpool, currently the Archbishop of Canterbury. We had met him before, on several occasions. When he saw my sadness he put his hands out to hold mine, and asked how he could help. Ken and I explained and I said that I needed to 'commit my sister to God'. It was an unusual request I imagine, but, in an act of great kindness *and generosity, he set aside time in his busy schedule to personally arrange and conduct a funeral service, in the small Chapel of the Holy Spirit within the cathedral, attended by family and a few special friends, at the precise moment of Lizzie's cremation, thousands of miles away.*

The last word on the subject of faith should come from Ken himself. He said this in a BBC TV religious programme called *The Heaven & Earth Show* in 2002, talking to Alice Beer: "I believe in the afterlife. I sing a song every night in the show called 'Absent Friends'. When I'm singing that song I'm singing it to some very special people, to all the people I have loved, to all the good friends who have passed on. I'm singing it to them. You never lose anybody. They are always with you. So you say 'goodnight' to them and you say 'good morning' to them, and I say 'hello' to them every time I do a show and sing that song."

That's a heartfelt sentiment which I think probably resonates with most people of any faith.

Chapter 17:

A DIFFICULT TIME

In 1988, when I worked with Ken Dodd at the BBC in Manchester, on the comedy panel game series *A Question of Entertainment*, I found I got on very well with him, and spent a lot of time chatting to him, but he did always seem a little withdrawn and pre-occupied. Although I had no idea why at the time, it turns out he was.

With my love of showbusiness those programmes were a sheer joy to make. The after-show drinks in the Green Room were always a real treat, with a bunch of famous showbiz professionals sharing their anecdotes, latest jokes and hilarious experiences. Ken was a great story-teller, but he was also a good listener. There never seemed to be any big egos at play – they would all take their turn, and then sit back to enjoy somebody else's story. I absolutely adored those evenings, and will remember them fondly for the rest of my days.

On one of those evenings, after a studio recording, I must have been very tired, or knew I had an early start the next morning, because, against all instincts, I had to leave slightly early, while the banter was still going on. I'd left Ken in full flow in the Green Room. It must have been around 11pm, and I went down to my car in the eerily quiet dingy underground car park, beneath the BBC building, and drove out into the night. Normally at that hour that part of Manchester was quiet and I could just drive out of the BBC gates and into Oxford Road, unnoticed, on my long journey home to Yorkshire. That particular night I was shocked to see a large throng of excited-looking people clustered around the BBC gates. Slowly I tried to inch my car through them, but they blocked my way, banging on my roof and windows. It was a little unnerving, to say the least. I had by now spotted cameras, tape recorders and notebooks, and realised they were journalists, baying for blood. Whose blood I didn't yet know. I let my window down just far enough to talk to them, as they clearly weren't going to let me pass until I did. There were shouts of, "Is Ken Dodd still in there?" I had no idea what this was all about, but it obviously wasn't good, so I lied and said, "No... Sorry... He went home about an hour ago..."

I didn't have to wait long to find out what the pandemonium had been about. The next morning every British newspaper carried front page headlines about Ken Dodd being under investigation by the taxman.

Out of professional courtesy and respect we never mentioned the breaking news to Ken next time we saw him, and, understandably, he never discussed the matter with us. We all just carried on making the programme as though everything was fine. Which means, like the rest of the country, I knew no more than the sensationalist sound bites and column inches the media chose to toss our way.

Only Anne knows what it was like to be right there in the eye of the storm:

At that time the Inland Revenue seemed to be targeting a few famous people, as a warning to the others. In 1987 the famous jockey Lester Piggott had been sent to prison as a result of the Inland Revenue's investigation into his tax affairs. Ken found this very sad at the time. He and his dad loved watching horse racing on the television and Lester Piggott had been their hero on the race track over many years.

After Lester Piggott I think they were looking for another high profile name, this time in showbusiness. In many ways it was just bad luck that it happened to be Ken.

Ken's accountant at that time was a jovial sort of chap. When they met up they would swap jokes before, and even during, business discussions. However, unbeknown to us, it turns out he had recently been charged with, and found guilty of, six counts of false accounting. The suggestion we heard was that he had taken on too many clients and his work had become sloppy and careless.

Looking back we realised that Ken had perhaps been a bit slapdash about keeping financial records, but the accountant didn't seem to mind. Ken would go in with carrier bags full of receipts, but they accepted them and appeared to sort them out for him. In fact Ken thought his accountant was a bit of a joker. He was always trying to be funny. With the benefit of hindsight perhaps that should have sounded alarm bells, but we carried on using him. We had no idea his company was under investigation for false accounting, until it was too late.

Naturally enough, after the accountant was found guilty, the Inland Revenue took a look at the list of all his clients. Of course when they spotted Ken's name on the list their eyes lit up. You can imagine can't you? They must have thought all their birthdays had come at once. In fact, during the case, one of the tax inspectors, with whom we were unfortunately having to share a lift, actually said to us, off the record, "We have to make an example of somebody. It's nothing personal Mr Dodd." Nothing personal? With great difficulty we held our tongues…!

They could have picked on just about anybody in showbusiness at that time, but Ken just happened to be the unlucky one who came on to their radar, because of his lackadaisical accountant.

It was certainly true that the tax inspectors could have picked on just about any top entertainer at that time. This was nothing to do with Ken Dodd, per se. The Inland Revenue were just keen to make an example of somebody high-profile in showbusiness, in the hope it would bring all entertainers into line regarding their tax affairs. If they found somebody – anybody – to splash all over the front pages in a major tax investigation then it would frighten everybody else into toeing the line.

It's perhaps important to set all this in the historic political context of eye-wateringly high taxation, which, understandably, led everybody earning a decent income in the UK to seek ways of minimising their tax liabilities – not just jockeys and entertainers.

The rot had set in during the 1960s and 1970s, when the top rate of income tax was over ninety per cent, so high earners were understandably keen to keep their taxable profits as low as possible. Showbiz and sports stars were high earners, but those high earnings could be short-lived, so they were justifiably anxious to hang on to as much of their hard-earned cash as they could, while the good times lasted.

The honest truth though is that every single one of us tries to pay as little tax as possible, whilst, of course, keeping within the letter of the law. Put it another way – nobody on Earth wants to pay more income tax than they absolutely have to. That's how accountants and financial advisors make their not insubstantial livings.

Showbusiness agent Laurie Mansfield says that Ken's tax trial totally transformed the way the whole of the entertainment world did business, and, consequently, most entertainers started paying more income tax from that day forward. That was of course the Inland Revenue's intention all along. Ken was the unfortunate sacrificial lamb who gave them the means to realise that plan. He was just collateral damage – a means to an end.

As the tax inspector said, it was nothing personal. They weren't out to get Ken, and didn't mind that, in the end, he was acquitted of all charges. They were just keen to grab headlines, put the fear of God into other entertainers, and deter tax evasion and slipshod accounting throughout the business. Job done.

Back to Anne, who puts a fresh perspective on the headline-grabbing fact that Ken had a large quantity of cash lying around 'Oak House' when the taxman came calling:

Ken, like all entertainers, had that terrible insecurity about income. They could earn good money, but there was no guarantee it was going to last. He had no idea then that he would still be working at the age of ninety. We'd heard many stories of fellow successful showbiz professionals who had gone out on spending-sprees, living the high life, then got caught without enough money to pay their tax bill at the end of the year. It happened a lot. Ken was always canny, so he made sure he kept plenty of money back for both the taxman and for a time when he might not be earning so much. He wasn't interested in living a lavish lifestyle anyway, so long as we were comfortable.

There was a period when high rate income tax was running at eighty-three pence in the pound, and, if it was income from investments, they took another fifteen per cent. That meant that for every pound a high-earning investor made in interest the government took ninety-eight pence of it, so there really was no point in bothering to invest money at that time.

There were also rumours in the turbulent political times of the 1970s that the entire British banking system might crash, so it seemed to make sense to keep spare cash savings well away from the banks and building societies.

The charges in court were 'intent to defraud', and that was never Ken's intention. His only intention ever was to carry on working and making people laugh. Yes, he had perhaps been a bit haphazard in some of his business dealings, and slapdash with his record-keeping when he was busy, but he certainly never set out to defraud anybody. He was just getting on with making a living in an uncertain business. He kept extremely busy, which is why he was so disorganised about money affairs. And of course he managed to prove that. Which is why he was acquitted on all charges.

When the tax inspectors came calling in 1986 we of course signed up with a different accountancy firm in Liverpool, but they were very unfriendly, verging on hostile. They treated Ken like a child, bullying and belittling him and giving him instructions about what he had to do. I remember Ken was doing a summer season in Eastbourne, where we'd hired a little cottage, and we had to spend every day filling in endless forms and doing book-keeping exercises about what we spent on this each week, and what we spent on that. It took about a year to re-do all Ken's books. Unfortunately the Inland Revenue still weren't happy and gave us the awful news that they were going to prosecute. Of course that was a terrifying thing to hear. We were devastated, but the new firm didn't seem to care that this was inevitably going to attract a lot of media attention. I suppose a high-profile tax trial was good publicity for an accountancy business.

One morning Ken was having a heavy meeting with his new accountants and the tax inspectors, who suddenly announced that they wanted to see our house that afternoon. Ken told them that it wasn't possible as he had to be at the home of a half-cousin who had died, to register his death and make the arrangements for his funeral. The relative wasn't somebody the family were particularly close to, but his wife wasn't in a position to sort things out herself. Because Ken was the successful one, it had fallen to him to organise and pay for the funeral. So he told the tax inspectors they'd have to make an appointment to come to the house some other time. They tried to insist that they were coming immediately, that afternoon, and Ken was insisting that they'd have to make an appointment, or at least leave it until the next day. Well of course you're not supposed to talk to tax officials that way. They didn't like Ken's attitude, and he didn't like theirs, which didn't help matters. In fact Ken told them that he thought they were behaving like the Gestapo.

It was quite amusing in court because George Carman, Ken's QC, called one of the tax officers to the stand – a weedy little fellow – and asked him why he had left out of his 'contemporaneous notes', which were supposed to be a complete and accurate record of every meeting, the fact that Mr Dodd had accused them of behaving like the Gestapo. The man said, "Well, we get called a lot of names..."

A year or so before the trial we still hadn't quite realised the enormity of what was going to happen, although we didn't like the way things were going, and the accountants weren't being particularly reassuring or helpful. Of course they don't want to alienate the Inland Revenue, because they have to deal with them all the time, on behalf of their other clients. You soon realise that they're not actually on your side when things start getting tricky.

The next big shock was when the Inland Revenue, as it was still called then, wrote to Ken, saying that they were going to press charges and take Ken to court, advising him to get legal representation. Up to that point we thought the accountants could sort it all out, so we hadn't taken any legal advice. I remember Ken opening that letter. There was a great string of charges they said he was going to have to answer, some of which were dropped before it went to court, but they create a long list in the hope that something will stick. The list of charges was eventually reduced to eight. That was a horrible feeling when we realised how serious things had become. The new accountancy firm admitted in court, under cross-examination, that they never warned Ken that any of what was going on might lead to criminal prosecution. They also admitted that they should definitely have done so.

The charges were that Ken had deliberately evaded tax – 'intent to defraud', as they call it. He had been disorganised and perhaps naïve at times about money matters, but we needed to prove he wasn't dishonest.

Ken had to appear before the magistrate's court in May or June of 1988, to have the summons read, and for the case to be referred up to a crown court. That's when the press got hold of the story for the first time, which was horrible for Ken. Despite all that stress he was still having to fulfil commitments for shows, including the BBC recordings of A Question of Entertainment.

After the magistrates' hearing, knowing the press would hound us, we stayed out of town for the night, but, the next day, we had to fly down south for Dave Forrester's funeral, Ken's agent. On our return, passing through Manchester Airport, a photographer lunged towards Ken and, instinctively, Ken put up his hands to defend himself, knocking the 'camera' to the floor. It was a put-up job to make him look bad. It wasn't a camera at all – it was a fake one, which was made to fall to pieces on the floor, but of course the photographer's mate then took a real picture of Ken "smashing up a press camera in anger". A reporter came up and asked for a quote. Ken didn't speak and I knew to be careful with any sort of a quote, so I just said, "Please – we've just come from a funeral," meaning show a bit of respect and leave us alone. That's all I said. Next day in the papers I was quoted as having said, "Well naturally he's in a bad temper and he's going to hit out, isn't he?" I took legal advice about appealing to the Press Complaints Commission, but I was told to let it drop or it would just extend a story that would otherwise be forgotten, and the photograph would be shown all over again. You can't win against the press.

With a crown court case looming we went to see a big legal firm in London, who had been recommended, but they turned out to be not very nice people, and, frankly, not very helpful or supportive. They were quite patronising towards Ken, and tried to blind us with big words and legalese. One of them did say something which was rather alarming though. He said, "I have no idea why the Revenue are taking this to court. It could have all been settled with a slap on the wrist and a fine, but they are obviously out to make an example of you. So you are going to have to fight this all the way." That really brought things sharply into focus, especially when he hinted that the Inland Revenue have a reputation for fighting dirty.

The crunch with them came one day when we'd taken a stack of papers down to London and we were walking along the road with them. I tripped on the kerb and dropped all these vitally important documents all over the pavement and in the gutter. Ken had to help me up and then we were in a bit of a panic, trying to gather up all the papers between us, and these three lawyers just stood by and watched. Not one of them even offered to help, or moved a muscle to get me back on my feet when I fell over. They just carried on talking to one another as though nothing had happened. So we decided they were horrible people and we didn't want any more to do with them.

Ken auditioned another couple of QCs after that, but none of them seemed right for us. The law firms really went out of their way to sell us their QCs. One of them proudly boasted that the QC they had in mind for Ken had been a junior in James Hanratty's defence team in the notorious A6 murder case. I turned round and said, "But they hung Hanratty!"

Then I had an idea. My late father had been a lawyer and his business partner's son John had gone into legal practice, so I thought at least we'd be dealing with somebody friendly, and on our side. In fact John was the one who suggested George Carman as the QC to conduct Ken's defence in court. Of course that was the best thing to happen in the whole sorry business. Like most people at that time we'd heard the name George Carman on the news, and in press coverage of high profile cases, but we would never have thought of him for defending Ken, and, to be honest, we didn't know much about him. But, from the moment we met him, we were extremely impressed by his quick mind and his sharp brain. He had a good sense of humour as well. When we told George about my response to the QC who had been on the Hanratty case he was most amused. George was terribly clever though. We'd have long meetings, discussing the case for hours, and he had the knack of encapsulating everything we'd told him in one erudite statement. We knew right away we were in good hands. Ken, without hesitation, said, "That's the man for me."

George was brilliant with words, and could see through any waffle, or bluster, cutting right to the chase, and to the kernel of the truth.

He told us in an early meeting, "This case will be won on facts. I want facts and information on everything, so you are going to have to work hard with me, but we can win this."

He asked me one day if I could make a list of every appearance that Ken had ever made for no fee whatsoever. I enlisted the help of Ken's brother and sister to go through mountains of old press cuttings with me, dating right back to 1954, writing down places and dates of all the hundreds of times Ken had done shows and appearances for nothing. It took us ages. Then I mounted all the relevant cuttings, wrote notes underneath about each one, putting them all in date order in ring-binders. It took me a long time, but it was actually quite therapeutic during that stressful period. I filled six huge ring-binders in the end. I was quite offended when George didn't seem terribly interested in reading them, and said he didn't even need to look at them, but again he knew exactly what he was doing. One day, during the trial, he asked me to bring the ring-binders along and set them out on a table at the front of the courtroom. That day George made a statement to the court saying that Mr Dodd had worked hard and made a lot of money, but he'd also made time to do any number of things for nothing. He waved his hand dramatically towards the ring-binders and said that every one of them contained literally hundreds of press cuttings showing evidence of the many times Ken had done things for no fee, and for charity, and pointed out that those were just the ones that had made it into the newspapers. He said that if any member of the jury wanted to have a look they could do so. That's all he said, but it must have made a dramatic impact on the jury.

George also had me make a similar file on all the theatres which Ken had selflessly helped and saved from closure.

One of the charges related to Ken trying to smuggle cash off the mainland and evade tax by hiding it offshore in a bank on the Isle of Man. That all came about because of a misleading advert by the Manx NatWest bank, which had appeared a few years previously in a newspaper which Ken happened to see. It implied that you could invest your money tax-free with them on the Isle of Man, which turned out not to be true. Our loyal friend and driver at the time, Roy Boardman, actually managed to find an old copy of the advert for George Carman to use in court. Ken had taken the ad at its word and invested a sum of money on the island, believing that any interest earned on the cash would be free of British tax, and therefore didn't have to be declared. Again maybe he was naïve, but he wasn't being dishonest. He believed it was a perfectly legitimate way of paying less tax on invested money. We actually heard from a man who was a senior advisor to a top politician at that time, who told us that, ironically, he had fallen for the exact same advert, and had made the same mistake as Ken, which must have been rather embarrassing to somebody advising the government of the day.

The Inland Revenue summoned a spokesman for NatWest to appear in court, expecting him to say their advertisement had been clear and transparent, and not open to any misinterpretation. The prosecution QC, Brian Leveson, must have regretted calling him though, because the spokesman from NatWest surprised us all by admitting that particular advert had unfortunately been misleading and, with the benefit of hindsight, they now regretted publishing it. His apology completely undermined the prosecution's case on that count. Leveson tried to play the NatWest man's admission down, but it was too late – he'd said it for all to hear.

And to say Ken had smuggled the money over there covertly was utter nonsense, because the local Manx NatWest management team made a big fuss of him when he took the cash in a briefcase into their Isle of Man branch, in person. He even posed for photographs with the staff. Hardly a top secret cloak and dagger mission!

In fact the prosecution had a couple of things backfire on them. They called one of the juniors from the original accountancy firm, asking her if Mr Dodd had ever asked for anything to be hidden, or falsified, but she said, on oath, that he hadn't ever suggested anything like that. Then they found out we'd done two or three shows in Porthmadog in North Wales and had taken small payments in cash. Ken occasionally would do somebody a favour and do a gig for a reduced fee in cash, mainly to pay the musicians and support acts. It was perhaps ill-advised looking back – he should really have made them pay the full amount, but he was trying to help them out.

The Revenue were suspicious because these Welsh shows were paid 'cash in hand', but when they interviewed the nice chap who organised those shows, they realised that he wasn't going to say what they wanted him to say, so they decided not to call him to the witness box after all. On that basis George thought he might be useful for us, so we subpoenaed him to be a witness for the defence instead. We had no idea what he was going to say, but we took along a Welsh *slate clock that he'd presented us with, inscribed in gold lettering to Ken, by way of thanks. Sure enough he said how grateful the town had been to Ken, because the proceeds from the shows had paid for essential maintenance to their hall, and they wouldn't have been able to afford any show, never mind a big star name, unless he'd accepted such a small cash payment. Of course he remembered presenting Ken with the inscribed slate clock as a token of their gratitude for all he'd done for them. This man, who had almost been a witness for the prosecution, ended up being a superb character witness for Ken's defence.*

One thing we did discover during the case – in a crisis like that you find out who your real friends are. Di Brooks and Roy Boardman, who toured everywhere with us, were marvellous, and so was Ken's friend Peter Rogan. They were in court with us every day and were a real support. They were always there for us. Laurie Bellew, a former scriptwriter for Ken and his publicist, turned out to be another loyal supporter during that difficult time. He was very good at handling damage limitation with the press.

George had said it would be a good idea to have a few celebrity chums who would come along as character witnesses, speaking on Ken's behalf in court. Some said they'd be happy to help, but never actually did anything, or backed out at the last minute, because they were afraid the taxman might start looking into their own dubious money affairs.

The true friends who did speak on Ken's behalf in court included: Eric Sykes, Roy Hudd, theatre critic Michael Billington, and TV producer John Fisher. There were a few other less high-profile, but equally compelling character witnesses.

Comedy writer and performer Eric Sykes and Ken had a lot of mutual respect and, although they didn't get together too often, living at opposite ends of the country, they liked one another and they would always support each other with new ventures. Eric, who was profoundly deaf in later life, once said that Ken and he were 'a right pair' when it came to appearing onstage: "I don't know when it's time to go on, and he doesn't know when it's time to come off!"

Sykes spoke so fondly of Ken's talent in court that he told the judge Ken Dodd should be available to everyone on the National Health, as a tonic.

Comedian and actor Roy Hudd also had great respect for Ken, and had been a close friend for a long time. The BBC went down to talk to Ken in his early days of fame, during a summer season in Torquay, and Ken told them, while they were down there, they should go along and take a look at a very promising young unknown comic called Roy Hudd, who was appearing in nearby Babbacombe. Roy never forgot that kindness and generosity, and was for ever grateful for where it led. *The News Huddlines* alone ran for twenty-six years on BBC radio. Hudd found giving evidence in Ken's case a nerve-wracking experience, far more so than going onstage. Others commented on how nervous Roy was before he was called to the stand, pacing anxiously up and down the waiting area, but he wasn't going to let his old pal down. Roy himself told me he was shocked at the famous friends who did let Ken down, but, diplomatically, avoided naming names.

Michael Billington and John Fisher had met Ken through work, but had become friends, and were big admirers of his prodigious talent, so they were people who understood his dedication and professionalism, and also knew of his sometimes chaotic lifestyle.

John Fisher described Ken to the judge as the best stand-up comedian in the country, and the most life-enhancing person he'd ever known. He also spoke of Ken's consummate professionalism and tireless work ethic.

George Carman got Michael Billington to speak to the court about Ken's comic genius, and how meticulously well organised he was when he was onstage, but how shambolic and disorganised he could be in his private life, which maybe explained some of his carelessness with his book-keeping. Another character witness was less famous, but equally powerful in Ken's defence. Sheila Murray, secretary of Clatterbridge Hospital cancer research trust, told how Ken, as a patron, had helped them raise a staggering ten million pounds. It was movingly revealed that this was the hospital where Ken's fiancée Anita had died of the brain tumour.

All the character witnesses confirmed Ken's standing in the business, his dedication to charitable work, his disorganised and sometimes chaotic lifestyle, and indeed his unusual attitude towards money. This all helped to prove George Carman's point that Ken could, at times, be shambolic, careless and naïve over financial matters, but never dishonest.

In his erudite and concise summing up, at the end of the trial, Carman reemphasised these attributes of his famous and somewhat eccentric client, before making a dramatic point, criticising the prosecution for not calling Ken's former accountant to the stand, because "the disgraceful way he kept accounts" was in fact the reason Ken's tax affairs had ended up in such a mess. Carman then raised a laugh with his much-quoted (and often misquoted) crack: "One thing we have learned from this trial is that comedians are not chartered accountants... but sometimes chartered accountants are comedians..."

There had been other moments of levity and even laughter during the trial. Ken himself, despite maintaining respect at all times, couldn't resist making the court, even Judge Waterhouse, laugh from time to time. In fact, on one occasion, the judge had to gently remind Ken that this wasn't a performance. Another amusing time came when Eric Sykes was asked his age. He grimaced and said, "Let's just say I'm past my sell-by date..." Despite these lighter moments, Michael Billington remembered glancing across at Ken from the witness box: "He looked understandably worn and fatigued, and uncertain as to what the future was going to be... I think that the tax trial must have been agony for Ken." Billington observed that many aspects of the trial were particularly difficult because Ken was normally such a private person offstage, and here he was having his personal circumstances and domestic life laid bare before the packed courtroom and the media: "It must have been hell for him to go through…"

Anne talks candidly about the effect it had on Ken:

Ken hated the intrusion into our lives, but it was a price we had to pay to win the case. Whatever George Carman told us to do – we did it. I had to stand in the witness box and talk about our failed attempts to have children, and the emotional stress that put us both under. George said it was relevant to the case, and would play well with the jury, but it wasn't very nice having such a sad and highly personal thing brought out in front of the nation's media. It was our greatest regret that we couldn't have children. At the time I was trying to conceive it genuinely felt like the most important thing in my life, but we didn't want it all over the front pages. Of course it was misreported by the press. They tried to say I'd been undergoing IVF treatment, which simply wasn't true. George was pushing the whole thing, because I think he wanted the court to see me in tears, to gain sympathy, but I didn't want to be seen crying and feeling sorry for myself. This wasn't about me.

The defence team had filmed in and around the house – especially the attics, outhouses and our garage, which, at that time, were all cluttered with props, costumes, books, memorabilia, tapes, scripts and a lifetime's paperwork. George then showed the six-minute video to the court to show the chaotic, eccentric life behind the creative genius. They also wanted to prove that we didn't live an extravagant 'Hello Magazine' celebrity lifestyle – quite the opposite in fact. Ken had always guarded his privacy so carefully, and yet here was this massive intrusion, and nothing he could do to stop it. That wasn't his biggest concern though – he was more anxious at that point about the outcome of it all.

Ken obviously couldn't work during the court case and Anne poignantly told me that they hadn't booked in any work for immediately after the trial either. Presumably fearing the worst… or at least not wanting to tempt providence…

After almost five, long, gruelling weeks the jury were sent out to consider their verdicts on the eight charges of intent to defraud the taxman. They deliberated for over nine hours, which included an overnight break. All that time Ken and Anne sweated and agonised over the jury's potentially life-changing decisions. George Carman had done a good job, and the case had gone well, but juries can be fickle and sometimes unpredictable. I once sat on a jury myself and was shocked at the idiotically flippant attitude of some of the jurors to such a momentous decision. One woman seemed to be treating it like a TV talent show, saying, at the start of our intense deliberations in the jury room: "That prosecution man's not going to get my vote – I don't like the look of him!" It was the prosecution barrister she "didn't like the look of" and wasn't going to get her "vote"! Nothing whatsoever to do with the case itself, or his compelling evidence against the vicious bully in the dock. Terrifying!

Anne vividly recalls the distressing emotions as they were eventually called back into court to hear the jury's verdicts:

I felt terrible… weird… Terrified, if I'm honest. Ken was standing there. I knew he was feeling the same. A young comedian called John Martin, who was a great friend, was sitting by me – shaking and in tears because he was so fond of Ken, and was so worried. On the other side of me was 'Big Stan', Stan Clarke, who was the keyboard player we were using in the show at that time. A gentle giant of a man, and a great friend. He took my hand as the foreman of the jury stood up. Then it came – the verdict on the first charge – "Not guilty!" Well I sort of convulsed, like an electric shock had jolted through me. I lurched back in my seat. Stan said I tightened my grip on his hand so much that my nails dug in and drew blood. I did the same on the next "Not guilty"… and the next. I was counting the charges in my head, jerking backwards involuntarily as each one was cast aside. It was almost as though I was having some sort of seizure. When it got to the jury's eighth and final "Not guilty" I

THE DIDDYMEN...

Ken's Great Uncle Jack, his inspiration for the Diddymen

Early sketches created with artist John Geering

One of the first Diddymen dancers

Ken Dodd & the Diddymen, BBC TV, circa 1968

The onstage double act with superstar
Dicky Mint

Ken & Dicky receiving the Honorary
Fellowship at the Liverpool John Moores
University

OBE at Buckingham Palace, 1982

Knighthood, 2017

FAMOUS FRIENDS AND PEERS...

Norman Wisdom

Spike Milligan

Eddie Izzard

Eric Sykes

Close friend, Roy Hudd

Ken's idol, comedian Ted Ray

Ken as jester Yorrick on the set of Kenneth Branagh's 1996 film *Hamlet*, with Brian Blessed

Getting ready for a
TV recording

Getting ready for
another stage show

David Cobley's
painting in
the National
Portrait
Gallery, 2005

ON STAGE, WHERE KEN BELONGED...

At home in the garden of 'Oak House'

With sister June and brother Billy

Ken & Boodle

Ken & Prince

Ken & Doodle

THE SQUIRE OF KNOTTY ASH... & HIS LADY...

The look of love, Berlin

Anne's first panto with Ken, 1980, *Dick Whittington*, Birmingham

Anne, the country singer

Onstage together in later life

Celebrating Ken's knighthood in London

Celebrating Ken's 90th birthday

90th birthday civic reception at Liverpool Town Hall

Top: Reunited with Hilda
& Maisie Fallon, *This Is
Your Life*, 1990

Above: Ken & Anne
bringing in the New Year
with close friends

Right: Ken the family
man

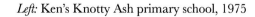

Left: Ken's Knotty Ash primary school, 1975

Below: Anne by the renovated and extended building, now 'The Sir Ken Dodd Happiness Hall for Church & Community'

remember hearing this massive cheer, then a ringing in my ears, and I collapsed unconscious, slumping down off my seat, on to the floor. I don't remember any more. When I came round the courtroom was empty. Stan was attempting to get me up, there was a woman trying to give me a drink of water, and of course an elated Ken was coming over to see how I was. What a blessed relief!

What Anne missed during those moments of unconsciousness was Ken looking up to heaven, and his police escort patting him on the back, by way of silent congratulation. An emotional Ken then turned to the jury and mouthed, "Thank you." Some of the jury were in tears themselves, such was the relief all round.

When Anne had recovered and emerged from the courtroom with Ken, a free man, acquitted on all counts, the press were naturally desperate for a statement. Ken said, "Thank you all. Thank God it's over. Thanks to all the people of Liverpool and Merseyside who have said their prayers for me. God bless you all."

Anne was so traumatised she doesn't remember much immediately after they left the court:

Obviously we hadn't dared to organise a celebration beforehand, but somebody, I'm not sure who, very kindly made some quick arrangements and we ended up in a Liverpool hotel drinking champagne with George Carman. I was in an absolute daze. The press were all over us, as you can imagine. Laurie Bellew came over to me and said the Daily Mirror *want to ask you a question. I wasn't in the right frame of mind, and I didn't really do interviews, but Laurie said they'd been pretty supportive throughout the case, so I agreed to one question. The reporter came over and asked the obvious, "What's it been like Miss Jones?" Without thinking I just said, "It's been... a trial!" and walked away.*

Ken had to pay a substantial sum in back-tax, penalties for late payment and considerable legal costs, but he had been acquitted on all eight counts of deliberately defrauding the Inland Revenue. Despite the 'not guilty' verdicts though it had been a distressing and upsetting time, as Anne recalls:

People do go through bad patches and problems and that was ours. At one stage Ken said to me, "Do you know, I haven't had a single happy day for three years," and that, to me, was heart-breaking, absolutely heart-breaking, because nobody deserves that.

It was relentless. We'd try to relax, but the phone would ring and there was something else, and it would bring it all back. When George Carman came on board he was always asking us to dig out something, or prepare some paperwork for him. It never stopped for those three years.

We got through it. It wasn't an easy time. The sort of thing that kept Ken going was saying to himself, "I'm not dying, I haven't got a terminal illness, I've just got to get on with it."

I remember at the lowest point, after one of those heavy meetings in London, we were driving back up the motorway and Ken turned to me in the car and wearily said, "Oh, do you know, I can see why people commit suicide…" I quickly said, "Now don't be ridiculous! Things could be worse. You said yourself you're not ill. We can get through this…"

You do get strength from somewhere. And I'll be absolutely honest, I think faith helps. I know Ken would say his own quiet prayers, for help to cope with it all. We boosted each other. When he was feeling particularly low, I'd say, "We're just going to have to get through this together. I'm here… we'll survive it…"

Anne can't say this, but I can. Not for the first time Ken was extremely fortunate to have such a calm, understanding and capable partner for support and to keep him sane during a prolonged period he movingly described in court as "torture". For a man who had always put such importance on happiness, and had given so much happiness to others, you can see why Anne thought it was heart-breaking that he had been completely deprived of any happiness himself for such a long period.

Anne found those three years as stressful as Ken did, but she stayed strong for his sake, helping him battle through it. I think she was like a pressure cooker, bottling all that stress up, so that Ken didn't see it. Anne's almost inevitable physical reaction at the end of the trial was the ultimate release of all that built-up pressure.

Anne fondly remembers the more happy aftermath:

Ken was keen to get back to work and draw a line under the whole unpleasant business. Phil King, the Head of Tourism in Southport, who was a good friend, and had supported us in court, came to the rescue. He arranged a date, at short notice, at the Southport Theatre, to put on a celebratory show. It was a venue Ken had enjoyed playing many times, so it was like going home. It was a wonderful night and we had lots of superb support acts, who were all keen to appear with Ken on this special occasion. Of course the moment Ken walked out on to the stage the whole place erupted. He received massive cheers and a standing ovation, which moved him greatly. The audience was tremendously supportive all evening, especially George Carman, who was highly amused when one of the Diddymen came on in a little grey wig and black gown, waving a bunch of papers.

One of the next things that Ken did, after the Southport show, was to accept a booking at the London Palladium, a few months later, to do a three-week season. Of course that was another of Ken's favourite venues, so he was looking forward to enjoying life again.

Keith McAndrews, who had been booking theatre dates for us around the country at that time, quickly filled the diary with what Ken used to call his "Window Cleaner's Round". That was his affectionate term for playing all the many theatres around the British Isles.

Understandably a bond had formed between George Carman and us during the case, and he came along one night to the Palladium show as well as the Southport one. Afterwards I was chatting to him, and he said he had just recorded Desert Island Discs *with Sue Lawley, so we listened to the programme when it went out. Quite unexpectedly Sue asked him, "Did you like Ken Dodd?" After the briefest pause George replied, "Anyone in Ken Dodd's company for half an hour or more would find it very hard not to like him." That was lovely.*

Shortly after the trial TV producer John Fisher, who had made such an excellent character witness in court, secretly approached Anne about the possibility of Ken being the surprise subject of a special 500th anniversary edition of ITV's *This Is Your Life*. That is a whole story in itself, covered in a later chapter.

As a return favour for Roy Hudd's kindness in speaking on his behalf in court, Ken readily agreed to be the guest of honour and keynote speaker at that year's annual Water Rats Ball, held in November at the opulent Grosvenor House Hotel in London's Mayfair. The Grand Order of Water Rats is the renowned charitable fraternity of British entertainers, and, that year, Roy Hudd had been elected King Rat. A great time was had by all. Ken was back on form and enjoyed a wonderful reception from his peers, which made a very satisfying end to a very difficult year.

Many current comedians seem to rely on laying bare their own lives for material, and just talk about themselves. Ken had never done that. His comedy was extracted from a whimsical world of grannies at the doctors, camels talking, inverted Scotsmen in kilts and three-legged chickens. The tax case was the first and only time he allowed his own life to creep into the act. I suppose the public had been subjected to so much in the press about the trial that he felt he couldn't ignore it onstage. And of course it was a rich seam of comedy to mine. Anne says he was careful not to make jokes directly about the Inland Revenue though, and he didn't want to be seen to be gloating over his acquittal, but, pretty soon, he was doing some hilarious material about accountants and income tax. Here are just a few noteworthy examples:

He'd introduce himself onstage as:

"Kenneth Arthur Dodd – playboy, artist's model and failed accountant…"

"I have thought about going into politics… The job I fancy is Chancellor of the Exchequer… At least I'd be reunited with my money…"

"The tax office have this thing now called self-assessment… I invented that!"

"I've written a book on how to teach yourself accountancy… Oh yes. It's based on my own personal experiences… It's called *The Mysterious World of Numbers*… If you buy one before the end of the month you get a free eraser…"

"I had this big firm of accountants called Doolittle, Diddlem & Ripoff. They advised me to put all my money into land. I asked the fella what he meant and he said, 'Bury it in the back garden'…"

With good reason it was actually accountants who came in for Ken's comic ire, with uncharacteristically barbed jokes like:
"What's black and brown and looks good on an accountant? … A Rottweiler!"

However this is my personal favourite, and arguably the best:
"Two hundred years ago this barmy MP – he's sitting there in Westminster with nothing to do. Oh, he thinks, I know – I'll invent income tax. And so he did, two hundred years ago… In those days it was tuppence in the pound… *(sniff)*… I thought it still was…"

Chapter 18:

AN AUDIENCE WITH KEN DODD

In an interview for the prestigious arts documentary series *Arena* Ken said how he had always much preferred playing to a live audience, explaining that his stage act was really a double act – "me and the audience", adding, "On television you're just performing to a set of wires, or a camera…"

He once told Terry Wogan on his teatime chat show: "When you go to watch a live show – you don't just watch the show – you're in it. I love playing to a live audience. It's a one-to-one experience." He then pointed to the camera he was on and added with unconcealed disdain: "There's not all this scrap-iron in the way!"

That neatly sets the scene for the uphill struggle the TV production team faced in 1994 when they invited Ken to be the next star of *An Audience with…*

An Audience with… was a simple but very clever idea created by ITV, as far back as 1980. The premise was to take a seasoned and much-loved star performer, who was at the top of their game, and give them an hour to showcase the talent they had honed over the years, in front of a sea of well-known faces – an audience of their peers and famous friends. The springboard for each nugget of their performance was a question from a relevant star in that celebrity audience. Of course the questions were prearranged, so that the performer had a witty answer ready, but it gave the impression of a freewheeling conversation between star and star-studded audience, creating a glittering occasion.

The shows only happened periodically when the right star was available, which meant that each individual episode became a major television event. Some of the early protagonists were: Dame Edna Everage, Peter Ustinov, Billy Connolly, Joan Rivers, Kenneth Williams, Mel Brooks, Victoria Wood and Dudley Moore. By maintaining a policy of casting only 'A-list' stars it became viewed as a showbiz accolade and a rare honour to be offered the chance to headline the show – even more so than being the subject of *This Is Your Life*.

In the mid-1990s, when youthful alternative comedy was at its peak, and was dominating television, somebody at ITV had the bright idea of using their *Audience with* format to showcase and pay tribute to some of the biggest and most talented names from the old mainstream, who had been shunned in recent years by TV executives, but were still hugely popular with the public. These veteran national treasures proved they still had a huge amount to offer – Ronnie Corbett, Bruce Forsyth, Bob Monkhouse and of course Ken Dodd all made stand-out appearances on *An Audience with*.

Ken, as we know, was deeply mistrustful of television, so he didn't leap straight in when he was approached about the show in 1994. He didn't need the exposure. He was filling theatres everywhere he went anyway. He didn't like the constraints TV usually placed upon him. He didn't like television bosses telling him what to do – he'd now been his own boss for a very long time. And he didn't particularly relish the prospect of the hard slog of coming up with new material of sufficient quality, or, worse still, giving away his best tried and tested stage material. On the plus side, however, he had always said it was prudent to reinvent yourself as a comedian every decade or so, and this would put him in front of a new audience. I'm sure it also appealed to Ken's ego as a top performer to be chosen for this 'A-list' accolade. It was undoubtedly a sincere form of recognition in the entertainment business to be asked to star in this prestigious programme. Nevertheless he was undecided and so played hard-to-get. ITV producer Lorna Dickinson was sent to woo him.

Lorna told me it took a long period of cajoling and persuasion before Ken finally agreed to do the show: "It took many months of discussion and during those months I went to see a lot of his shows. At five hours a time, he knew I was serious. We spent a lot of time getting to know each other... He was never going to sign on the dotted line until he thought he understood the team and he trusted us. That's why it took so long... Ken was his own man. You could never ever persuade him to do anything he didn't want to do. In the end he made the decision it was time to do another television show. He didn't have to, he could have carried on playing the theatres as he always did, but I think he liked the idea of doing something different."

The appointed studio director was the splendid Patricia Mordecai, somebody I knew well and worked with a lot. Sadly Pat is no longer with us, but I had a huge amount of respect and fondness for her. She didn't take any prisoners, didn't suffer fools and didn't stand any nonsense, but she knew the television business inside out, and was very good at what she did. Pat's language could be quite colourful, and she was capable of reducing a big hairy cameraman to a gibbering wreck with one lash of her tongue, if the need arose, but she had a wicked sense of humour, and I loved working with her. Lorna Dickinson's associate producer (her deputy, if you like) was also female. Lorna says Ken was a bit taken aback by dealing with an all-female team at first. He'd been used to standing up to macho male producers throwing their weight around, having to assert his authority and, if necessary, engage in quite robust arguments. His old-fashioned chivalry made that difficult with a female team. He got used to the arrangement however, as Lorna says: "I think after a while he just thought – this is different, but I quite like it..."

Ken was perfectly benign when it came to television chat shows and panel games, but, when it came to showcasing his comedy, Ken had always viewed working with TV people as an 'us against them' situation, or, in his case, 'me against them'. He was used to his demands being met with, "That's not possible – we'll do this instead."

Everything always seemed to be a battle or, at best, a compromise. He therefore found working with Lorna and Pat rather refreshing. He hadn't realised that the whole ethos behind *An Audience with* was to create and customise a comfortable environment which allowed the star to shine. The aim was to enable them to make the best possible showcase for their talent. Whatever they wanted, they got, within reason. Ken loved this unaccustomed 'no problem' attitude.

Ken told the team he found television studios starkly clinical places – he was much more relaxed in the warm familiar atmosphere of a theatre, so Lorna and Pat commissioned a sumptuous studio set to be built with a raised stage, an ornately decorated red and gold proscenium arch, plush red velvet tabs (theatrical curtains), and a cleverly disguised audience seating arrangement which emulated a Royal Circle. Ken loved it.

He said he liked to be able to see his audience – he didn't want a wall of cameras forming an impenetrable barrier between him and them, so Pat concocted a way of discreetly tucking the cameras as far away as possible in small dark booths, and she made all the camera operators and crew dress in black, so that Ken barely noticed they were there.

He said he hated technical hitches, recording breaks and re-takes, which often plagued television productions. Once the show started it had to keep rolling, warts an' all, or he would lose his momentum and the audience would go off the boil. This is where he was fortunate to have Patricia Mordecai as his director. Pat had done her training and gained all her early experience directing on ITV's *World of Sport*. Directing sport for television is very much a world of 'you snooze, you lose'. You can't very well say to a footballer, "You couldn't just score that goal again for us could you darling? I'm afraid we weren't quite ready." Or to a golfer, "Do you mind teeing off one more time? We didn't know you were going to hit the ball that hard and our camera missed it!" Pat was able to tell Ken, with absolute confidence, that he could keep 'motoring', as he called it, and she would capture whatever he did.

The only minor disagreement in the early stages was over wardrobe. Lorna said she wanted to put Ken in more fashionable clothes, but he was stuck in his ways and didn't feel comfortable in the new designer suits he was persuaded to try on. Lorna sensibly backed off and let him wear his old familiar stage outfits. Ken was hardly a fashion icon, and his quirky look was all part of the Dodd package, so it made sense to leave well alone.

Selecting the comedy content of the show proved a little more tricky. Lorna had seen the four hours of material Ken did every night onstage, and felt she knew what would work well on television, but Ken wanted to make those sort of decisions, and he had always been wary of giving away his best stage material to a vast TV audience. Lorna told me: "Ken had a strange relationship with television, because he was used to being his own boss. When he was doing his theatre shows he was in charge of everything. He wasn't a malleable person. He would only ever do what he wanted to do. Ken could be difficult, he could be awkward, but, having said that, he was very likable. Understandably he was protective of his material, but he really needn't have worried about people stealing it because no one could deliver his jokes like he did. What took time was making him understand that this was going to be a programme that would preserve his act for posterity. A show that future generations could look at and see what he did. Once he understood that was our approach, he was willing to let go of some of his hard-earned material. He was an absolute control freak when it came to his work, but the more he got to know us as a team, the more he accepted that we knew what we were doing."

Eventually a compromise was reached and Ken agreed to use some of his best tried and tested stage material. Naturally enough, Ken being Ken, he wanted to record far more than the fifty minutes which was required to fill an ITV hour, including adverts. They all knew he'd overrun. Lorna Dickinson had to warn him of the consequences of staying on too long: "The real relationship Ken had trouble with was time. There's Ken time and there's everyone else's time. I made it very clear, before we went into the studio, that at some point the lights will go off. We have unions and that is what will happen. I think I might have also suggested that if we did get into overtime, which meant double pay for all the crew, that might have to come off his fee."

Wisely she had factored into the tight studio schedule a degree of over-recording, and Ken inevitably did stay on longer than was required. The televised version of the show is around fifty minutes long, but the DVD release contains all the extra material which Ken performed, and runs at around ninety minutes.

I asked Lorna how Ken was, just prior to the recording that night: "He was very nervous, very tense before the show, because it was a good few years since he'd been in a television studio. We did everything we could to make him feel reassured and that we were going to make it work for him, but we couldn't stop the nerves. However once he got out and he could see the audience, as usual, something happened with him. What he had there was an audience of his biggest fans and his biggest famous fans. He could see all those faces enjoying what he was doing. In a theatre, often the audience are in the dark, so he couldn't see it. He was seeing them all laugh, and the more they laughed the more it spurred him on, and so I think that exchange of energy invigorated him to do the best show that he could have ever done. Like a vampire he feeds off the energy of the audience and it energises him. The audience wanted him to do well that night, he wanted to do well, so he was pushed on to heights that maybe Ken had never reached before in a television studio."

Comedy actor Miriam Margolyes was in that audience. She got her first big television break on Ken's BBC shows, and had become a close friend of Ken and Anne. Miriam had always observed the same thing of Ken in his preferred environment – a theatre: "The minute he comes onto the stage, he feels the warmth of those lights and tastes the audience out there and he lights up from inside, it's almost a spiritual thing." For once he had felt as relaxed, and found that same energy, in the more clinical atmosphere of a TV studio.

Lorna continues: "He was jubilant at the end of the recording and he was so relieved. After all those *Audiences with* we had great parties and so he got to meet everyone in the audience and it was just the best party he could ever have had, and he loved it."

Once the euphoria had died down the overrun that night led to the next problem. Editing it down to the rigid time slot allotted by ITV. Forty minutes of perfectly good material to discard. Director Patricia Mordecai sensibly invited Ken to visit the editing suite from time to time, so that he felt involved in the process, and didn't feel he was being railroaded into bad decisions. As Lorna said, "He accepted that we knew what would work on television, but the edit took forever, as you would expect. We had plenty of discussions over what would work best, but I was able to reassure him that everything we cut out of the ITV version would go into the video/DVD release. In the end I think what you get is a Ken Dodd comedy masterclass."

Lorna admits there were quite a few very long days and some frustrating negotiations in the edit suite, but she is understandably proud of the fact that, ultimately, they earned Ken's trust and respect, and ended up with something they could all be proud of. For once here was a television show which did Ken justice.

The reaction to the programme was tremendous. It had a large viewing audience and received rave reviews from both critics and public alike. The Museum of Television & Radio immediately approached ITV for a copy to preserve for posterity in their archive of classic broadcasts.

Ken was ecstatic and extremely grateful to Lorna and her team, but it didn't fill him with any desire to make another TV series. He had enjoyed the rare freedom the *Audience with* format gave him to make television on his own terms, but he was still wary of the medium, and knew its limitations for him as an artist. However it had done what he had hoped and reinvented him as a comedian, in the public's eyes. It did introduce him to a whole new younger audience who had never heard of Ken Dodd. It also reminded his older fans, who hadn't visited a theatre to see the stage show, that he was still going strong and was even funnier than they remembered. And I'm sure it was gratifying for Ken to show the young new wave of comedians that he still had what it takes, reinforcing his long-standing reputation as the comedian's comedian.

This was, without doubt, the closest a television audience ever got to seeing Ken at his hilarious best, in a theatre. Not quite as good, but close. Theatre impresario Nick Thomas, who was very familiar with the sheer joy of Ken's live performances, commented, "I'd never thought he was at his best on television, because he was very big and very bright, and somehow that wonderful charisma and huge personality didn't really come across on a small screen. But, I did think he was at his best on *An Audience with*. It is just a classic piece of Doddy TV."

The *Audience with* programmes, by their very nature, were really one-off tributes to stars and couldn't easily be revisited or duplicated. However Ken's edition had been so successful that, in 2002, they invited him to make a sequel: *Another Audience with Ken Dodd*. He was at first unsure whether he had sufficient good material left to fill another show, but of course he had, so he agreed. This put Ken in an even smaller elite handful of just four or five stars who have done the show twice.

Ken was reunited with director Patricia Mordecai for the second show, but had a different producer. This time Paul Lewis was running things.

I asked Anne how Ken felt about plundering his stage act for these shows:

To be honest I was surprised how much he did allow to be used. On the first one he said there were bits he could afford to let go, because he'd been doing them for a long time, and the regular fans of the live shows had heard them before, and would be happy to hear them again. On the second one he and his writers did put quite a lot of new bits in.

On both shows, even the first one, which was mostly familiar material, he did have it all up on 'Autocue' as a prompting guide. He knew all the bits off by heart, but things were in a different order, and out of their usual context, so he thought it would be safer to have it all there in front of him. Of course he did stray off the 'script' occasionally, or did a gag in a different way, but it was reassuring to have the words there, just in case.

With the editing they kept Ken involved. They sent him all the studio rushes (VHS copies of the unedited master tapes) so that he could decide what he particularly wanted to keep in, and what he thought should be left out.

Lorna Dickinson and the ITV team really chose which celebrities asked the questions, because they wanted contemporary television faces, as well as Ken's friends, but he was quite happy with that. I can remember when they sent Ken the impressive guest list of all the other famous people who wanted to come along just to watch the show. He was very flattered actually.

What a lot of people don't know about that programme is that not all the audience were stars. That big ITV studio accommodated over 500 people, so they split the seating into two layers – celebrities at the front, and then they filled all the back rows with non-famous members of the public. Of course you never saw them. The cameras just focussed on the famous faces. I asked for all the tickets for the back rows, because I knew I could fill them with friends, family and Ken's loyal fans, who would not only love to be there, but would also guarantee a warm welcome for Ken and a good reaction. I had a mailing list of over three thousand people who used to write to Ken requesting our list of future engagements. These were the loyal people who regularly attended the theatre shows, so I was able to contact them fairly easily, and knew they would make a good receptive audience. The TV production team weren't too keen on that idea at first, because they were worried they wouldn't turn up, especially as they were going to be travelling from all over Britain. Apparently, because television audience seats are free, a lot of even local people back out at the last minute and don't show up, so they always send out more tickets than they can actually seat, in order to be sure of filling the place. If they ever do happen to end up with an overflow situation they put the extra folk in a hospitality room, give them a drink by way of compensation, and allow them to watch the recording on a big screen. I had to insist that none of my guests would be stuck in that room, as they were travelling the length and breadth of the country to get there. Sure enough all my ticket holders showed up, and the studio was packed with Ken Dodd supporters, which was great.

Ken was terribly nervous before he went on for that first one. We were alone together in the Green Room at the back of the studio, waiting for the audience to be seated. Normally I didn't say much to Ken before a show, but, as this was something special, I did the old theatrical tradition of saying 'break a leg', rather than 'good luck', and then I said, "You know everybody is behind you with this. It's going to be wonderful. All your family and lots of people have come here to support you." He said, "Don't tell me that – it makes it worse!", so I changed tack and said, "Just go out there and do it. It's going to be great." I wanted him to know that he had lots of support, but perhaps it was the wrong thing to say at that moment. Having to impress friends and faithful followers simply added to the pressure he was already feeling. He just wanted to get out there, so I gave him a quick kiss, as I always did before any show, and he went on. The moment he stepped out to a huge welcoming roar of appreciation from the crowd, and could see that everybody was on his side, he started to relax and had a ball...

Once he was on it was his show, and nobody interfered. The good thing was no one rushed him or tried to hurry things along, like they often do in television studios, so he was able to enjoy it. In fact he relaxed so much he started throwing in the odd ad-lib.

Ken was very happy with the show and it did bring him to the attention of a new younger audience. In fact we were surprised how young. We got lots of letters from kids and from parents who told us how much their little children had enjoyed the Dicky Mint spot. Ken liked that.

On the second Audience with show we had a friend of ours who made a guest appearance – Joan Hinde, the brilliant trumpet player. The gag was that Dora Bryan begged Ken to sing a song all the way through without pulling faces or telling jokes, so he launched into a beautiful ballad – 'The Very Thought of You'. Joan Hinde and her husband Ken were sitting on the front row, wearing ceremonial chains, posing as visiting dignitaries – the Lord & Lady Mayoress. As Ken started crooning Joan stood up in the audience, pulling a trumpet out from under her seat, and launched into a strident lead trumpet line, which completely overshadowed Ken's voice. He of course pretended to be horrified at this annoying and inappropriate intrusion stealing his thunder. He kept going, but Joan's trumpet playing got more and more dominant, drowning Ken out completely. The louder she got the more Ken looked as though he could throttle her.

During rehearsals Paul Lewis, the producer, approached Ken and said he didn't think the routine was very funny and perhaps Joan should pepper her playing with a few 'bum notes'. Ken didn't like that idea and assured Paul the routine would work fine just the way it was. A few minutes before the recording Joan came round to Ken's dressing-room, looking very anxious, asking to see Ken. I told her that he was keyed up and didn't want to see anybody just before the show, so she told me what was troubling her. Paul Lewis had just taken her on one side and told her to play some 'bum notes' during the song. She really didn't want to do it, and she didn't think it was a good idea, so she wanted to check if the change of plan had come from Ken. I didn't even want to tell him what was going on, so I just told Joan that the instruction definitely hadn't come from Ken, and she should stick with the original plan and play it exactly as they had rehearsed. Joan was very relieved. Of course the routine got more and more laughs as it built, all based on Ken's comic reactions to Joan's rowdy (but perfect) trumpet playing, and 'Lady Mayoress'

Joan got a massive round of applause at the end when Ken introduced her properly and thanked her.

Rule One there of the entertainment producer's handbook – never try to tell a veteran comedian what is funny.

Here is what Lorna Dickinson said when I asked her whether Anne had a visible role to play on the first *Audience with*: "Anne to Ken was his tour manager, his stage manager, his production manager, his tour travel coordinator. She did everything, as well as being psychiatrist, coach and comforter. He didn't make a move without her. She made his job possible, so she was with him in every one of our production meetings. You never saw her in front of the camera. She would never take any of the shine off Ken, because her role in life was to make sure he shone. She was the best possible partner he could ever have had because she was there all the time for him. They might have argued occasionally, they might have not agreed on everything, but she was always there for him."

By the time they came to make *Another Audience with* Ken was obviously keen to see Anne's unseen, yet vital contribution recognised. She was credited at the end of the programme as 'production associate'. You have to look carefully, and indeed know what you're looking for, because she appears in the end credits as Sybil Jones, her real given name.

The more you peel away the layers of Ken's extraordinary life and career the more you realise what a fundamental role Sybil Anne Jones played in it all. I am reminded of Ken's nephew John Lewis's insightful words about Anne, which I used in the introduction to this book: "Quite frankly I don't believe my Uncle Ken could have retained his fame to that degree, and for that length of time, without having someone alongside him who was so close to him, so loyal to him... She was his rock, there's no doubt about that. She was monumentally important."

And Ricky Tomlinson's words, likening them to a double act: "She was his right hand. It really should have been Doddy and Anne..."

An Audience with Doddy & Anne. I would have watched that...

Chapter 19:

ARISE SIR KEN

Honours and awards come in many guises, shapes and sizes. In a career as long and as successful as Ken's there were a plethora of accolades bestowed upon him by a large number of bodies for a huge variety of reasons. They all meant a lot to him in different ways.

The music room in 'Oak House' is filled with trophies, awards, scrolls, clocks, trinkets, framed photographs and certificates, and lots of other decorative acknowledgements of Ken's many achievements in life.

In showbiz circles he was tickled to be named Showbusiness Personality of the Year by the Variety Club of Great Britain, way back in 1965. He was thrilled to be awarded gold and even platinum discs from the record industry during the Swinging Sixties. It was always an honour to be invited to perform before the Royal Family, something which Ken did often. He proudly accepted two university honorary doctorates – one from the University of Chester, and the other from the Liverpool Hope University; and he was also awarded an honorary fellowship of the Liverpool John Moores University, who dressed Ken and Dicky Mint in matching academic caps and gowns. In 2003 BBC Radio Merseyside and the *Liverpool Echo* jointly conducted a poll to determine the Greatest Merseysider, and Ken Dodd came in at number one. The *Sunday Express* conducted a nationwide poll to decide who was the UK's favourite comedian, and, again, Ken came out on top. He was deeply touched to be awarded not one, but two trophies at the British Comedy Awards in 1993, including one for Lifetime Achievement; and we have already established that it was a rare accolade to be the star of two editions of the prestigious television programme *An Audience with*.

One of the greatest tributes to people in the entertainment industry was to be the subject of the iconic TV show *This Is Your Life*. This was more of a problem for Ken because, by the very nature of the programme, being the unsuspecting star would be an invasion of his closely guarded privacy and would be an intrusion into his private life, so it was one tribute he actively didn't want.

However the whole point of the show was that it should be a surprise. Collaborating friends and family were sworn to secrecy by the producers, so that the host could get a big reaction when he pounced on that week's recipient, unexpectedly, to present them with the legendary 'big red book', saying, "Joe Bloggs – This Is Your Life!"

From his early days of stardom Ken had always told his friends and family not to cooperate and to warn him if there were any approaches about the programme. He was an obvious candidate in the 1960s, when the show was at its height, hosted as it was in those halcyon days by the legendary avuncular Irish broadcaster Eamonn Andrews. Sure enough there was an approach to the Dodd household, which Ken's mother Sarah had to rebuff, knowing Ken's strong feelings on the matter. I'm sure she would have loved to have taken part in the tribute to her worthy son, but she knew she had to respect his wishes.

Fortunately this attempt had been nipped in the bud at an early stage. Only two episodes of the UK version of the programme have actually got as far as the televised 'surprise', only to have the subject walk away and refuse to take part.

In case you're wondering – the first was in 1961, when footballer Danny Blanchflower refused to play ball completely. The other was *Doctor in the House* author Richard Gordon in 1974. He swore live on television, then tried to run away from Eamonn Andrews, so the live broadcast had to be abruptly cancelled. However, after a bit of arm-twisting and gentle persuasion, he relented and agreed to his episode being recorded for the following week. At least the Dodd family had been spared that sort of embarrassment, as the process was halted in good time, and the public were none the wiser.

In 1990, after the dust had settled from the court case, Ken's TV producer friend John Fisher had been put in charge of *This Is Your Life* and decided to have another attempt at giving Ken the big red book treatment. It was about time, he thought. Fisher had been very gracious of course in giving a glowing character witness statement during Ken's trial. He secretly approached Anne and mooted the idea. She was dubious at first, but John promised it would be a very special show, because it was going to be their 500th edition, and he had been given an hour by ITV, if he could get Ken, instead of the customary thirty minutes.

As John had been such a good and loyal friend, and understood Ken's desire for privacy, Anne decided they would be in safe hands. I'm sure she also agreed with him that this time-honoured TV tribute to the man she loved was long overdue.

Anne respected the secrecy of the programme, so that when Michael Aspel, the host at that time, confronted Ken with the big red book, it was a genuine surprise to him. Anne says that wasn't as easy as it sounds:

The elaborate plan was to tell Ken he had to attend the London Palladium to do a promo in the foyer for his forthcoming three-week season there. This was the day after a Sunday night gig in Wimbledon, so he couldn't complain about travelling all the way to London. When Ken arrived at the Palladium, for this non-existent press call, the idea was for Michael Aspel to step out with the big red book and surprise him.

It's all so top secret that even in the production office of the show they never write down the real name of the person to be surprised. They give them an alias, which is used for all correspondence and phone calls. Apparently Ken's codename was 'Stick'.

It was so difficult to keep it secret from Stick. My mother nearly let the cat out of the bag one day. She and her sister were invited along by the ITV team to be there. I told them that all their travelling would be taken care of. All they had to do was let me know if they could come, but I had to impress upon them that they must not, under any circumstances, discuss it with Ken. The next day Ken told me that there was a message on the phone from my mother, and started to play it. I was panicking, but all she said, in her strong German accent was, "Hello! ... Annie! ... Annie! ... Vell ve can go!" Ken looked puzzled, and was about to start asking questions, so I had to think very quickly: "Oh! That's good!" I said, "I've booked them on a coach trip and it looks like they can go..."

Somehow I managed to keep the secret from Ken right up to the day of the recording, but, unfortunately, that morning, one of the newspapers had printed a 'spoiler' about him being the special guest on the extended 500th edition of This Is Your Life. I hadn't seen it, but my sister Lizzie phoned me at the hotel to warn me. She knew where we were staying because all the family had been booked in there for that night, after attending the recording. Ken was in the room when I took the call, so I had to fake my end of the conversation. She asked me if I could talk, and I bleated an uncertain 'yes', which was meant to imply that I could really only listen. Lizzie told me about the spoiler and said I absolutely had to stop Ken from reading that particular newspaper that morning. I said, "Ah right – how are you darling? Nice to hear from you..." Ken wanted to know who I was talking to, as nobody usually knew where we were staying when we were away for a night, doing a normal gig. I managed to bluff some reason why I'd had to tell Lizzie which hotel we were in, then I had to rush down to the lobby, where a man had a stand selling daily papers. I spotted the pile of the newspaper with the spoiler and said I wanted to buy them all. The man looked really puzzled. I told him I'd pay for them, but I didn't want them. I wanted him to keep them. I said he could even sell them to other people, but he had to keep them hidden. The poor man looked even more puzzled. I told him

I couldn't explain, but, whatever happened, he mustn't sell one to Ken Dodd. I left him looking really bewildered, scratching his head, clutching a handful of money, watching the crazy lady dash back to her room.

A car came to pick us up to take us to the Palladium with Ken's friend Laurie Bellew. There was nothing suspicious about Laurie being around. It was perfectly natural for him to be there at a promotional event as Ken's PR guru. Ken walked straight past the newspaper stand, without buying a paper, and got into the car. On the journey though he asked the driver to stop at a shop so he could buy a newspaper. I nearly had a fit, and bossily told him we didn't have time to stop, so I did manage to prevent him from seeing the spoiler.

When we got to the theatre I let Laurie take Ken in via the stage door at the back, to meet John Fisher, who Ken thought was just popping by to film the press launch for ITV. In the meantime I'd gone round the front to sneak into my hiding place near Michael Aspel in the foyer. I was in this tiny little booth, which had been a small ticket office at some time I think. I could just peep out through a crack in the door.

Now you have to remember that Ken had always made it painfully clear that he never wanted to be on This Is Your Life, he'd managed to avoid their approaches in the '60s, and he'd made me promise that I would tell him if there was ever another approach about it. So, while I was waiting nervously in my cubbyhole, for what seemed like an eternity, I kept thinking, "Don't have a heart attack... and don't kill me..."

At long last Ken appeared with John Fisher, and was being shown the poster for his upcoming show. Suddenly he spotted Michael Aspel holding a red book, flanked by half a dozen leggy show dancers, and he tumbled what was really happening. I could hear him groaning, "Oh no, no, no..." So I quickly emerged from my cubbyhole, and smiled at him. When Ken saw me smiling he immediately relaxed. He could see that the surprise wasn't a shock to me, so I must have been involved in the planning. From that moment he was fine about the whole thing, because he knew I would have kept control over what was going to be said and what wasn't, bearing in mind we'd only just come through our most difficult time. He always trusted me, and he knew it would be okay if I'd been keeping an eye on things. I think if it had come as a shock to us both then he might just have walked away.

In the end of course he really enjoyed it and, secretly, I think he was glad it had eventually happened, despite his protestations.

It was good timing really because his brother and sister, Billy and June, were both still alive, so they came on, carrying Charlie Brown, Ken's first ventriloquist doll from when he was a boy.

My own younger sister and brother, Lizzie and Billy, were seated behind me on the stage, laughing and enjoying themselves. It is so lovely to see them on my treasured recording of that show, because it is the only video record of us all together. Sadly my brother Billy succumbed to multiple sclerosis, and Lizzie to breast cancer, just a few years after the show.

The production team had found Hilda Fallon, Ken's showbiz mentor from his teenage years, with her sister Maisie, and they'd even managed to record a sweet message from his infant school teacher, Miss Sefton, who was very old and frail by then. They had numerous acts we'd worked with over the years, and of course they wheeled on lots of his showbiz friends – Jimmy Jewel, who had been very kind to Ken when he first started, his former straight man, 'Diddy' David Hamilton, Vince Hill, Rosemary Squires, Frank Carson, Bernie Clifton, my mentor Miss Bluebell, Jimmy Cricket, Bob Carolgees, Roy Hudd, Victoria Wood, Bill Tidy, Danny La Rue, Bonnie Langford, and the final star guest to close the show was his old pal Eric Sykes.

Sykes paid tribute to Ken's genius, then advised all wannabe comics not to get their inspiration from watching TV, or they'd end up steeped in mediocrity. Instead they should save up to see Ken work live in a theatre because "this man is a Chippendale in a room full of G Plan furniture…"

Perhaps the most moving moment came when Michael Aspel brought on the least famous person of the whole evening – a very lame Audrey Simkiss from Blackpool. She was recovering from two long months in a coma in hospital, following a brain haemorrhage. Audrey had always been a huge fan of Ken, so her daughter managed to contact him, thinking a visit from Ken might trigger some response from her mother. Audrey movingly recounted the story of how Ken had come to the hospital where she was lying in her prolonged comatose state. He held her hand and talked to her. He even sang her a song, at the end of which she opened her eyes for the first time in two months, raised her arm a few inches, and whispered her first word – "Happiness". From that day, Audrey said, Ken had always affectionately called her "Doddy's Miracle".

A very different, and arguably more prestigious, form of recognition came in 1982, when Ken was invited to Buckingham Palace to be awarded the OBE, for services to showbusiness and charity. Ken did a lot of charity work, especially for cancer charities. This was almost certainly a direct result of watching his mother suffer this cruel illness, culminating in Sarah being taken from them prematurely in 1968. A particular favourite charity of Ken's was Macmillan Cancer Support. He embraced the idea of cancer-sufferers getting personal attention and support from sympathetic understanding nurses and home visitors, especially those who lived alone and didn't have an active support group of family and friends, or lacked the funds to pay for carers.

Ken kept a very low profile regarding his charity work, never doing it for personal glory, or to get himself into the headlines, as some celebrities do. It was only because Sheila Murray, secretary of Clatterbridge Hospital cancer research trust, had given a character witness statement on behalf of Ken during his tax trial, that we ever heard about his tireless efforts as a patron of the charity, helping them raise a game-changing ten million pounds. The only time Ken did court press coverage was if the charity would gain public awareness by his visible presence. Then he would happily pose for a photograph.

Anne of course was always by his side, helping him with charity work:

Ken was involved in several appeals to raise money for CT scanners, which were in their infancy in those days, but ground-breaking in the diagnostic process for cancer patients. In the early 1980s he helped a journalist from Blackpool called Pat Seed with her scanner appeal. He did a benefit show at the Blackpool Grand in fact. Through that he met a wonderful woman called Phyllis Ford who had been involved with Pat's appeal, but then set up her own appeal to raise money for a CT scanner for her local hospital in Stoke-on-Trent. Phyllis moved to Llandudno and became involved with raising money for Macmillan Cancer Support. She and her husband Frank were marvellous fundraising organisers and we did quite a few shows and functions for them over the years.

I remember one benefit lunch we did for Phyllis in Wales. Ken was trying to do a speech after the meal to entertain the 250 or so guests, but there was something wrong with the sound and he couldn't make himself heard. I called a chap over, who was helping, and asked him where the amplifier was. He said it was under the top table, where we were sitting, so he couldn't get to it. I said, "I can!" Looking back it wasn't very ladylike, but I slid off my chair under the table, on my back, grovelling round in the dark on the floor, knocking into people's legs, pushing handbags and feet out of the way, until I eventually found the amplifier. Unfortunately I couldn't see what I was doing, so I was trying to get somebody above me to shed some light down under the table. Ken stuck his head under the tablecloth and said, "What on earth are you doing?" I said, "We've come all this way – they're going to bloomin' well hear you!" And I pressed a few buttons and got it working...

Ken was extremely generous with his time for good causes. Anne would tell him that it would be a lot less hassle just to write them a cheque, but Ken didn't think that was the right attitude. She said he enjoyed doing things to help people, and he liked to see where the money was going, and meet the people involved. If somebody asked him to do something worthwhile, for no fee, his usual default position was to say 'yes', if he was available, especially if it was in his beloved Merseyside area.

After the tax trial in 1989, feeling benevolent towards the world, and more than ready to move on with his life, Ken formed the Ken Dodd Charitable Trust. He and Anne were official trustees, and the fund was managed by a third trustee, Ken's close friend Peter Rogan. The proceeds of the Southport show, to celebrate Ken's acquittal, launched the trust fund. Ken, like most celebrities, had regularly received letters asking for money for all sorts of causes. Now Ken, Anne and Peter could meet up periodically, to decide which of these requests was worthy of a donation from the fund, and also how much they should give. They had to be careful however, because Peter Rogan, as manager of the trust fund, received far more requests than they could possibly help.

Over twenty-two years the Charitable Trust donated almost half a million pounds to any number of good causes, but, when Ken died, the trust was dissolved, in favour of the Ken Dodd Charitable Foundation, which he had set up a few years earlier. Anne immediately placed a large proportion of her substantial inheritance into that Foundation. Her innate self-effacing humility makes her play this down, but a huge amount of Ken's money is now being used for the benefit of the local community, and for any number of worthy charitable causes. The intention being to honour Ken's original objectives when he first set up his Foundation.

In the late 1970s Ken found that he kept bumping into other Liverpudlian entertainers, often at funerals of older performers. Some of these people he'd remained in contact with, some he hadn't seen for years, but they were all people he knew and fondly remembered from his days in the Liverpool pubs and clubs. Comedians being comedians they couldn't resist telling each other their latest jokes or funny showbiz yarns, which somehow wasn't always appropriate at a funeral. In the end Ken and his comic actor pal Phil Kernott decided they should organise occasional get-togethers where they could all catch up and keep in touch, and also be able to let down their hair and have a good laugh, away from the solemnity of funerals and graveyards. Once these meet-ups started to become a regular fixture, enjoyed by all, they decided to give this all-male gathering an official title: The Good Turns Society. It was a delicious double meaning because a 'turn' is a showbusiness term for a variety act and, although it was never intended to be a charity as such, if they had any surplus cash left over after a get-together they would use it to do 'good turns' for friends or colleagues who were having a tough time.

Ken was the most high-profile of all the Liverpudlian 'Good Turns' and so was the natural choice for President and event host. They would meet around two or three times a year, always on a Tuesday, in a venue near Knotty Ash. Latterly the Devonshire House Hotel became their unofficial home. They would also organise a gala Christmas function where wives and partners were invited along.

Ken looked forward to these gatherings and, like everything else in his showbusiness life, he threw himself into it whole-heartedly. However he hated red tape and committees, so it was all run informally and, at Ken's admission, as a benign dictatorship, with him telling his fellow organisers, especially his chum Peter Rogan, what he wanted and how the events (often lengthy luncheons) were to be formatted and planned.

Although it wasn't a registered charity they would occasionally hold 'fundraisers' for good local causes, or friends in need. The money would be donated discreetly and without fuss to maintain the dignity of the needy recipient(s). Of course, with Ken at the helm, they could attract famous guest speakers for these special events, the likes of Tom O'Connor, Jimmy Tarbuck, Norman Wisdom, Roy 'Chubby' Brown, Jimmy Cricket, Roy Hudd, Rick Astley, Stan Boardman, Ian St John, Gerry Marsden and 'Good Turns' regular Ricky Tomlinson. They were riotous occasions and they did some very 'good turns' for people, so Ken was justifiably proud of his uniquely benevolent boys' club.

Comedy actor Ricky Tomlinson became one of the stalwarts of the Good Turns Society, but he remembers meeting Ken for the first time at one of the early functions and thought Ken was a bit suspicious of him. They weren't sure they would get on because their politics were at extreme opposite ends of the spectrum. Ricky was famously an ardent Socialist and Union activist in the 1970s. However, they soon became good friends and Ken nicknamed him 'Rickety', taking the micky out of his acting abilities mercilessly, but always in a good-natured way, which Rickety himself found hilarious.

All of that charitable work, and his standing in the business, put Ken Dodd on the New Year's Honours List in 1982. He was to be presented with a well-earned OBE medal by the Queen in February of that year. He was of course thrilled. Anne, naturally enough, remembers the day with great fondness:

A single person receiving an OBE was allowed to bring two guests to Buckingham Palace to witness the ceremony. I was one of them, and June, Ken's sister, was the other. We had gone down the night before, and it was one of the few times we didn't think it was appropriate to have the dog with us. June's husband Reg drove us into the palace grounds and Ken was horrified to see lots of dogs running around. He said, "Isn't that disgusting?! All these people that have brought dogs, letting them run wild!" Of course we soon discovered they were sniffer dogs belonging to the police. We hadn't ever witnessed that level of security before.

When we went into the palace Ken was taken off one way to be instructed on what to do and about the ceremonial etiquette, and

June and I went a different way to the audience seating. We were like two kids in a sweet shop looking round and getting this privileged peep inside the Queen's humble abode. We asked to use the loo, just to see a bit more, because obviously you are strictly shepherded around and corralled into particular 'safe' areas. We were really surprised that certain other areas weren't quite so grand. The toilets were big antiquated things with wooden seats. June said they were so big her feet didn't reach the floor. All the brass fittings and wood were all beautifully polished of course, but very old-fashioned. I suppose even the Queen has to keep to a household maintenance budget.

It was all very exciting though, and Ken was extremely proud of the honour, even if he did always joke that OBE stood for one boiled egg...

Closer to home, and perhaps even more gratifying to such a loyal and flag-waving Liverpudlian, Ken was delighted to receive the Freedom of Liverpool in 2001. This put him in an elite bunch of less than a hundred venerable Scousers to be given this honour since 1886, a highly revered list which included numerous politicians, cabinet ministers, magistrates, judges, military chiefs, three Earls and all four Beatles.

Anne confirms that particular honour was important to Ken:

The Freedom of the City meant a lot to Ken. He really was delighted to receive that. Partly because it was his beloved home city honouring him, but also because it was an honour bestowed by the council. Back in the militant left days of Liverpool Council in the 1980s he had been shunned and even banned from the town hall. Ken's perceived links with Maggie Thatcher were misconstrued and the militant Labour council said he was 'too blue' for them. The council really was hard left in Derek Hatton's days. They even abolished the title of Lord Mayor of Liverpool in 1983, although it was reinstated a few years later. So Ken was thrilled that all that was behind him and the council were now embracing him as a key Liverpudlian figure.

The giving of the Freedom of the City is a big deal actually. Lots of traditional pomp and pageantry. The Lord Mayor presided over the ceremony and presented the actual scroll to Ken, but there were all sorts of civic dignitaries there, plus our friend James Jones, the Bishop of Liverpool. There were formal speeches, and Ken made a less formal speech, which went down well. We'd even taken along the Diddymen, who, at that time, were children from the Russell Leite Theatre School. They danced and sang, so, all in all, it was a lovely colourful occasion, and an honour which Ken was particularly proud of.

In interviews, when asked why becoming a Freeman of Liverpool meant so much to him, Ken would grin and say, "Because I'm allowed to drive a flock of sheep up Dale Street every Tuesday morning… They presented me with this beautiful mahogany casket. Inside was a lovely scroll, which said – 'Present this at any pizza parlour before January 1st and receive a free portion of garlic bread'…"

He wasn't being facetious, or denigrating the honour, it was just Ken being Ken. If there was a laugh to be wrung out of anything he'd wring it. And, in fact, the bit about driving a flock of sheep up Dale Street is true. Ken had researched what the Freedom gave him, and, in some ancient statute, that particular inalienable right of all Liverpool Freemen was there in black and white.

Strangely, for a lifelong resident of Knotty Ash, Ken also received the Freedom of the City of London in 2017. Anne remembers it as quite a different procedure:

The Lord Mayor of London is a separate job from the Mayor of London. The Lord Mayor is the only person who can bestow the honour of making somebody a Freeman of the City. The way it works is totally different from the way it's done in Liverpool, where it's in the gift of the council to select their Freemen. In the City of London you have to be proposed and seconded by two prominent people 'of note'. One night, after a show in Watford, two very distinguished looking silver-haired gentlemen came to the stage door asking to see Ken. One of them introduced himself as somebody high up in the running of the Tower of London, so I took them round to the dressing-room. They cut straight to the chase, saying they would like to propose Ken as a recipient of the Freedom of the City. Ken was a bit confused because he'd already seen how it worked in Liverpool, but he said he'd be honoured and made all the right noises. The men then politely left, saying we'd hear from them again.

Sure enough, a few days later we received a letter asking Ken to send in an application to become a Freeman of the City of London, along with a cheque for a hundred pounds. I began to think it was some sort of scam or a con, but, when we enquired, it was confirmed that this was all part of the official procedure. You had to apply for the Freedom, and pay for the privilege. Apparently it was an old tradition, dating back hundreds of years, when merchants and craftsmen from outside London would buy the freedom to sell their wares in the city. Hence the payment.

Ken was a bit taken aback at first about having to pay to apply, but I egged him on to do it, partly because the two men who proposed him were such nice people. But, I have to admit, half of me did think we'd pay the money and then never hear another thing from them again. We did get a second letter however, saying we would be informed of the date in a future correspondence, but it gave a long list of instructions, telling Ken where he'd have to go and what he'd have to do when he got there. The letter went on to say the whole ceremony would only take a maximum of fifteen minutes, and the final paragraph said that, for an extra thirty pounds, he'd get to keep the scroll after its presentation. Ken's first reaction again was to forget the whole thing, because it all sounded so strange, and he still wondered if it was some sort of elaborate con trick. But, soon after that, when we'd pretty much decided not to bother, Ken received a much more important-looking letter from the Lord Mayor himself, *formally inviting Ken to the Mansion House, on the 20th January 2017, where he himself would present Ken with the Freedom. Apparently the Lord Mayor didn't always preside over the ceremony in person, but, when he'd seen Ken's name on the list of recipients for that day, he'd decided to do this one himself. Not only that but, just for Ken, he was going to turn it into much more of an elaborate ceremony, like the one in Liverpool. The ceremony became such a big occasion we even had to arrive early to have a rehearsal beforehand. In the end it was wonderful – lots of pageantry and people all dressed up in red and black robes, draped in gold chains. The Lord Mayor then invited us all for lunch in the magnificent dining room of the Mansion House, his official palatial home. So, from a slightly odd start, we ended up having a lovely day, and Ken was very proud to become a Freeman of the City of London.*

Like the oddities of the Liverpool Freedom Ken was amused to find that the privileges the Freedom of London gave him were an entitlement to drive his sheep over London Bridge; the right to have a silk rope for his noose if he was ever executed by hanging; and apparently if Freemen are caught drunk by the police in the city of London they are entitled to be put in a cab home, rather than being banged up in a cell for the night.

Whatever else happened his sheep were going to be well travelled.

Despite all these great honours, awards and tributes, there was still one major one which was eluding Ken – a knighthood. His fans thought he deserved one, and there had been various campaigns over the years, lobbying the government to give Ken that ultimate honour. It is said that Ken was actually nominated for a KBE (Knight of the British Empire) on more than one occasion, but the Cabinet honours committees didn't approve the nominations. There was a growing feeling that the honour was being unofficially withheld as a consequence of Ken's tax trial. This didn't seem very fair as he had been acquitted of all charges.

In fairness it's only in recent years that pop stars and entertainers have been seriously considered for knighthoods. There never was a Sir Eric or Sir Ernie, Sir Tommy Cooper, or Sir Ronnie Barker. Bruce Forsyth, like Ken, had to wait until he was an octogenarian before becoming a KBE.

And, although we now have Sir Paul and Sir Ringo, there was never a Sir John or George. Pop musicians presumably get knighthoods in part for their contribution to the British economy, via the export market, selling millions of records all over the world. This doesn't normally apply to comedians, who are less exportable, with the honourable exception of Sir Billy Connolly.

One campaigner, who lobbied endlessly for Ken to be properly recognised, was a remarkable lady called Norma Hornby from Runcorn. Norma has dedicated her whole life to voluntary work for charity, helping with the rehabilitation of young offenders, working tirelessly with troubled teenagers, and supporting deprived youngsters who haven't had a great start in life. She has enriched so many damaged young lives by giving them purpose, responsibility and a sense of fulfilment, not to mention fun. She told me she finds it terribly rewarding, but these are not easy people to handle, and I take my hat off to her. Ken came across Norma forty years ago and was so impressed by her that he became patron of one of her main charities and worked with her right up until his death. Norma says it can be very lonely as the head of a charity, so having Ken's support meant the world to her. She also says how generous Ken was with his time, and how good he was with these troubled young people, who she says worshipped him. Norma said his kindness shone through everything, but, equally importantly, his presence generated badly-needed funds. She estimates around half a million pounds a year for forty years. Norma, who had been awarded an MBE herself for her incredible work, felt Ken had earned a knighthood just for this selfless dedication to her charity alone. She actively lobbied both Gordon Brown and David Cameron, while they were Prime Minister.

Anne, like Ken Dodd's many fans, also thought he deserved the honour:

I must admit, for two or three years before it eventually came, I had started thinking it would be nice for Ken to receive a knighthood. I knew how proud his mother and father would have been of him, and he had earned it just as much as some that were being doled out, perhaps more.

The honours committee notifies recipients around six weeks before the honours list is published, presumably to make sure they aren't going to turn it down, which does happen occasionally. So every April and November I would have half an eye on the post, looking for an official-looking letter. If it hadn't come by May or December I knew that was another honours list Ken hadn't made, and I'd have to forget it for six more months.

Fans were for ever writing to him, asking why he hadn't received a knighthood, and saying it was about time he did. A lot of fans wrote to Buckingham Palace, but they'd get polite letters back saying it wasn't the Queen's decision, the honours list was drawn up by the appropriate Cabinet committee.

I suppose we both thought it might come one day, but we didn't lose sleep over it. Ken never really talked about it actually, and he never complained about being over-looked, although I'm sure, deep down, he was wondering if it would ever happen.

The funny thing is that the year it did come I'd really given up hope and had forgotten to look out for the letter. So, when an official looking envelope arrived from the Cabinet Office in November 2016, I didn't realise what it was and passed it straight over to Ken, without giving it much thought. It was marked 'private & confidential' so I left him in the room to open it on his own. When I came back in, a few minutes later, I asked if it was anything important. He didn't say a word – he didn't really look at me. He just handed me the letter to read. I started skimming through all the formally worded small print and then got to the critical line about the Queen and the knighthood. I was so thrilled for him. I gave him the biggest hug and said congratulations and 'love you'. Ken just said, "That's the right reaction." I don't know quite what he really meant by that, but I was so delighted for him and of course he was delighted too. I think he was pleased that my first reaction was so genuinely emotional and not centred on what him receiving a title might mean for me.

When the New Year's Honours List was published in late December his public reaction was, "I hope I can live up to it," and I used to say, "You've already lived up to it. They are giving it to you because of what you've already done and everything you've achieved over the years."

During the six weeks between receiving the letter and the publication of the list, just before New Year's Eve, you are sworn to secrecy. You can't tell anybody, which is really difficult, especially when so many people around us were saying that he deserved it and were getting cross that it hadn't happened.

I shouldn't have done, but I did tell one person. Norma Hornby. She had worked so hard to get Ken knighted. In fact technically I didn't tell her. I just phoned her and said, "I'm ringing you about something rather special that has happened..." and she guessed. She screamed with delight, and said, "Oh, that's wonderful!"

On Boxing Day that year we were hosting a Christmas get-together for Ken's nephews and nieces at 'Oak House'. There would have been about ten of us I think. There were still a few days to go before the news of the knighthood was published in the press, but Ken gave me a look, and then said he had an announcement to make. I could tell he was dying to break the news, and simply couldn't wait any longer. Everybody was so thrilled when he told them he was about to become Sir Ken, and I just burst into tears.

I suppose we were a bit naughty about the 'absolute secrecy' thing. Twenty-four hours before the official announcement we were doing a show and somebody shouted out, right at the end of the night, "Why haven't you got a knighthood?!", and Ken said something about they should keep an eye on the newspapers. Well I heard the roar from right down in the dressing-room. This huge cheer went up.

When it finally became public knowledge it was lovely. People kept coming up to him in the street and hugging him and shaking his hand. The people of Liverpool were genuinely delighted for him.

The actual investiture ceremony was on Thursday 2nd March 2017, so we went down to London the day before and stayed in a nice hotel near Buckingham Palace. We were allowed to bring two guests with us to the Palace, so Ken's nephew John Lewis and his wife Linda came along. On the morning of the ceremony I'd got my special outfit all laid out on the bed, including some beautiful expensive silk stockings I'd bought years before, and had been saving for a special occasion. I did my make-up and my hair, and got dressed, feeling like a million dollars in these lovely stockings, which had a real elegant sheen to them. Last of all I put on my dress. I'd deliberately left that until last, because I didn't want to sit down in it and make creases. When I put it on I couldn't do up the zip – it was stuck fast. I asked Ken to help, but he couldn't shift it either. Men are hopeless at those sort of things, and I was worried he'd force it and break the zip, so I decided to get Linda to help me. Off I went down the corridor of this posh hotel, looking for John and Linda's room. There I was with my dress undone, trying to look calm, speaking politely to all these well-heeled strangers along the way. Linda was brilliant and managed to zip me up properly, without any problem, so I dashed back to our room, thinking all I needed to do was put on my hat and coat and go off to Buckingham Palace. Ken took one horrified look at me and said, "What on earth's that??!" I looked down and both my best stockings were rolled up in wrinkles, like a couple of deflated balloons, down round my ankles. I looked like Nora Batty from Last of the Summer Wine on a bad day! They were supposed to be elasticated 'hold-ups', but I'd kept them so long the elastic had perished, and weren't holding up at all! I shrieked, "Oh my God!" The stockings were so lightweight and sheer I hadn't even noticed. Fortunately I had some less glamorous, but brand new tights to wear instead. Now – if my zip hadn't happened to get stuck I would have just finished getting dressed and got straight into the car. Those bloomin' stockings would have probably fluttered down to my ankles while I was walking into Buckingham Palace! I'll let you imagine the headlines!

It was a lovely day though. Prince William conducted the ceremony in the Palace. Ken was nearly ninety by then, so he'd joked that when he knelt to have the sword placed on his shoulder he might not be able to get up again. I was so proud of him when he was introduced and called forward with the words: "Sir Kenneth Dodd, for services to entertainment and to charity." It just sounded so right. I had a little tear in my eye as I watched him kneel in front of the Prince. When his investiture was complete Sir Ken came to sit next to me. Unfortunately I got a tickly throat and started coughing. There was serene music playing softly, Prince William was quietly talking to the next recipient, and here was me coughing my head off. It was embarrassing, so I went to the back and asked if there was any way I could get a glass of water. A very distinguished looking naval gentleman in dress uniform gallantly came to my rescue. We went down this great long beautiful hallway – it's the one you see in news items when foreign dignitaries visit the Palace. It was magnificent, with a long red plush carpet and paintings on the wall, but then he took me off into this big untidy side room. It was full of upended tables and piles of tablecloths – like a hotel storage room where they keep all the stuff for functions. No wonder they keep saying the Palace needs a lot of money spending on it. He managed to clear a small table and sat me down while somebody went to fetch my water. How the other half live!

After the ceremony you move into the Palace grounds for photographs and interviews. Of course Ken didn't have a tickling-stick with him, but he felt naked without one for press photos, so he turned to one of the TV crews and asked if he could borrow their microphone, which had a long fluffy windshield round it. So, if you look at the press photos from that day, the slightly odd-looking charcoal grey tickling-stick which Ken is brandishing is in fact a BBC microphone.

I had arranged a celebratory champagne afternoon tea in the hotel where we were staying for when we got back from the Palace. I'd invited about thirty close friends and family from far and wide. I hadn't told Ken, so it would be a nice surprise for him. First though we went back to our room and Ken said, "Oh God, I can't wait to get this lot off!" and, with a sigh of relief, started stripping off his morning suit and tie. I had to stop him, saying, "Oh no! Don't get changed yet! It'll be nice to keep your finery on while we have a cup of tea with John and Linda, and then they can take a few photographs..." Fortunately he agreed and we went downstairs. The surprise on his face when he saw everybody made it all worthwhile. He kept spotting people he loved, and he was so pleased to have them all there. He didn't normally like surprises, so it wasn't the kind of thing I would normally do, but this was a very special day, and he loved every minute. I'm so glad I did it. Ken's press officer Robert Holmes was a great help handling and looking after Associated Press journalists who turned up. In the end they remained very discreet and actually took some excellent photographs. There was a lovely moment when Sir Ken 'knighted' Roy Hudd, who went down on one knee to have the ceremonial Knotty Ash tickling-stick placed on his shoulder. In a BBC interview about his investiture Ken said it was the best day of his life.

I think he viewed the knighthood as the ultimate lifetime achievement award, but he was always keen to point out that it was also for everybody around him who had helped him get there.

He'd had a long time to wait and, sadly, at the age of eighty-nine, he didn't have too long to enjoy it, but Ken was extremely proud of becoming Sir Ken. It had been an extraordinary journey from leaving school at fourteen to join his father's coal round in Knotty Ash, to Buckingham Palace and receiving a knighthood.

Chapter 20:

TEMPUS FUGIT

Just like when he was onstage, in life and in his career, nothing stopped Ken Dodd going on and on. He was often asked if he would ever retire. Sometimes the question would amuse him, and then be cut dead in its tracks, by Ken wryly enquiring, "Is that an offer?" However, in more contemplative mood, Ken would say, "People retire when they stop doing what they don't want to do and start doing what they do want to do. I'm doing what I do want to do. I'm still stage-struck. I love it…"

That'll be a 'no' then.

Theatre impresario and friend Nick Thomas summed it up: "Being a comedian wasn't work to Ken Dodd, it was a life, and he could never have retired. Why would he? Because he loved what he did."

By his 90th birthday Ken had got a little more benign about the question of retirement. The *Liverpool Echo* asked him if he was still refusing to retire. He answered, "That sounds very arrogant, doesn't it, that I refuse to retire. No – but while I can still do it, I will still do it…"

That was only four months before he died, but he did still have a few shows left in him. Ken's last ever show ended up being on 28th December 2017, but he was planning more, even from his hospital bed.

Like many things in Ken's private life, he had always been quite secretive about his actual age, usually trimming a couple of years off, or refusing to give a serious answer to the question, with a quip like, "I'm thirty-five – well, in my head, I'm always around thirty-five…" Even his official *Who's Who* entry was two years shy of the truth, regarding the year he was born. However, like many people, as they get older and wiser, Ken became quite proud of his survival to a grand old age and began to tell the truth. I would say this turning-point was around his 80th birthday, which he happily talked about, even in public. Although Anne says he didn't particularly care for the birthday cards he received with the number 80 starkly emblazoned across the front, something she tactfully avoided.

On that momentous milestone birthday in 2007 Ken said, "I don't want to grow old. I don't mind growing older. But I don't want to grow old. So long as I can keep thinking, even if they're just crazy funny thoughts… As long as I can keep my sense of humour – I'm fine!"

His own Good Turns Society threw Ken a lavish all-star party at the Liner Hotel in Liverpool, to celebrate his 80th birthday. His peers and celebrity pals came along, as well as family and friends. Danny La Rue, himself old and frail by then, sang a moving rendition of 'Somewhere Over the Rainbow'. Camp comic Duncan ('Chase Me!') Norvelle did a memorable spot, Andrew Sachs (aka 'Manuel' from *Fawlty Towers*) said a few words, and Ken's good friend, motormouth Irish comedian Frank Carson was scheduled to make a speech. Ken and Frank had bonded during the making of their joint BBC radio series, *Pull the Other One*, where the banter between them was hilarious and unstoppable. Unfortunately Frank was having such a good time he rather overdid the liquid refreshments during the meal, and had to retire to his room just before his 'turn'. Most unusually for Frank he remained speechless that day.

Ken's 80th birthday was a special day, but his 90th birthday celebrations were phenomenal. Three huge parties were thrown to mark the occasion. Despite not being a showbiz party animal Ken thoroughly enjoyed all three of them. He was thrilled to have the opportunity to see so many old friends, and, let's face it, we all like having a fuss made of us.

The British Music Hall Society honoured Sir Ken at ninety –
he had been knighted by this point – with a fun-packed celebrity
get-together in the opulent Lansdowne Private Members' Club in
London's Mayfair, organised by society President Roy Hudd and
other members of the BMHS. The night before the party, in the hotel
where they were staying, Ken took the opportunity of having a long
chat with Roy about the business, which he thoroughly enjoyed.
Roy had always been Ken's closest showbiz pal, but they rarely
got chance to meet up, as they lived hundreds of miles apart. Anne
fondly remembers how good it was to observe the two of them
locked in such a deep and enjoyable conversation on the eve of the
90th celebration. That party was to be the last time the two friends
would see one another, although they would have one last brief
telephone conversation just days before Ken passed away. At the
party itself there were heart-warming tributes from many acts who
had worked with Ken over the years, and Anne says it was a truly
hilarious afternoon, which Ken loved.

On the actual day of Ken's 90th birthday the Lord Mayor of
Liverpool organised a lavish afternoon tea celebration in the Town
Hall. There was a ukulele band, a children's choir singing and signing
'Happiness' to Ken, along with lots of pomp and civic ceremony, not
to mention a massive birthday cake.

The third and final 90th party was laid on by his pals from the
Good Turns Society. A special surprise video tribute was shown of
some very famous people, who couldn't attend, wishing Ken a happy
birthday, including no less than Sir Paul McCartney. Anne even read
out a goodwill birthday message from HRH Prince Charles:

> Having heard a rumour that you were celebrating a
> rather remarkable birthday I just wanted to send you my
> warmest and kindest wishes on such a special occasion.
>
> Since you first went into showbusiness over sixty
> years ago you have become in so many ways a national
> institution, and have given so much untold pleasure

and sheer happiness to countless numbers of people – including me! And the fact that you are still performing to capacity audiences all around the country is clearly an astonishing tribute to the miraculous properties of the tickling-stick!

I shall never forget an occasion, years ago at Balmoral, when I bumped into a coach party of very jolly people who, when I asked them where they came from, said proudly, "Knotty Ash." Until that moment I always thought you had invented it!

I pray that you will have a thoroughly memorable 90th birthday with endless happy returns of the day. This brings you special blessings and immense appreciation for all you have done for so many charitable causes throughout your life.

HRH The Prince of Wales

There was a moving moment when Ken stood up and sang to all his friends who had attended. It was a song appropriately entitled 'My Thanks to You'. It had become an almost concluding part of his stage repertoire in Ken's later years, as though he was wanting to thank all his audiences and many fans for their loyalty and friendship throughout his life.

Anne recalls:

After singing 'My Thanks to You' at his 90th birthday party Ken said some very touching and kind things about me, thanking me for everything I had done for him over the years. Blinking back the tears he reached out for my hand, thinking I was still there. Unfortunately I had slipped away from the party to let the dog out and I completely missed both the poignant song and his personal tribute. I'm so sorry I missed those particular words, but I have a pretty good idea what he said. Over the years he'd left me loving notes around the house, and on birthday cards he would always express his gratitude and appreciation of my loyalty and hard work. I didn't actually need to be thanked though. I loved every minute of my life with Ken.

Like many people in their later years there were health issues to contend with for Ken. As far back as 1989, during a medical examination requested by George Carman, prior to the court case, Ken had been diagnosed with tachycardia, which is an abnormally rapid heart rate. It was thought this may have been a result of prolonged use of medication for his long-term asthmatic condition. Cynics suggested this declaration of ill health was merely a ploy to gain sympathy, but it came as a huge shock to sixty-two-year-old Ken, who was genuinely alarmed by the news. It did cause a short delay to the start of the trial whilst the ramifications of Ken's condition were investigated, but it was decided that he had lived with it up until then, and it had never bothered him, so the trial went ahead. Tachycardia is a relatively common condition which sufferers just have to live with.

More seriously, in 2004, when Ken was seventy-seven, he suffered severe kidney damage, as a result of an enlarged prostate. Like many men Ken hadn't bothered to get the prostate problem nipped in the bud, so the condition worsened and caused complications. In the end his specialist had to call Anne, telling her that if Ken didn't attend his surgery immediately, to get this sorted out, it could be fatal. Naturally Anne ensured that Ken saw the specialist right away, but his kidneys and bladder were already damaged. This meant from that day, and for the rest of his life, Ken had to wear a catheter bag strapped to his leg. His first alarmed reaction was that he would regrettably and reluctantly have to stop performing onstage. Of course it was going to take something much more debilitating to keep Ken off the stage for very long.

I saw the live theatre show quite a few times in that period between 2004 and 2018, and I had no idea that Ken was doing those marathon shows wearing a catheter bag – in fact I was astonished when Anne told me. Such was the dogged determination of Ken

Dodd the performer.

Anne and I did discuss whether or not this little-known intimate medical detail should be included in this book, but, after careful consideration, we both agreed that the clinical fact in itself is not essential reading, but it does offer an important insight into the measure of the man.

Let's not forget that he had suffered chronic asthma since childhood, something which would have curtailed the live performances of many entertainers, especially singers. He had discovered the abnormally high heart rate, then he was beset by the prostate and kidney problems and the unpleasant consequences. None of those things were going to stop Ken getting up onstage for hours on end.

It wasn't always easy, as Anne recalls:

During the last fourteen years of Ken's life there were several occasions when he suffered acute pain from the malfunction of the catheter. This usually seemed to happen in the middle of the night, when I would have to rush him down to the A&E department at the Royal, if we were at home. On the odd occasion I'd have to find the local hospital if we were working away in another part of the country. He'd always apologise for waking me, but of course I would be up in an instant, and tick him off for not alerting me earlier, when he had already been suffering a lot of pain. The staff were always so caring and professional at these difficult times, whichever A&E we were in, and Ken was so grateful that they were there and able to treat him, along with all their other emergencies. Despite being in intense pain he would somehow always find the strength of will to crack a few jokes with the doctors and nurses.

At the end of 2007, eighty-year-old Ken had to have a hernia operation, which he'd delayed, against all his surgeon's advice, because of Christmas and New Year theatre commitments, which he insisted on performing, despite acute discomfort. The operation was eventually carried out in the Royal Liverpool Hospital on New Year's

Eve. Anne recalls pushing Ken, with tubes, wires and contraptions still attached, in a wheelchair, to a large window, because he wanted to watch the midnight firework display, which heralded Liverpool becoming the European Capital of Culture in 2008. Undaunted by his recent additional health issues, as part of the Capital of Culture event diary, just a couple of months into 2008, octogenarian Ken performed three solo charity gigs in Liverpool's magnificent St George's Hall, celebrating his Liverpudlian Heroes of Comedy, from past and present.

Ken Dodd's resilience was astounding. Nothing, but nothing, was going to keep him off that stage. Anne says in all those years they never cancelled a single show through Ken's ill health.

When he was well into his eighties Anne had persuaded Ken to reduce the number of shows he performed every week, but she could never persuade him to cut down the length of the shows. She had managed to reduce the time it took to get in and out of theatres, although the latter could still be two hours after coming offstage, but Ken's work ethic never diminished. Although, as Nick Thomas rightly said, Ken didn't consider it as work anyway.

When he was onstage he'd always had a tendency to suddenly think of something and go off at a humorous tangent, before finishing a longer joke. In his younger days he always remembered where he was in the act, and would eventually get himself back on track. In his later years his brain was still sharp, although, occasionally, Anne says he didn't always remember to finish a joke, having broken off with some ad-libs in the middle of it, but the audience didn't mind, or would sometimes remind him. He found he actually enjoyed these comic senior moments, and so did his fans.

The only concessions he and Anne made to Ken's advancing years were odd logistical things, like not travelling too far to do a show on a Friday, when British traffic is notoriously at its worst. Similarly they would try to tie a couple of gigs together, when they were travelling long distances, perhaps scheduling a leisurely day off in between, but Ken never lost the will to perform.

And he wasn't resting on his laurels either in his twilight years. He was still adding new material all the time. From around 1986 his main writer had been Midlands-based Barry Reeves. They talked on the phone almost every day, right up to the end of Ken's life, and Barry would send reams of material, based on those discussions, so that Ken would always have a dozen or so new jokes to try out in each and every new show. The ad-libs were still being noted down every time Ken performed. He would always make copious notes after shows, regarding any new material. His meticulously scientific approach to the work never diminished.

Incidentally I once witnessed Ken's forensic approach to his comedy first-hand, which I found fascinating. It was during BBC recordings of *A Question of Entertainment*. We always had what they call a 'warm-up' comedian in the studio, who would literally warm up the audience before the recording started, telling a few jokes, before the real stars of the show made their entrance. He would also be on stand-by to fill in with the odd gag during any recording breaks, or, God forbid, technical hitches. One day, when Ken arrived at the Manchester studio, he approached me and said, "Would there be any chance of me going on early tonight young man, and doing part of the 'warm-up'?" (I was still a young man then.) I said that would be no problem at all, and the audience would love it, which of course they did. Ken explained to me that he was doing a talk in a couple of nights' time, not his normal full show, and he had some new specially-written funny material he wanted to try out. Sure enough Ken appeared as soon as the audience had settled down, carrying a clipboard to read from. The 'warm-up' comedian introduced Ken to a huge round of applause, then Ken explained he was testing new material so not to worry if they didn't like anything. He then read over a hundred brand new, quick-fire jokes from the clipboard, using a pen to mark each one as he gauged the audience reaction. Ken showed me the clipboard afterwards. There were pages of the typed jokes, with columns down every page, headed with things like: No good / Needs re-working / Quite good – change words / Little laugh / Big laugh, etc. He had put a tick in one of the columns after each joke. Ken said, "Thank you very much young man! That was good – I think I got 20 or 30 there..." And we had a well warmed-up audience...

Octogenarians understandably become a bit more reflective about life, and perhaps people become a little more reflective about them. It was when Ken was in his eighties that fans and supporters started the campaigns to secure his knighthood, before it was too late. I think it was also at this ripe old age that Merseyside started to fully appreciate their local hero's loyalty to the area and to the people there. Most Liverpudlians who had found fame had done a mass exodus to London and the home counties – The Beatles, Cilla Black, Jimmy Tarbuck, Freddie Starr, and countless others. Ken hadn't joined them. He'd enjoyed his temporary stays in London, both in 1965, when he was resident at the Palladium for forty-two weeks, and again during his similarly long and successful season in 1967. Of course it was the height of 'Swinging London', Carnaby Street and all the excesses of the '60s, which were centred around the capital. He said he met some wonderful people – and some rather strange people as well. Ken admitted that period of his life was great fun and extremely exciting, especially as he was very much part of the fashionable Liverpudlian 'in-crowd', and could get in anywhere. But he still couldn't wait to get home. He was terribly proud of the north-west, which he always heralded as 'the cradle of comedy', citing great stars from as far back as Stan Laurel and Frank Randle, through the likes of George Formby, Arthur Askey, Ted Ray, Eric Sykes, Eric Morecambe and Victoria Wood, to current top comedians like Peter Kay.

The former Bishop of Liverpool, James Jones, understood better than most what Ken meant to Merseyside: "I was often asked what the special relationship was between Ken and the people of Liverpool, and the answer can be summed up in three words. 'He never left'. He had fame, he had fortune, he filled the Palladium for weeks and weeks, but he never left, because he was faithful to the people of Knotty Ash, to the people of Liverpool and to the people of the north-west, and they loved him for it, because he remained faithful to them, right to the end of his life."

Liverpudlian actress Claire Sweeney told me, "The first thing you're greeted with when you get off the train at Lime Street station is a statue of Ken Dodd. He's there. He stayed in Knotty Ash, in the house that he was born in. Scousers love it when you stay in Liverpool… Ken was very, very good to the city. He'd always turn up at events, he supported the hospitals. His heart was very much in the city. He stayed there… even after he became a legend…"

Ricky Tomlinson feels much the same: "The people of Liverpool adored Doddy. If you're a special person and you're good to them, they will be so good to you. They will back you to the hilt. Doddy was what we call a real Scouser. Because there have been other famous Scousers, who made the grade, and became a celebrity, and you never saw them again. They're called plastic Scousers…"

This recognition in his beloved Merseyside led of course to Ken becoming a Freeman of the City in 2001, something he was particularly proud of.

Old age had its downsides for Ken, as it does for anybody. His hearing was beginning to fail, especially on his left side, as Anne recalls:

Like most people who start to lose their hearing Ken would complain that people were mumbling, or speaking too quietly, and he didn't like wearing hearing aids. I'd have to tell him to put them in, but he hated messing around with them. He tried all sorts of different gadgets. We spent a fortune on some tiny little ones which claimed to be 'invisible'. They were so invisible he promptly lost them! They were no great loss though because they never seemed to work. The best hearing aid of course came from the National Health, but he still didn't like using it.

It actually became quite funny onstage because Ken would often ask a woman sitting a few rows back to tell him her name to use her for a gag, but it got that he couldn't hear the answer. She'd say, "Joan!" ... and he'd say, "What was that? Janet? Josephine?" ... "JOAN!" ... "Joannne??" ... "JOAN!!!" ... "Jean??" ... and the audience would start yelling out the name until he got it. When he did get it right he'd get a huge cheer.

Despite the minor limitations imposed by advancing years, Ken had no intention of giving up. Even in hospital, towards the end of his life, there were the ever-present notebooks by his bed. He was still planning new shows and tours, reluctantly admitting he might have to cut them down a little. He was still scribbling down new ideas and making notes about new gags for Barry Reeves to work on. He was even planning a new album of songs he'd like to record... and of course he was still promising to write the autobiography, which never was...

At a gathering of friends and family on New Year's Eve 2017, at 'Oak House', ninety-year-old Ken suddenly felt quite ill and was having breathing difficulties. Anne quickly dialled the NHS emergency number 111, and the visiting paramedics wanted to take him to hospital to be checked out, but Ken refused, so they gave him antibiotics. A subsequent chest X-ray showed that his lungs were reasonably clear. A few days later though he felt worse, even telling Anne that he thought he might be dying. This time she dialled 999. An ambulance whisked Ken, reluctantly, off to the Liverpool Hospital A&E department, where they stabilised him. The next day he was transferred to the Liverpool Heart & Chest Hospital at Broadgreen, where they could give him specialist help for his breathing problems.

Ken had to stay in hospital for seven long weeks. Anne says that, fortunately, she was able to be with him the whole time:

The first night I fell asleep in a chair at his bedside, and the kindly staff found me a small foldaway bed and agreed to let me stay all night. In fact I ended up spending the entire seven weeks sleeping in that bed at Ken's side. I'd pop home to feed Rufus the dog and let him out, and do odd errands, but I was able to be with Ken nearly all the time. It was wonderful – the staff were so kind and considerate. There was one alarming day though. They had to transfer Ken to the Intensive Care Unit. I felt that they were preparing me for the worst, but they were able to stabilise his condition and, thankfully, he survived that episode.

Back on the ward he could walk a little, using a frame, but he wasn't eating and was losing weight. He was still making notes though about the act, and planning new shows when he came out of hospital, knowing that he'd have to ease back, but he was constantly thinking of ways of being able to get back onstage, despite his frailty. One of Ken's first priorities was to put on a show for Malcolm Kennedy, the Lord Mayor of Liverpool, as a 'thank you' for his 90th birthday celebrations. He was determined to live and get back to work.

During that seven-week hospital spell, a few of the hierarchy from Liverpool Cathedral came to visit him, including our previous vicar, Roy Doran. He hadn't felt well enough for normal visitors, but when the senior clergy phoned to see if it would be alright to make a visit he agreed. It was lovely actually, because they are so used to those kind of visits, and know exactly what to say. Our vicar Julia was very thoughtful too, and said the right things when she made a number of visits to Ken in hospital. George Perera, who was chaplain at the hospital, also came to Ken's bedside on several occasions, to conduct Holy Communion for both of us.

I'm reminded of a poignant joke Ken told on Songs of Praise. *A little girl went to her father and asked, 'Why does granny keep saying her prayers and reading her Bible?' and her dad said, 'Oh, she's cramming for her finals...'*

Eventually, thank goodness, the doctors said Ken could go home.

Most of us, when we leave hospital, can just quietly slink off home, not having to worry about how we look, or what people will say, but Ken knew that the press would be watching him leave and keen to scrutinise how he looked. In this case the journalists and TV news crews weren't behaving like bloodthirsty vultures, but inevitably they were indeed curious to check he was alive, see how he looked, and to help his fans celebrate his return home. Ken was no fool and planned his own hospital discharge, knowing the public would be watching, so he wanted to make it a mini-event. He asked Anne to arrange for Norah Button's stage school pupils, dressed as Diddymen, to be there to wave him off. The reception staff, at first, didn't take too kindly to loud music being played in their area, but relented when they saw the exuberant Diddymen singing for Ken, with lots of happy photographs being taken. Ken also got his nephew John Lewis to arrange a hired Rolls Royce to take him home in style, but they couldn't hide the fact that he was now looking increasingly weak and fragile. Anne remembers it all too well:

When they eventually let him out of hospital he had lost a lot of weight, and was very frail. However he put on a brave face, and even cracked a few jokes for the press, but it was a struggle for him. I know it was.

I thought he'd rally though when he got home – he was such a fighter, and he'd been talking about new shows, just as soon as he was strong enough. We certainly hadn't given up. He was so pleased to be out of hospital, back in 'Oak House'.

In preparation for his return home I'd put a stairlift in; I'd had rails put around everywhere; I'd bought an enormous television for him to watch; I'd even invested in this wonderful adjustable hospital-style bed that helps the patient get in and out more easily. I'd gone out and filled the house with all sorts of different bits of equipment and paraphernalia that would make Ken's life easier and more comfortable while he was getting better. I'd brought him home to live, but it wasn't to be. Sadly he passed away just eleven days later...

Chapter 21:

THE FINAL CURTAIN

Anne, the new Lady Dodd, was understandably numb the morning after Ken's sad passing, just two days into their married life. John Lewis, Ken's nephew, had come round to 'Oak House' to comfort her. Word of Ken's sad passing had already been announced to the media by Ken's press agent Robert Holmes, as a short factual statement. Newspaper reporters, photographers and TV crews had quietly and respectfully been gathering outside the gate since 6am, hoping for a personal comment from somebody. It was a horrible, cold, dark, wet, March morning, matching everybody's spirits. John said to Anne that somebody should go out and say something to the news people. He offered to do it, but Anne insisted on sitting down at the computer and typing a statement herself. The words just came tumbling out. She hardly changed a syllable, because what she had first written was straight from the heart, and felt right. John offered to go out and read it on her behalf, but Anne got changed into a smart plum-coloured suit, put a comb through her hair, and insisted on venturing out into the rain to read it herself. John, out of solidarity, took her by the arm and led her out to the gate, gallantly holding a large umbrella over Anne's head. There were already row upon row of heartfelt floral tributes lined up against the low front wall, left by grieving fans and neighbours. By this time the rain-sodden army of cameramen, photographers and journalists had swelled to fill the entire pavement outside. Bravely the new Mrs Dodd straightened herself up, faced them all, and read the following, with conviction, and with barely a tremor in her voice. It must have been one of the hardest things she'd ever had to do…

"I have lost a most wonderful husband. We first met when I was in *The Ken Dodd Christmas Show* in 1961 at the Manchester Opera House. I have had the supreme joy, and privilege, of working and living with him, as his partner, for the past forty years. The world has lost a most life-enhancing, brilliant, creative comedian, with an operatically-trained voice, who just wanted to make people happy. He lived to perfect his art and entertain his live, adoring audiences. I have been overwhelmed by the love and affection, which I've already received from dear friends, and the public, and I thank you all for being here. Thank you…"

Then she added, off-the-cuff, with the self-effacing modesty I have learned to know, and her genuine caring for others, despite her own grief:

"… I'm not used to this… Sorry to keep you in this rain – it's awful…"

John thanked the gathered press for their respectful patience, then he and Anne posed for a few photographs and went back indoors, to what must have felt a very empty, bleak 'Oak House'.

Anne was right when she said she wasn't used to this. It was the first time she had ever spoken publicly about Ken, and she had rarely even been photographed with him. Ken would actively keep Anne out of photos and never let her be interviewed – to protect her privacy. The first widely-seen photo of them together was at Buckingham Palace when Ken received his knighthood, although Anne had of course been seen very publicly at his side on Ken's *This Is Your Life*.

Merseyside was already starting to grieve. John Lewis said, "After my Uncle Ken passed away the city mourned him, immediately, on a huge scale. Outside the house became like a shrine. People used to come from far and wide, fifty people at a time, just walking round. I was there every day before the funeral, and people get to know that you're a member of the family. They'd come up and talk to me, and talk about my Uncle Ken, and burst into tears. This was something I found quite overwhelming, because, at the end of the day, we're just ordinary people with a celebrity uncle. But this was very much a city in sorrow. And his passing really did affect so many people in so many ways..."

Then came the mammoth task of organising an appropriate funeral. This was no mean feat as there were so many people to please. The obvious venue, in many ways, would have been St John's Church, Ken's local place of worship, just round the corner. However the vicar there, Julia Jesson, had been forewarned when she was approved for the Knotty Ash job: "You have a famous parishioner, now getting on in years. We hope he will be with us for a lot longer yet, but, when the time does inevitably come, it won't be down to you, I'm afraid – we will be giving him a suitable send-off from the cathedral." Anne knew nothing of this pre-destiny, but of course the powers-that-be in the Merseyside clergy were absolutely right – the only place big enough for Ken Dodd's funeral was indeed the colossal Liverpool Anglican Cathedral.

There was a lot to consider. Ken had been a man of faith, so Anne felt strongly that it had to be a proper religious service for family, friends and the public. However, she was also acutely aware that, because of who Ken was, it would be expected that there should be some light-hearted moments. One solution, often employed by celebrities' families, is to hold two separate services – a private closed funeral, just for immediate friends and relations, followed a few weeks later by a memorial service for showbusiness colleagues and fans, allowing them to celebrate the life of the deceased star. Anne and her team of helpers very cleverly managed to combine both aspects into one unforgettable and extremely moving occasion.

John Lewis told me: "I was involved in the arrangements of the funeral, and I've never been involved in something so big, which happened so quickly. Everybody did their bit. Liverpool City Council were marvellous. They were very supportive in crowd management and traffic supervision. That's something us ordinary folk don't normally have to think about when we're arranging a funeral – crowd control! And it was done with such professionalism. The people at the cathedral itself were marvellous. The organisation was something I've never witnessed before or since. It was amazing…"

Sir Ken's funeral took place on Wednesday 28th March 2018. It was probably the biggest funeral Liverpool will ever see. It was broadcast live on British television, something which usually only ever happens for state funerals. The weather was awful, another cold, miserably-wet, sleety, rainy day, but that didn't stop literally tens of thousands of people from coming out to pay their respects to Liverpool's favourite son. To paint a true and accurate picture of that extraordinary day here are the words of some of the key people who were actually there to witness it first-hand:

Anne:

"As a child Ken was always around his family's horses and carts, so we thought it would be appropriate to have two beautifully groomed shire horses, pulling a gleaming glass carriage, to carry Ken to the cathedral. Funeral horses usually wear black plumes, but I specifically asked for white plumes, which looked beautiful. We had about eight or nine cars to accommodate everybody, following the carriage, and, from the moment we came out of the house, there were crowds in the streets…"

Peter Rogan, Ken's best friend:

"The day of Ken's funeral was one of the most remarkable days that I've ever experienced. To say it was a splendid occasion is to completely understate what actually happened. My wife Colette and I left Knotty Ash, following the hearse, and I just couldn't believe the crowds of people that were out lining the streets, for miles and miles, sometimes ten deep… There were people waving tickling-sticks, people crying, people cheering, everybody was applauding.

And, as you got nearer the city, the crowds got bigger and bigger, and noisier and noisier..."

John Lewis, Ken's nephew:

"On the day of the funeral I was escorting Anne and we went through the streets of Liverpool, right from Knotty Ash. It was a six-mile route to the cathedral. There must have been over 30,000 people lining the streets on that journey. All clapping, all throwing flowers, roses, all shouting, 'Thank you for the happiness!'..."

Anne:

"There were literally tens of thousands of people waving. At first we were just going along quietly, and I didn't want to wave or anything, and then I suddenly realised that, although they're paying tribute to Ken, we're the car behind and they're actually waving at us, because they want to offer their sympathy and support, so I started waving back. It was the most incredible journey..."

Michael Billington, theatre critic, Doddy fan, and friend:

"The streets were lined with loyal Liverpudlian followers and fans. It was rather like a state occasion actually. I've never been to a private ceremony that was quite like that. Tickling-sticks were adorning the railings. This was a true national figure that had died, and Liverpool wanted to pay their tribute..."

John Lewis:

"When we arrived at the cathedral there must have been two thousand people outside. They'd queued for hours and hours, in the rain and cold, to watch the service on a massive TV screen. The Press were there, TV cameras were there, the Red Rose Band was outside playing a medley of all my Uncle Ken's songs, there were lots of Norah Button's kids dressed as Diddymen. It was almost like a carnival, but it was right, it was fitting... Respectful, but not miserable...

"When we walked up the steps of the Anglican Cathedral I remember linking arms with Anne and saying to her, 'Stop, take a deep breath, then let's do this'… Because it was hard… But there were so many respectfully emotional people around, and literally millions of eyes on us. It was something that most people never experience at a family funeral, but we had to make sure we walked in there in the right manner, with dignity…"

Anne:

"I was sort of carried along by everything really. It was all very emotional, but, strangely, I only cried during one little bit… I was just carried along by this tremendous feeling of love that day. Those people didn't just admire Ken, they loved him…"

Stephanie Cole, comedy actress and close friend of Ken and Anne:

"The cathedral was absolutely packed. It seats three thousand, but I'm sure there were more than three thousand in there that day. It was just phenomenal. It felt as if the whole of Liverpool had managed to get into or around the cathedral… And it was a wonderful service. Ken and Anne were great believers, so it was very traditional in many respects, but beautiful. Absolutely lovely and very moving… I started to think it was like a state funeral. But there is a big difference. A state funeral you're there because of a sense of duty, but we were all there because we absolutely loved Ken…"

The service was conducted by the acting Dean of Liverpool, Myles Davies, in the presence of Bishop Paul, ably assisted by Julia Jesson, Ken and Anne's local vicar from Knotty Ash. The organist was Ken and Anne's friend Ian Tracey, the cathedral's Organist Titulaire. The whole cathedral was packed with stars, plus the great and the good, who had come from all over the country. There were far too many to mention, but they ranged from Miriam Margolyes to Roy 'Chubby' Brown; Lord Michael Grade and Lord John Birt to Roy Hudd; Ricky Tomlinson to Les Dennis; Tom O'Connor to Claire Sweeney…

Many of the guests commented that they had never seen so many clergy in one place before. Ken had been such a strong advocate of the Anglican Church that all the Merseyside ministry had wanted to be there. Not only that but, because of the respect he'd had in Liverpool, where there is such a huge Roman Catholic community, all the Catholic clergy had wanted to attend as well, to pay their respects, including their bishops, Archbishop Malcolm McMahon and Bishop Tom Williams.

Even the Archbishop of Canterbury, Justin Welby, a former Dean of Liverpool, sent a personal message: "I will miss Ken Dodd. He attended Liverpool Cathedral faithfully while I was Dean there. Always friendly, always wise, always funny. May he rest in peace and rise in glory."

The sad, yet uplifting occasion was full of Ken's favourite hymns, psalms and church music, peppered by moving and sometimes amusing eulogies from: Stephanie Cole; Irish comedian Jimmy Cricket; Ken's great nephew, RAF serviceman Alex Otley; Peter Rogan; Jimmy Tarbuck and TV producer John Fisher. John Lewis said the whole service over-ran, but then astutely pointed out that it wouldn't have really been appropriate for Ken if it hadn't.

Showbusiness agent Laurie Mansfield:

"The service was an incredibly moving mixture of sincerity, humour and Ken's Christian beliefs. I've never seen that so cleverly put together before at a funeral. The balance was absolute perfection.

The music that was chosen; the people who spoke, from the great and good of showbusiness, to his own friends and family; made as good a show as Ken had ever been in during his life.

The love that was in that packed cathedral and from the crowds outside, for one of Liverpool's own, was heart-warming. It was a sad event, but you realised that Ken's truly was a life well-lived, and, in a strange way, I came away from his funeral feeling good."

Peter Rogan:

"I think my most abiding memory of the funeral itself, was actually at the end, when 'Happiness' struck up on the organ and Ken was carried back down the length of the cathedral, to tumultuous applause. Louder I think than he ever got, even in a theatre! Absolutely remarkable… It was a day that I'd rather hadn't happened at all, but it was a day that I shall treasure and never ever forget…"

Comedy actor and friend Miriam Margolyes had rightly predicted a year or so before: "I don't think that Ken will ever stop performing until the breath leaves his body. He will die and that is the only way he will stop." After the funeral she said, with pride, "Ken was the funniest man in the world… and my friend…"

Several hundred select guests were invited back to a wake at Ken's favourite Good Turns Society haunt, the Devonshire House Hotel. The Squire of Knotty Ash, quite rightly, had a send-off fit for a king…

Chapter 22:

THE LIVING LEGACY

Before we discuss the not-inconsiderable material legacy which
Sir Ken left behind, let's look at his massive and enduring
legacy of laughter. Of course there are the DVDs of *An Audience
with*, *Another Audience with*, and *Live Laughter Tour*, to act as
permanent reminders of the comedic skills of a master at work, but
there are a million-plus people out there, who were fortunate enough
to see Ken's live stage show. They all share fond memories of one of
the most joyous and hilarious nights they've ever spent in a theatre,
and quite possibly the longest!

Lord Michael Grade summed up that incredible experience from
behind the scenes: "One of my great joys, when I was in that business,
was standing at the side of the auditorium. Out of the corner of one
eye, I could see Ken working his magic, and with the other eye I'd
be watching the audience. It was one of the most joyous sights you
could imagine, watching the audience hanging on his every look, his
every gesture... and me too – I was completely helpless."

Ken Dodd's legacy of laughter lingers in less tangible ways as
well. The influence he has had on future generations of comedians
is immeasurable. It's not for nothing that he was known as the
comedian's comedian. Consciously, subconsciously, directly and
indirectly, other comics reflect Ken's genius. With some comedy
performers it had simply been by an unconscious process of
osmosis, others were more directly influenced. Tim Vine happily
acknowledges what a great influence Ken has been on his style of

quick-fire performance. Stars like Dara O'Briain were just reminded by Ken why they got into the business in the first place, by watching Ken's sheer joy of performing.

A handful of entertainers were lucky enough to directly learn from the master. Many comedians covetously guard what they have learned, and are jealous of new talent. Ken was the opposite. He was extremely generous and encouraging with other performers, especially young newcomers. He had benefitted from help and encouragement when he was starting out, and he liked to pass it on. Ken would often tell of his pre-show nerves, standing in the wings, clinging on to his script, waiting to make his first ever radio appearance on *Workers' Playtime*. The star of the show, 'Cheerful' Charlie Chester, spotting that Ken was nervous, came up to offer some encouragement. He asked to look at Ken's script, then smiled and said, "That's better than mine lad! Get on there and do your best..."

A fresh-faced boyish Joe Pasquale made his first television appearance in 1987 on ITV's iconic talent show *New Faces*, hosted in those days by comedienne Marti Caine. On the panel of three judges that day was Ken Dodd. The judges got their first look at all the acts during dress rehearsals in the afternoon, so that they could start making notes for their critiques in the evening, after the actual performances. Joe was a little wet behind the ears regarding performance and was incredibly nervous. Somehow he managed to stagger through his short spot for the cameras and for the judges, which must have been unnerving for a raw young comedian in an empty echoing theatre. He then went into the make-up room to get ready for the real thing, in front of the audience. After a few moments Ken came into the same room and sat next to Joe, who was quite awestruck at the close proximity of this major star and a personal comedy hero. Joe told me, in typical Pasquale style, "It gave me the willies!" Ken was charming and introduced himself, shaking Joe's hand, then asked if he could give him a bit of advice. Nervously Joe said, "Yes please Mr Dodd," and was amazed when Ken produced a notebook where he had jotted down every detail of Joe's act. Ken then proceeded to give him the benefit of his many years of experience, suggesting changes to the order of gags, slowing down on some, and speeding up on others, cutting an unsuitable gag, and suggesting bits of comic business to prolong a laugh, or even elicit a double laugh. He shifted the whole order around to make the whole act build. Ken said, "If you take my advice and do this, you'll win tonight son…" Joe was overwhelmed and thanked Ken profusely.

Ken always said it's the easiest thing in the world to give advice, but it's much harder to take it. He had given lots of advice over the years that had fallen on deaf ears. However Joe Pasquale is no fool, despite his act suggesting the contrary. He went back to his dressing-room and re-wrote his entire spot, exactly as Ken had suggested. When he went out there that night Joe stormed the place and came out as the overall show winner, as Ken had predicted. Joe fondly remembers Ken giving him a thumbs-up from the judges' box at the end of the show. He never forgot Ken's generosity, and was tremendously grateful for such a priceless lesson. Joe told me, "The one thing I learned from Ken that day was take no prisoners. When you're out there, it's you against them. It's like a boxing match, or a football match. Every moment counts. It's you against them and you have to win every time…"

A very young Liverpudlian club comic called Jimmy Tarbuck was standing in the wings of Ken's show in 1961, in awe of his older mentor, learning from the best. In fact Jimmy's perennial catchphrase 'boo-boom!' was influenced by Ken's classic big bass drum routine.

By 1965 Liverpudlians were ruling the roost in London, not just because of The Beatles, but, while Ken was starring in his record-breaking run at the Palladium, Tarbuck was just down the road doing a late-night residency at the fabled West End cabaret spot The Talk of the Town. He also took over the Palladium from Ken on Sunday evenings to compere ITV's blockbuster variety show, *Sunday Night at the London Palladium*.

Comedian Alex Horne, famous as the creator and co-host of comedy show *Taskmaster*, and as the frontman of The Horne Section, was brought up in a family of Ken Dodd lovers, and became a massive fan himself. When Alex appeared on *Celebrity Mastermind* in 2011 he came second, thanks to his encyclopaedic knowledge of his specialist subject, 'Ken Dodd'. It seemed natural therefore, when Alex was preparing for an Edinburgh Fringe show in 2004, with his then comedy partner Tim Key, to see if Ken could help them. They were doing a big piece about body language and there was a slapstick/physical comedy section where they felt they needed some expert advice. Alex wrote to Ken, not really expecting an answer, but, sure enough, Ken came back to them and suggested meeting in his dressing-room in Nottingham the following week. Alex and Tim went along and enjoyed the full five-hour Doddy show, then waited patiently to see him afterwards. It was long after midnight before Ken could actually see them, but he still gave them a couple of hours of his time. Alex said, "It was amazing. He wanted to know what we were doing with our comedy, and he gave us advice. We even filmed him and used it in the show. It was such a special moment. There was no hesitation he would help us. He was very keen to help not the next generation, but four generations down the line..."

First he gave us a comedy lesson in how to slap someone in the face, while the other person makes the 'slap' noise. It was all about the timing. Obviously he was very meticulous about it. He'd learnt from the greats, and now we were learning from one of the greats. And then he taught us how to do the perfect custard pie in the face, which involved all three of us. I still have it on video. It truly was a comedy masterclass..."

I asked Alex if Ken's comedy advice was still relevant today: "His advice to us was mainly to keep it fresh and keep writing and that's absolutely relevant today, because it's all about the passion, and believing in your comedy and delivering it well. I think comedy is the same no matter how old you are. You're just trying to make people laugh and however you do that is up to you, so it's a pretty pure art form. Either they laugh or they don't. So I think his advice was absolutely valid today…"

Alex also praised Ken's sheer industry, even in his eighties: "I was really struck, when we met him, that he had new jokes scrawled on his hands. Both hands were covered with jokes. Some were jokes about things that happened in the news that day. Comedians like me are lazy and we don't write jokes about what happened today. I should, and Ken always did, which is so impressive…"

Ken gave a different type of advice to Liverpudlian actress Claire Sweeney when she was starting out as a teenage singer in Merseyside, during the mid- to late-1980s. He'd occasionally put her on as a support act in his shows, and he'd give her guidance about the business, keeping a paternal eye on her, and talking to her about the stage and showbiz, generously sharing his years of experience. Claire was also going to theatre school at the time, but she says that she learned far more from performing alongside Ken and watching a true master at work. She told me just standing in the wings watching him perform taught her so much about stagecraft and holding an audience. Again she freely uses the word 'masterclass'.

One bit of advice Claire didn't heed, however, was a suggestion from Ken to get elocution lessons and lose her broad Liverpudlian accent. The next year she got the part of Lindsey Corkhill in Channel 4's soap opera *Brookside*, which was to change her life. A part she wouldn't have been given without her broad Liverpudlian accent…

Nevertheless Claire takes every opportunity of thanking Ken for the support and encouragement he gave her during her formative teenage years.

Liverpudlian comedian John Martin literally learned at the master's feet. Ken took John under his wing at a very early age and spent time with him, teaching him all about comedy and the correct way to tell a joke. John particularly remembered Ken's tip that you don't tell a joke, you sing a joke. A joke must have a rhythm and a beat all of its own, just like a song. One word too many, or one word too few and it destroys the rhythm and the joke doesn't work. John was coming up through the business as a mainstream comedian at a time when it was perhaps more fashionable for a young comic to be 'alternative', but Ken praised him for that and would stick his neck out for John, mentioning him as someone to watch out for, at every opportunity.

One minor shortcoming which Ken did have when it came to advising new younger comedians was that he rather expected them all to end on a song. He'd always done it and it had certainly worked for him. It's probably different though when you recorded the third best-selling single of the 1960s, but somehow it's hard to imagine Sean Lock, Dara O'Briain or Ross Noble picking up a top hat and cane and wrapping up their two-hour set with a melodious rendition of 'Give Me the Moonlight'…

Almost a year after Ken's sad passing the tabloids all ran headlines about Ken's financial legacy. As Lady Dodd, Ken's widow, Anne had inherited the entire fortune, reportedly over twenty-seven million pounds. I'm far too gallant to ask if that amount was correct. People seemed surprised it was so much, but I confess I wasn't. Ken had worked solidly and worked hard for over sixty years in a business where the rewards can be high. He'd had a sustained and successful chart career at a time when being a pop star was particularly lucrative. And, let's face it, Ken hadn't blown huge amounts of money on a glamorous celebrity lifestyle. There were no sprawling Surrey mansions with swimming pools, luxury yachts, Rolls Royces, sports cars, private jets, helicopters, villas in the south of France, or stables full of racehorses. He hadn't spent it.

Anne was suddenly faced with the huge responsibility of deciding what should be done with all that accumulated money. And, as far she knew when he died, Ken hadn't written a will. Although she does remember the subject being discussed:

A few years ago Ken did say to me that I should write a will. He said everybody should write a will, otherwise it can all go to the government, and it gets terribly complicated. I suppose I assumed that he must at least be thinking about writing a will himself at that time. I never really knew whether he got round to it or not, and I'd certainly never seen a will. Once we were married it wasn't too complicated, because everything goes to the surviving spouse anyway, and I'd a good idea what Ken would like me to have done with the money. However, a few months after his passing, I was going through a cupboard where Ken kept a lot of his private paperwork. Out of respect I'd never gone in there while he was alive. Suddenly I spotted an envelope marked 'very private', which contained a draft will. It was extremely vague in detail, but it had the name and number of a solicitor scribbled on it, so I phoned her. She'd actually changed companies, but I managed to track her down and, within twenty-four hours, she'd come back to me saying that there was a completed will and that I was welcome to come and pick up a copy. He had actually written it around seven years earlier, at the time he had mentioned about me writing a will. The will was written when we weren't married of course, and referred to me as Anne Jones, not as his spouse obviously. In fact I was the named executor of the will. I was mentioned on every page, with detailed instructions to carry out, which is strange as I didn't really know it existed, or where it was.

I do remember, around that same period, Ken was busy setting up the Ken Dodd Charitable Foundation, so he was obviously thinking about what was going to happen to the money after he'd gone. I helped him with all that and signed piles of papers as joint trustee, in a solicitor's office. But this was still more to do with what happened to the money tied up in his various trusts, rather than the traditional personal family will, which was done through a different legal firm.

The personal will, when I eventually found it, did in fact mention some pretty large amounts of money to be allocated to a few select charities which Ken had always supported. It also detailed the family members who should be financial beneficiaries. I found the will a helpful guide, and I feel he would have been happy to know I was following his wishes. In addition Ken's will mentioned that I should be allowed to live in 'Oak House', if I so wished, for the rest of my life. And it said I was also entitled to his chattels, whatever chattels are.

I must admit I found the responsibility of inheriting the entire estate, and putting it to good use, a pretty daunting prospect, to be honest.

To his credit, long before Ken eventually wrote the will, and even longer before he married Anne, he had always instructed the family that she had to be protected and looked after, in the event of anything happening to him. I get the impression he hadn't relished the prospect of actually writing a will until very late in life, because it meant facing up to the unpalatable reality of his own mortality. Let's be honest, none of us are particularly good at that.

In truth Anne didn't really need to find the will. She knew the sort of charitable things Ken wanted to do with the money, and the individual people he would have wanted to remember. However, as Ken's wife, she inherited everything, superseding any previous will anyway. A greedy widow could have kept the lot and not respected Ken's wishes to give something to his family. To a principled person the will did help confirm some of Ken's wishes, so that Anne could honour them nevertheless. In fact it's clear that Anne has been far more generous with the money than the legal specifications of the will would have required, even if they hadn't got married. She is also enjoying doing all sorts of good deeds, making large charitable donations, and financially enabling worthwhile ventures for the local community and other Merseyside and national causes. She modestly says that it isn't really her money, so she shouldn't take too much credit for her generosity. Of course it is her money now, and, more to the point, she doesn't have to be so generous with it, but there is no doubt that judiciously and thoughtfully donating vast amounts of her financial legacy is giving her a lot of pleasure and personal satisfaction. Of course she is also pleased that her noble gestures are helping keep Ken Dodd's name and memory very much alive.

Tellingly Ken's accountant, and his lawyer, used to advise Ken to marry Anne to simplify legal considerations and for financial reasons, if nothing else, and he used to say, "I will, I will! But she'll give it all away! She will you know!" How well he knew her…

Anne said to me:

He was right of course. It gives me such pleasure though. It's brilliant. There are wonderful things happening right now, because I've been able to help. It's lovely. The funny thing is I still make sure I collect all my Nectar points, and get the senior railcard discount fares on first-class off-peak travel. Ken taught me well!

The truth is I loved the relatively modest way we lived. I never wanted for more. We did have the odd argument about money, but not that he wouldn't spend it on me. I'd tell him to treat himself and he wouldn't. He did enjoy buying some good designer suits and stylish jackets, but he hardly ever wore them. He liked to relax in corduroy slacks and sweaters, always favouring comfort and warmth over sartorial elegance. Anything nice he'd keep for use on the stage. In the early years, if he was travelling on his own, he'd travel standard class on the trains. When I started making the bookings he did enjoy the extra comfort of first-class travel, but luxury really didn't interest him. He'd look at me sometimes and say, "You and I have a different attitude towards money."

I have been fortunate enough to witness some of Ken's money at work in the local Knotty Ash community. The clock in the beautiful gothic bell tower of St John's Church had stopped many years ago, and it had never chimed since. The repairs were expensive, and not a high enough priority for the limited church funds. Ken had been keen to help, so Anne has had the whole clock stripped down, professionally cleaned and repaired. The elegant face of the clock has been given a striking gold leaf and black makeover to restore it to its former glory. I happened to be there, interviewing Anne for this book, when she heard the clock chime for the first time in decades, and I went round the corner to the church with her, to witness her cutting the ribbon across the entrance to the clock tower, to formally acknowledge the church clock being put back into regular use.

Right opposite the church is a red sandstone building, dated 1837, which was in fact Ken's infant school, back in the day. It became the St John's Church hall, but fell into such disrepair it ultimately became unsafe for public use. Anne is paying for renovations, improvements and a major extension. The hall, unlike the church, is not a listed building, but it is in a conservation area, and any alterations have to be approved by the local planners. When it is finally completed, within these strict parameters, it will be put to good use by St John's Church and the local community, for any number of activities and events. At the time of writing Anne was thrilled to tell me that the Parochial Church Council had just unanimously agreed that the former infant school should be renamed the Sir Ken Dodd Happiness Hall, for St John's Church & Community. I have been keeping an eye on the ongoing (very costly) work every time I have visited Knotty Ash, and have witnessed Anne's growing pride in saving this historic building, and returning it to the Knotty Ash community.

I was also there to watch Anne cutting the ribbon on a recently converted state-of-the-art heart surgery wing of the Liverpool Heart & Chest Hospital, which she has helped fund. It's the hospital which nursed Ken towards the end of his life. The event was rather touching as several of the nurses who were present at the ribbon-cutting were the staff who had looked after Ken in his last few weeks, and were clearly very fond of him. A significant donation has also been made to the new Clatterbridge Hospital and Cancer Centre, to equip 110 bedrooms with televisions and radios. Clatterbridge was always one of Ken's favourite charities, as they had cared for fiancée Anita at the end of her life.

In the arts world Anne is heavily involved in Shakespeare North, which is a brand new purpose-built complex in Prescot, east

Liverpool. It includes an Elizabethan-style, 350-seater playhouse, plus an educational centre for Shakespearian stagecraft, as well as a performance garden. Ken's charitable foundation is funding the entire performance garden project, which will be named in his honour. This ambitious venture includes an open air theatre in the Greek/Roman style, which resonates well with Ken's love of both Shakespeare and those historically-preserved and acoustically-perfect semi-circular amphitheatres which he loved to explore all over Europe.

Anne, together with the trustees, is planning to help fund some modernisation to the entrance of the Liverpool Anglican Cathedral, making it more wheelchair-friendly. She gets terribly excited when she talks about all these projects and clearly loves being able to help. The cathedral I suppose holds a very special place in her heart, as they gave Ken such a magnificent send-off.

Other beneficiaries from Ken's charitable foundation trust are Merseyside homeless associations; local animal welfare charities; theatre schools; the Strawberry Field Salvation Army Centre; Parkinson's UK; plus the military charity, Combat Stress, which cares for and rehabilitates service veterans who have been left with PTSD. All causes which were dear to Ken's heart, and Anne is helping, in his name.

It's very endearing to see how animated Anne becomes when she's talking about all the people who are benefitting from Ken's charitable legacy. There are so many she finds it difficult to keep track of them all.

Ken was absolutely right when he predicted that Anne would give his money away. It is her intention that the Ken Dodd Charitable Foundation will continue to fund a great many good causes, ensuring that Ken's name lives on, and will continue to do so, long after she herself has gone.

There is one further legacy of Ken's life and career and that is down to Anne herself. She has taken to giving talks and after-dinner speeches about her life with her legendary husband, peppered with her funny anecdotes and fond memories. Ken would be justifiably proud of her. She is really enjoying the feedback from her enthusiastic audiences, so the Doddy laughter lives on.

Chapter 23:

A LIFE WELL LIVED

There have been other books about the Ken Dodd story, but Anne and I have always known that there never has been a book like this before. The reason is simple. Nobody knew much about the offstage Ken. He only ever tossed inquisitive journalists titbits about his life, and he always declined to cooperate with biographers, so there was little they could say about the real man behind the comedy legend, or his personal life. Ours was always going to be the intimate biography that nobody else could possibly write.

However, when I first sat down with Anne in 'Oak House' to start work on this exciting project, I was extremely aware that there were three known quirks of Ken that would have to be addressed, or readers would think I'd failed to uncover the real Ken Dodd. Worse still, you might think I was sugar-coating or deliberately overlooking his human idiosyncrasies. We all have them, but Ken's were of course his unconventional relationships with time and money, and his intense privacy, to the point of secrecy, about his private life.

I worked with Ken intermittently for a year and people used to ask me what he was like to work with. I truthfully said that he was very professional, not in the least bit difficult, and he was good, chatty, amusing, amiable company. My only criticism was that I felt I knew no more about the real Ken Dodd on the day the series ended than I did on the day I first met him in the Adelphi Hotel, twelve months earlier. That's unusual in the television/entertainment industry. One of the enjoyable and gratifying aspects about working in that world is that spending a lot of time in close contact with the stars, working intensely with them, is that you do usually get to know them quite well, and find out what makes them tick. I should just add though that, unbeknown to me, Ken did have a lot on his mind during the year I knew him. It was the year of the tax investigation, prior to the trial.

Writing this book was a delicate balancing act for me, because I had no intention of being crass, or offending Anne with my questions, but I did want to learn the whole truth. I am satisfied that we have addressed those issues. She has been disarmingly honest and open about many things, and I think I understand Ken much more as a result. Hopefully you do too.

His attitude to time we have covered in great detail, and we have talked a lot about his perhaps slightly over-zealous need for privacy. The money is probably the best known of Ken's idiosyncrasies and arguably the most complicated, as I have discovered.

There are undoubtedly many funny stories about Ken and his carefulness with money. Roy Hudd told me about the time when Ken came to see him in a theatre bar after a show to ask him if he'd be a character witness at the tax trial. Ken offered his best friend Roy a drink by way of a thank you for promising this massive personal favour. Roy said, "That's very kind Ken. I'll have a beer with you." Ken then apparently beckoned to the barman and said, "Half a bitter for Mr Hudd..."

There are also many myths about Ken and money. In the end I took the bull by the horns and asked Anne, the person who knew him best, how she would sum up Ken's attitude to money. As ever she gave me a full, frank, and I think revealing answer:

He said to me once, "To me money is purely a measure of success. It proves I've achieved something."

He also told me many times that the creativity has always been more important than the riches it provided. He certainly was never interested in a millionaire lifestyle.

In one of my first conversations with him, when we first met, I found it curious when he told me that he didn't know how to spend money. He mentioned a fellow entertainer, Joe 'Mr Piano' Henderson, who Ken said did know how to spend money. Joe told Ken he shouldn't be staying in theatrical digs – he should be staying in the best hotels and eating out royally, because it's all tax-deductible when you're on tour, but that didn't interest Ken. He liked to live modestly. He never ever craved the trappings of wealth. And of course he'd seen other performers who had lived life to the full, splashing money left, right and centre, and then couldn't pay their tax bill at the end of the year, because they'd spent it all. He couldn't live like that. With all professional performers there is always that nagging fear that it might all be over tomorrow, so Ken also saved for that unthinkable eventuality.

Not only that, but, to the day he died, he lived like he'd always been brought up – to value money and what it could buy. He always thought back to his parents and how they'd had to make every penny count so that he and his siblings wanted for nothing. I know, when the subject of money came up, he'd always think back to his mother and father and what they would do.

Sarah, his mum, used to go round door-to-door, collecting the money owed to the coal business his dad ran, and one night she got mugged. All the takings were stolen and she was obviously very shaken up. Ken could never forget that, and always felt guilty about it. He was out, in his early days, performing in a pub or a club in Liverpool, and there was his mum being attacked in the street for the money to keep the family household going. That haunted him for a long time. In fact it never left him.

He was also very practical. I remember he once talked about getting a Rolls Royce, but then he decided against it. Not because of the cost, but for practical reasons. He didn't think he'd be able to park it anywhere and it would draw the wrong sort of attention, so he didn't bother.

Ken did like nice cars though. I remember, many years ago, in a moment of madness, he bought an enormous turquoise blue American car, a Pontiac, which was long – very long! He loved it, but I only ever drove it once, after a lot of encouragement from Ken, with him as an increasingly nervous passenger. I drove a short distance, but I didn't dare try a tricky parking manoeuvre to stop, because it was so long, despite his firm, "You can do it, you can do it!" In the end I had to do a circuit of Knotty Ash in one gear, without stopping, and line it up to the kerb outside the house to park. Which is precisely where I left it, shaking from the experience, saying with a wry laugh, "It's all yours mate!"

Ken always bought brand new cars. He had a beautiful new Jaguar when I first knew him. He had several other Jags actually, until he ended up with a faulty Mark Ten. The floor leaked, which led to Ken christening it a 'Friday night car' – hastily built on a Friday night when everybody's in a rush to get home for the weekend, so, despite being brand new, it's far from perfect.

The last car, and my favourite, because it was such a pleasure to drive, was a beautiful leather-upholstered 'R Class' Mercedes. After Ken passed away I gave the Merc to Nigel, our keyboard player, who has spent time and money restoring it to its original immaculate glory. Over the years I had given it several 'jewels', as Ken would call them – a euphemism for minor dents and scratches. There was also a large patch of shredded cladding on the inside rear door, which Rufus, our ten-week old puppy, proudly showed me after a particularly long boring journey! Nigel was delighted to receive the car. I wouldn't have wanted it to go to a stranger. Nice to pass fond memories on to friends.

In the touring years we also had a succession of estate cars and then big seven-seater 'people-carriers', purely for practical reasons. We could get so much in them when we were on the road. With the seven-seaters we'd take out the back row of seats to give us more room for carrying props, and we'd put in a clothes rail for costumes. As well as the bigger practical vehicles we each had a smaller run-around car for local use. Ken enjoyed driving locally and appreciated going about his business somewhat incognito, driving *something inconspicuous. Having said that, he was always happy to talk to anybody who did recognise him.*

One book about Ken said he never went on holiday. That simply isn't true. We went all over the world. We couldn't always go too far afield for long periods because of the dogs, although, over the years, we got as far as San Francisco, Las Vegas, New York, the Bahamas, the Caribbean, Niagara Falls and the Canadian Rockies. We travelled a lot in Europe, and he loved that. A cruise down the Nile in Egypt was a real adventure, as was the Holy Land, which was spiritually moving for both of us.

Of course Ken was recognised nearly everywhere we went. There was no real escape. In Bethlehem he got down on his knees to say a prayer at Christ's birthplace in the Grotto of the Nativity. Suddenly this woman stood next to me, spotted Ken kneeling there, head bowed, and said in a broad Brummie accent, "Ooh, is he looking for the Diddymen?"

We would fly 'club class', if it was available, purely for the comfort of extra space, but we rarely travelled first-class though. I usually made the bookings, and it wouldn't really occur to me to pay so much extra for a journey.

The truth is Ken never thought about his wealth. I remember once a very close female friend offended Ken when he said he wanted to pop into a shop to buy a lottery ticket. The lottery had just started and it was all a bit of a novelty. She looked at him and said, "Why do YOU need to buy a lottery ticket?!" Ken looked quite wounded and said, "Am I not allowed to have the fun that everybody else is having in taking part?" It wasn't the winnings he was interested in, just the fun of the chase – a bit like his dad and the horses I suppose. She didn't mean to hurt him, but I could see he was clearly offended by that jibe and what it implied.

People say the house had been allowed to get run-down, which it had I suppose, back in the late 1970s and into the 1980s. The problem was Ken's father was a bit set in his ways and, like a lot of elderly people, he didn't like change, or the upheaval of home maintenance as he reached old age. When Mr Dodd died Ken had the whole house re-roofed and re-wired, because the electrics were potentially dangerous. We could also start to change and modernise things, and do all the things we had wanted to do for some time.

When it came to improving and extending the house, adding the summer house and the conservatory and sorting out the garden, they were usually my ideas. I don't think Ken would have bothered if he was living alone, because his was a single-track mind, and all he thought about was work. That was his life, but he always happily paid for all the improvements and appreciated what I'd done. He never once objected to any of my ideas. He'd say, "Oh you've done so much here. I do love it." In effect I had carte blanche. I didn't always tell him how much things were going to cost of course. He'd joke about it with Tony Hayes, our builder: "Oh no! What's she doing now?!", but it was a joke. He didn't stint on paying. Quite the opposite in fact.

In later years we got 'The Two Steves', a father and son building team, to completely rebuild one of the old outhouses, on the 'footprint' of the initial building, using all the original bricks, as a library for Ken's vast collection of books. He loved this creation, which was built during his last year. My friend Jean and I struggled with his favourite enormous swivel chair down two flights of stairs from the attic, where it had been stored for years, collapsing in fits of laughter every time it got stuck over our heads on each tight corner of the ancient 1782 farmhouse staircase. Ken was a great help, giving us instructions on how to do it properly. "Up a bit, down a bit..." He was never a particularly practical person. At long last though I had the great pleasure of watching him enjoy his own 'topping out' ceremony. That's a traditional builders' term for celebrating the placement of the final beam of a construction into place. Raising a glass of champagne, Ken placed the first book on one of the shelves – his favourite novel from childhood, The Wind in the Willows. *Sadly he didn't live to see his library as it is now, full to the brim with books, all beautifully displayed in subdued lighting.*

Ken asked me once if I wanted a swimming pool in the garden, but I just didn't want the hassle and worry of having one. He would have been happy to pay for it though.

He even offered to buy me the lovely five-bedroomed house, in which I'd been brought up as a child, when it happened to come on the market. It had been immaculately maintained and extended, but I didn't want it. You can't go back. I think Ken was maybe wondering if I might want to move out of 'Oak House' when he died, and have somewhere more my own. It was a thoughtful suggestion, but I wanted to stay in Knotty Ash. All my memories are in this house, but I really appreciated the kind offer. I think Ken was pleased though when I told him I wanted to stay here.

Of course that brings up the question of what happens to 'Oak House' when I'm gone. Ken had often talked about a museum of comedy in Knotty Ash, so that's perhaps a thought. That way people could use the library.

I have been fortunate enough to go into the library, and I have never seen so many books on comedy and comedians in my life. I thought I had a good collection of comedy biographies, but Ken's extensive library is mind-blowing. And Anne tells me there are as many books again, still up in the attics.

Apparently Ken had started making plans for a comedy museum on some land opposite 'Oak House', but that fell through. I hope Anne will live there for a lot longer yet, but it would be a fitting tribute if Ken's family home did end up being the chuckle museum he dreamt of.

Ken himself made jokes about his legendary carefulness with money. He would often say, "I've got money I haven't even used yet!" However, there is one final observation, which Anne confirms. For all the jokes and stories about Ken and his money, he was extremely generous with his time. Sometimes that is a far more precious commodity.

Personally I think it's a shame that Ken guarded his private life quite so closely. Fans love to find out about the human side of their idols – hence the constant demand for celebrity reality shows, at-home-with-the-stars-style glossy magazines, TV chat shows, biographies and autobiographies. He had nothing to hide. I think we'd have all liked 'the other Ken Dodd', just as much as we liked the performing Ken Dodd. Perhaps the whole package would have made him even more lovable to the great British public. It's probably why he was so genuinely well-loved in and around Merseyside, because those people did actually get to see glimpses of 'the real Ken Dodd'. I have been privileged to learn so much about the human side of Ken from Anne, and I find that I like him much more now, even though I worked with him quite happily for a year of my life. I am so pleased Anne has allowed me to share what I have learned with his many other fans, and I hope you have come to know the real man, and understand him better too.

Like most people I fell for the exaggerated tabloid stories of Ken's eccentric and unusual domestic lifestyle, plus his offbeat relationships with both time and money, but, now that I understand him more, I don't think any of it was anywhere near as strange as the press had us believe. Ken had his own logic regarding things, and I can now see where that slightly left-field logic came from. We all have our peculiar foibles. My wife would be quick to confirm that I have hundreds of them! Ken's lifestyle wouldn't have suited everybody, but it suited him and Anne, and that's all that matters.

One thing I did find surprising was Ken's tardiness in marrying Anne. It seemed slightly at odds with his Christian morality for one thing. These days living together is considered no big deal, but, back when they first co-habited, after 'Oak House' became Ken's, it was very much frowned upon. Anne says in one hotel where they stayed in their early days together they had to have separate rooms, because the hotel wouldn't put an unmarried couple in the same room. It's hard to imagine now how taboo living and sleeping together, out of wedlock, was back then. It was often referred to as 'living in sin'. Fortunately Anne's mother didn't seem to mind them sharing a home, even though she could be quite old-fashioned in her thinking. I'm not sure Ken's parents would have been quite so broadminded.

Marriage between them was occasionally discussed and joked about. Ken would say to Anne, "Maybe we'll get married when we're getting on a bit…" Of course he was saying that when he was already getting on a bit…

Perhaps there was a little typically-male reluctance to commit, but, if Ken did make fiancée Anita a rash promise on her death-bed that he wouldn't marry anybody else, then it explains an awful lot. Of course one could ask why he didn't marry Anita, despite their long engagement. He always said he was too busy to think about marriage, but I somehow feel it was never meant to be, and, arguably, they should never have rushed into an engagement at such a young age. I have heard from various sources that their lengthy relationship was not always the easiest.

Anne told me this about her occasional discussions with Ken on the subject of matrimony:

I suppose we thought a bit more seriously about getting married while we were trying for children, but marriage was never the be-all and end-all for either of us.

One of the legal team thought we should get married before the tax trial so that, as the defendant's wife, I couldn't be asked to give evidence against Ken, but I felt that wasn't the right reason for a wedding. I was my own person, and I wasn't afraid of standing up in court. In any case marriage really wasn't that important, so I was never going to coerce him into marrying me. The main thing was that he was a very loyal person, and I believed him when he told me that he'd never let me down. And he never did…

I asked Anne about any regrets that Ken might have had. I wondered if he'd ever hankered after international fame. He did in fact do a few gigs in Canada, but that was mainly to ex-pats, who made a very appreciative audience. Anne said they wanted to physically touch Ken after the show, because he reminded them so much of home. I think though he knew that his humour was quintessentially British, and he never played the world's entertainment capital Las Vegas, or even wanted to. Very few UK comedians have ever cracked America, and, in any case, Ken enjoyed a wonderful and gratifying career in his beloved homeland.

As Anne is often keen to point out, she's incredibly proud of the fact that Ken, the son of a coalman, rose rapidly to the top of the bill in the late 1950s and never was anything less for the next sixty years, and he created it all from nothing:

The thing I'm most proud of though is that he was still a normal person underneath, with normal values, good values, and could talk to anybody, from royalty to ordinary people in the street, and was comfortable. And, somehow, in amongst all the madness of showbusiness, he kept sane, totally sane. He didn't have any 'side' to him. We used to get so many wonderfully heart-warming letters from every level of society. There were any number of moving and touching stories of how Ken had helped people through their darkest hours of ill health and bereavement, by making them laugh again, allowing them to carry on living. I continue to receive such letters to this day. That makes me very proud of him.

Ken was always a great listener. Fans and friends would frequently share their problems in life with him, especially loneliness. He would always have words of comfort and he'd say, "Have a purpose in life. The secret of happiness is to be creative. Plant a seed and watch it grow. Grow a family, grow a business, grow a garden, grow a friendship. Give yourself a purpose in life." He understood that loneliness affects all age groups, but older people are especially vulnerable, and he would never refuse to help when asked to visit a care home or a nursing home. When I was in hospital myself with a broken hip he would visit every day, but, when he arrived, he'd chat to all the surrounding patients to cheer them up, and then eventually get to me!

He would use his clowning skills to connect with less fortunate people. He would go over to a local home for handicapped children and they would all run up and hug him. With his eccentric looks, his hair all stuck up, a big toothy smile and his air of harmless visual fun, they would all gravitate towards him, because he made them laugh. That was lovely to see.

Another great joy for me was sitting with Ken by the television and watching him rock with laughter at something he found hilarious, as far back as Bilko *and* I Love Lucy, *up to more recent comedy classics like* Doc Martin *and the long-running American series* Frasier. *He was a big fan of* Peter Cook & Dudley Moore, *and he always loved* Dad's Army. *He would fall about laughing at Arthur Lowe, especially when he was playing a drunk. Another one who always made him laugh was his friend Eric Sykes. Eric was a clever writer, but he was also a great comic actor who was particularly good at physical comedy 'business'. Ken loved that. More recently he found the surreal freewheeling stand-up comedy style of Ross Noble hilarious, and he always made a point of watching Derren Brown's TV shows, having been a fan of good stage magicians all his life. He loved magic and would say, "If I'm going to be conned, I like to be conned in style!"*

The Magic Circle actually made him an honorary member, and he was very proud to be elected President of the Blackpool Magicians Club, who famously hold an International Magic Convention every year. Ken would go on the final day, buying props and yet more books from the magic dealers. He would then host the Gala Show, presenting magic awards and entertaining the many professional and amateur magicians who attended. He looked forward to seeing old friends there, and relaxing with fellow pros. It was a pleasure to witness his enjoyment.

This was Anne's only thought on regrets:

I suppose our only regret, in an otherwise very happy life together, was not having children. It was 1978 before we were properly living together, by which time I was thirty-seven, so the old biological clock was ticking, as they say. From that time on we did try for kids, but nothing happened. We both had tests and there was no reason why I shouldn't conceive, but I didn't, for whatever reason. We weren't so obsessed about having a family, but it would have been nice.

A friend of mine at church recently said, "You are given no more than you can cope with, and you cope with what you're given." It would have dramatically changed our lives if I had become pregnant. I wouldn't have been able to be at Ken's side all the time when he was working, so maybe it wasn't meant to be. And I did always want to be there with Ken – even while I was still working for BEA. It was never a duty or a chore. It's where I wanted to be.

Sometimes I look at mothers with young children and think, 'Wow – that's hard work!', but I'm sure I would have enjoyed motherhood, if we had been so blessed. Ken, I suppose, almost had a surrogate son in Dicky Mint. He loved that cheeky character he'd created, so I'm pretty sure he would have made a good father.

From my privileged insider observations of the inseparable Ken/ Anne partnership it seems to me that children might have completely derailed the well-oiled machine, to mix metaphors. To get to the top in the cut-throat world of showbusiness you have to be a little bit selfish. I think it's fair to say that Ken needed Anne alongside him every bit as much as she wanted to be there. They worked so well together they were almost like conjoined twins. How could that finely-tuned, well-organised working relationship have coped with late-night feeds, nappy changing, early morning school runs and needy teenage tantrums?

Perhaps all they ever needed for a happy and fulfilled life was one another, plus of course an audience.

Laurie Mansfield's observation that Ken Dodd's was a life well-lived is very apt, but, of all the people who I talked to about the Squire of Knotty Ash & His Lady, perhaps comedian and Doddy fan Alex Horne hit the nail on the head most succinctly: "Ken's home was onstage and he performed right to the end. That was so inspiring. I was left with the impression of a man in his ninetieth year who was still having fun, driving round the country, with his best friend, to theatres to make thousands of people laugh. And if you can be doing that your entire life, there really is nothing better…"

Television journalist John Stapleton once asked Ken what he was most proud of. This is what he said: "I'm proud that I've mastered some of the art of comedy. When I stand on a stage and see the audience literally rocking backwards and then rolling forwards with laughter – then I'm proud. It means you've learned your craft."

Then John asked Ken how he'd like to be remembered. Ken thought for a moment, then modestly said, "He made us laugh! … That'll do…"

Well of course Ken you achieved that in spades. However, I think for somebody who put so much store in the emotion of happiness, your greatest legacy is how much happiness you gave to others.

On behalf of all your many fans – thank you Sir Ken Dodd, Squire of Knotty Ash… for all the happiness…

P.T. Barnum, arguably the greatest showman who ever lived, once said:
"The noblest art is that of making others happy."

POSTSCRIPT

by Michael Henderson

Ken Dodd was the last link to the music hall entertainers. He was also the greatest of the music hall entertainers. There is no precise way of measuring that judgment because people will always have their favourites, and there's no accounting for taste. But there is no denying the fact that, in seven decades of inspired clowning, the Squire of Knotty Ash trumped both his predecessors and his peers in longevity, generosity of spirit and sheer plumptiousness.

In his case it was a plumptiousness that translated into genius, which is never a word one should use lightly. No matter what you may have heard, performers of that stature do not appear at the drop of a hat. So it is worth cocking an ear to Michael Billington, who retired in December 2019 after spending 48 years as the theatre critic of *The Guardian*. The biographer of Harold Pinter and Peggy Ashcroft, and the author of a book about the 'greatest' 101 plays in world drama, Billington reckons he has seen two performers of undisputed genius on stage: Laurence Olivier and Ken Dodd. Quite a dish to set before a king.

Billington's phrase, 'a planned fiesta', will ring bells with countless thousands who caught this great comedian in full sail. To watch audiences leaving one of Doddy's shows after midnight, looking discumknockerated, was really something. One evening, at the Congress Theatre in Eastbourne, I made a point of standing by the exit, observing people as they departed. The delight on their faces, mixed with bewilderment, might have kept a platoon of anthropologists busy for a month.

Doddy played every theatre in the kingdom, from Truro to Shetland, and there wasn't a hamlet that escaped his attention, and every show was an outpouring of love: the love of live performance, and the love of being alive. What Philip Larkin called 'the million-petalled flower of being here'. Audiences returned that love. They came back time and again, as witnesses, nay, as participants, happy to let a great comedian's skill wash away all cares and worries. Each night was a liberation.

He knew there was misery in the world. The evidence may be found every day. He also knew, in a way many modern comedians appear not to, that the world can be a magical place. There was no malice in his buffoonery; no nastiness, envy or spite. Nobody ever left one of his shows wanting to set fire to a building. Every night, for five hours, he served dollops of jollity in king-size proportions. As Eric Sykes noted, speaking for performers everywhere, Doddy should have been available on the NHS.

My personal connection with Kenneth Arthur Dodd began in May 1980 when, as a student journalist, I knocked on his dressing-room door after a show at the Crucible Theatre, Sheffield. The clock said 1am but Doddy had little use for the bonds of time. He didn't have to give me a minute – it was an exercise, not an interview for publication – but he gave me an hour: a proper hour, with full answers. It was the conduct of a courteous, civilised man, and I vowed to pay him back one day.

When I did, in a profile for *The Times* three decades later, it was back to the Crucible. Once again there was a man in a glass booth by the stage door, ready for his bed, and puzzled why others were not so keen to get to theirs. Once again Doddy talked in long paragraphs of bracing common sense, this time for two hours. He was pleased with the piece when it appeared, and urged me to 'come again', a privilege I accepted and tried hard not to abuse. I found a man who was kind-hearted, and sentimental in the right way. There was also a chip of ice. There had to be. He was a performer, and showbiz, for all the sugar coating, is a brutal world.

He was a creature of the stage, a front-cloth comic. Television audiences never saw the best of him because the camera reduces and Doddy was the live performer par excellence, a jester who contained multitudes. From his professional debut in Nottingham in 1954, right to the end, in the last days of 2017, when he turned 90, he proved an irresistible force for good.

'Do you believe in happy endings, boys and girls?' he would ask at the end of a panto.

'And what about you, mums and dads?'

'Good. Let's have a whip-round!'

Neville Cardus, the writer on cricket and music, said that Vladimir Horowitz was the greatest pianist, 'living or dead'. Those who were transported nightly to another world by the matchless brilliance of Doddy at full throttle and his powers of transformation, might say something similar about the last of the great music hall entertainers. What riches he bestowed, so freely, for so long. And how lucky we were to share the bounty of his talent. There will never be another.

Michael Henderson, author, critic and regular feature writer on entertainment, the arts and sport.

www.greatnorthernbooks.co.uk